Dr. M. Bozdag

Spiritual Sincerity Intelligence
7 Steps to Success

Translation: **Louis Mitler**

Personal Development: 1

1. Edition: August 2012

ISBN: 978-0-985452100

Published by Peninsular Publishing

Author: Dr. M. Bozdağ

Translation: Louis Mitler

Print House: Peninsular Publishing

2503 Jackson Bluf Rd
Tallahassee, FL, 32304
Phone: 1-800-2273725
www.roseprinting.com

Dr. M. Bozdag

Spiritual Sincerity Intelligence
7 Steps to Success

Translation: **Louis Mitler**

About the author:

Dr. M. Bozdag (born in 1967) has a PhD in Business Administration and Political Science. He is a legislative expert, public administrator and author of several books on personal development. His books which are printed in Turkish (Dusun ve Basar [Think and Succeed] , Ruhsal Zeka [Spiritual Sincerity Intelligence], Istemenin Esrari [Mysteries of Wishing], Sonsuzluk Yolculugu [The Journey of Eternity] and Sevgi Zekasi [Affection Intelligence]), have sold nearly one million copies. He is married with three children.

CONTENTS

INTRODUCTION

Have you thought about it? What commands, which are related to your future, are given to the angels from the Ruler[1] of the Universe to help your future? How can you ask about your future from the amazing wisdom of the Master of Destiny, rather than from the lies of the fortuneteller? Does not the Almighty Creator, who inspires even the bee, have important messages for you? How can you read the divine messages sent to you through worldly events? Do you know the language that spreads peace throughout the universe? Taken as a whole, what is your heart?

In the book that you hold in your hands, you will be able to search for answers to these interesting questions. Every chapter of this book will open a different pathway to your intellect, which is on the threshold of amazement and surprise. I am speaking about an interesting, exciting, reinforcing, new, unusual field of understanding. Be calm.

What is the most important means for gaining success and doing well in life? If it is intellectual quotient (IQ), why is it that so many clever people do not succeed in life? If it is emotional quotient (EQ), why is it that so many pleasant and respectable people are passed by in their corner and ignored? If it is hard work, why is it that fierce strivings of some people do not produce results?

1 The beautiful names, like "the Ruler of the universe, Master of Destiny, Almighty, All-Wise, All-Powerful Creator, God Almighty, Limitless Power, All-Merciful Creator, Limitless Mercy" all are refer to the same, One Creator of the universe.

Even if all of these factors are all important, there is one even more important dimension behind them: I am talking about understanding the profundity of destiny and metaphysics, which is the ability to look at the metaphysical dimensions beyond events. From now on, we shall call this ability the spiritual sincerity quotient (SSQ)[2].

Your mind is near the physical face of the universe and your heart is near the metaphysical face of the universe. The more spiritually sincere you are in applying the seven steps discussed in this book, the more effective, energetic, and happy you will become. What does this mean?

If what you do immediately crumbles, if what you produce quickly decays, if it cannot avoid contradictions, it means that your time to look at your spiritual sincerity intelligence is passing by.

Experts talk about so many different models for success, we try them, and each of us obtains different results because, behind these models, lay a secret dimension: The dimension of Destiny. This book attempts to seek out the entrance gate to this mystery.

Imagine you are beginning an important endeavor. The status and wages of this endeavor may be high and your family and friends may very much want you to attempt it. What can you do to pass the written and oral examinations for this endeavor? Let us answer this question from three different aspects of intelligence:

From the perspective of intellectual intelligence (IQ): You cultivate yourself for the abilities that the job requires. You train yourself in fields of discipline such as speech and visual comprehension and expressing yourself, logic and mathematics, music, apprehension of distance, and mastery of your physical movements. You read the necessary books on the subject and engage in training for the endeavor. The level of your intelligence also greatly affects your accomplishment of this endeavor.

From the perspective of emotional intelligence (EQ): You will learn to understand correctly both your own feelings and of those of the individuals with whom you will interact. You will practice expressing yourself

2 Please note that from this part on, we will prefer the word "intelligence" instead of the word "quotient."

in a well-balanced manner according to time and place. You will succeed in arousing empathy and easily and harmoniously get along with others. The nobility of your emotional intelligence will affect your advancement in your job more than simply being hired for the job.

Even if you do develop your intellectual and emotional intelligence, you may still fail; you may be unsuccessful, even if material conditions are in your favor. For example, you may have a car accident while on your way to the exam or, on exam day, you may suddenly experience stomach cramps, or there might be a fire at the company the exact day you are to begin a new job. Factors that you cannot even imagine may keep you from moving forward. In addition, sometimes, just the opposite may occur; there may be extreme and unexpected help such as seeing the answers in a dream.

How many highly intelligent people do you know that were swallowed up by failure and how many mediocre people have you witnessed rise to the highest heights? How many people have demonstrated success, rose to the peak of success, and, right after, were unsuccessful and wiped from the pages of history? Some philosophers have ended up in mental hospitals; some holdings have completely gone under. The dimensions of these events direct us to the mysterious realities of destiny. Yes, we are referring to spiritual sincerity intelligence.

From the perspective of the spiritual sincerity intelligence quotient (SSQ): If you believe that you can succeed and sincerely believe in the Almighty Creator, a secret energy will nourish your spiritual activity. Spiritual climates will envelope your surroundings, guide your life so you can receive the recompense according to your intentions. Your power of perception determines the strength and quality of the energy you radiate and, if you can believe and persist without worrying yourself over the obstacles, you will receive support under the appearance of coincidence. The support of energy and love, such as prayers directed to you, are means for destiny to allow you to play a good part in the world. Destiny weaves a web so you can achieve your role. Of course, you need to work diligently, but you will also experience support for amazing reasons that you could not never have imagined.

Let Us Compare the Three Ways of Understanding

IQ and EQ explain extraordinary events via the concepts of "coincidence, luck, and accident." SSQ perceives these types of unforeseeable events as being amongst the directions planned via the will of the Almighty Creator.

When you are confronted by difficulty, your IQ relies on the power of your knowledge and your machine, at the same time, your EQ relies on the power of your feelings, courage, and beliefs. However, the SSQ depends on the Unlimited Power who, together with these factors, continually makes the universe persist.

When you look for a way out of these difficulties, your IQ will put your objective intelligence to work, your EQ will analyze the feelings and emotions involved, and your SSQ will ensure that you are aware of the wisdom of the All Powerful Creator. While your IQ is blocked by impossibility, your SSQ is not concerned with such impossibilities.

According to IQ, happiness, wealth, fame, music, and entertainment are the physical pleasures that "fill the moment." With EQ, these concepts are the meanings that produce positive feelings. Further, according to the SSQ, happiness is spirituality, good conscience, loving creatures because of the Almighty Creator, and feeling ready to fly to heaven, whether one is experiencing pain or pleasure. Wealth or poverty do not matter, as no goal other than heaven and eternity, can satisfy the SSQ.

When the inevitable and inescapable moment of your life arrives, your IQ will leave you unable to react, your EQ will frighten you, and your SSQ will hasten you at the last second to plant the young seedling that you hold in your hands.

If you succeed, based on your IQ, you might say, "I succeeded;" if it is according to your EQ, you might say, "I did it together with my friends;" however, your SSQ will make you say, "The Almighty Creator approved and created what He wished."

The universe of the IQ and EQ has been delineated via positive science; they do not acknowledge any beings other than galaxies, atoms, and physical energy; here, man is merely a physical body. On the other hand, SSQ places man's spirituality in line with the universe. SSQ also describes a different universe that has a spiritual profundity and believes in the living beings of other dimensions such as jinni, angels, and spiritual beings. The SSQ invites humankind to the eternal life after this fleeting life.

The eyes of the SSQ are open to beyond the universe as travelers to eternity receive their rewards according to their efforts and the best reward is the reward of the Gracious Creator who governs the universe. As such, we should do things for eternity until our last breath. For this reason, those who want to achieve real happiness in this mortal, accident-filled, tormented, stormy world need to start to look at events through the window of destiny.

We live our lives like fish in an aquarium. How many people can go outside of time and place and look with the eyes of the heart at what is really happening in our world? To catch such a glimpse, is an accomplishment of the love of the Almighty Creator.

Seven Powers of Spiritual Sincerity Intelligence (SSQ)

No spiritual being speaks about the color of its eyes, height, house, or car in the spiritual profundity of the universe. There, your body is not given as much importance as a speck of dust. While worldly people are concerned with such matters, the angels' interest themselves in the underlying spiritual meaning behind matter. Your true value is measured by the Almighty Creator according to your spiritual meaning. Moreover, your spiritual meaning is the value that you add to your physical existence by means of your heart. The book you are holding is focused on seven spiritual values: your beliefs, your intentions, your emotions, your persistence, your spiritual influence and gaining the wisdom of the divine will.

The powerful effects that are directed from the spiritual climate to your life can be shaped according to your position in these seven fields. This means that your spiritual supports must increase or you will struggle with spiritual obstacles. From the aspect of these fields, you are in the wishing and working stage of life; the Almighty Creator is the One who will accept and create your wishes by approving or disapproving them. Let us expand a little on these fields.

Power of Belief. Power and courage flow throughout the universe via the channel of belief. You carry on with your life guided by your beliefs. If you trust, at a most basic level, in yourself, you will find support while you are tested. If you trust in the All-Merciful Creator, you will find support as long as you live. Further, once you have decided where to place your trust, you need to prevent your logic from conflicting with your future. Those who trust in their own powers may be worried, while those who depend on the power of the Almighty Creator will not be shaken.

Power of Intention. The great secret is this: The meaning and value of your efforts is bound in your intentions. In the last analysis, we receive the recompense of our intentions, not our efforts, both in this life, in the form of inner peace, and in the hereafter, as promised by Divine messages.

There might be a hidden difference in the intentions of two people who work on the same thing, in the same way, yet achieve different results. Before you allow yourself to be disillusioned, examine your heart and ask yourself the following questions:

- Why are you doing this?
- What are your grounds for what you are doing?
- Can your motives turn from good to bad or from bad to good?

Any great success might be diminished for a small reason and any small action may be exalted simply by the sincerity behind it. You will come to know the power of your purpose in the second section of this chapter.

Power of Emotion. This is the language of appearances, sounds, or smells. Emotion is the language of spirituality and, the more spiritual the message is, the more emotional the message is. In particular, the strength of positive feelings shapes the size and strength of your individual world. As such, the world of thought is narrow, while the world of feeling is wide. If feelings are coupled with intelligence, the lives of one thousand people can fit inside the life of one. In Chapter 3, you will discover your emotional system, which can be defined as the hand and tongue of your spirituality.

Power of Persistence. Divine Destiny tests every traveler on the road to success with obstacles, especially at the beginning and end of the road when Divine Destiny will seriously test your sincerity. The secret of success is concealed in your ability to persist until you pass beyond the limits of hopelessness. Further, persistence holds out until the last breath: Persistence is patience. Those who are defeated are those who cannot persist because there is no defeat while the struggle continues. Success is also hidden in works carried out continuously, even though these successes may seem small. In Chapter 3, we shall discover the subtleties of persistence that will play an important role in our lives.

Power of Contentment. Selfish ambition will cause people to exceed, suddenly, their capacity and efforts to get ahead. However, taking this road to success will end in a person who suddenly stumbles and falls. The world weighs down the shoulders of the ambitious but is under the feet of those who show contentment and persistent belief. The universe is the enemy of the selfish as it offers possibilities to those who will further distribute them to others. Success, which is the result of hard work and satisfaction with what one has, is concealed in the secret of contentment.

Power of the Spirituality. The spiritual face of universe has been created in a reciprocal fashion. Those who give receive, those who love are loved, and those who share experience sharing in return. Just as the human body is affected by its physical surroundings, so is spirituality affected by its spiritual surroundings. The spiritual energy that permeates the surroundings either breaks down or strengthens people according to their qualities. For example, ten people who are interdependent with their spirituality are more powerful than thousands of people who live cutoff from one another in every way. Chapter 6 will further reveal the secret of spiritual interdependence.

Power of Divine Will. The last secret of divine destiny, whose structure we will comprehend, states that the laws, will, and wisdom of a supreme Ruler rule the universe. People have not been left to their own devices; they have not been forgotten. Events such as good luck, accidents, and messages, like instinct and intuition, are directions that come from the Almighty. If the humans know the "Divine Will" that envelopes the universe and if they behave according to these forms of wisdom, the universe will enter into their service.

Your life goes on like an adventurous journey and, with this book, a new adventure begins. Your spirituality, which is the driver of the automobile of your life, will take you through a thousand and one environments. You could say that you are going on a world tour, as your spirituality will take you through a thousand and one climates of this world tour as you drive the automobile of your life. Are you ready?

CHAPTER ONE:

THE POWER OF BELIEF

I. WHY WE NEED THE POWER OF BELIEF?

INTRODUCTION

Are you ready to discover the first of the seven basic mysterious secrets of success explained in this book? We are talking about the depth of your belief, which is the first of your spiritual supports that affect success.

Let's say that you have decided to write down realistic, balanced, useful, and clear goals related to your family, profession, health, economy, abilities, and environment. You have also thought about how you will reach these goals and you move forward every day by your efforts.

Belief and anxiety represent the strengths and weaknesses of your life's automobile engine, which has begun on its world tour. The engine of the vehicle makes the car move along as if it were cruising sound and strong. However, an engine that is worn out by anxiety in time will give out.

To avoid such a break down, you need to trust in the justice of the All-Wise Creator, believe that you will succeed, be truly hopeful, and work with your positive feelings. Additionally, the stronger your beliefs are, the more motivated you will be, the more spiritual energy you will have, and the more spiritual support you will receive from your environment, which will allow you to move ahead rapidly.

After you have calculated everything and, if after making your decision and seeing what is right and wrong in your situation, you still have doubts, anxiety, fear, hopelessness, and mistrust in the All-Merciful Creator, you will have only succeeded in facilitating negative possibilities. **The spiritual support you will receive on the road to success is as great as your hope to succeed.**

1. BELIEF AND PROFUNDITY

Belief that produces excitement, trust, and determination is more definite, powerful, and goes deep. Those who have belief that the Almighty Creator will bestow on them a just and wise reward will reflect more energy. Now, let's discover the secret to intensifying belief and confidence.

a) Certainty of Belief

Every quality reflected in the universe depends on the name of the Master of the Universe: beauty, esthetics, mercy, power, and everything else. For us to purify ourself of doubt, we must open ourself to the quality of the "certainty" of the Creator. Conversely, doubt closes the door to psychic energies that flow into the physical universe. **Prayers or efforts given up in doubt are powerless.**

We possess a multi-phased process of perception that takes us from knowledge, comprehension, and our view and opinions to a verified belief of certainty. The instant that an opinion is energized is the instant it is converted into a definite belief. From their defense, the people who are certain scatter sparks around themself with their every word.

For example we believe that "fire will burn." However, the opinion of an inexperienced child on the quality of this burning fire is not as powerful as the certainty of burning in the fire.

Every natural law created by the Almighty Creator is a universal certainty: Fire burns; water cools. What forms the behavior of matter is the spiritual structure hidden behind it. Additionally, every one of these laws represents the spiritual form and belief of a kind of angel.

In the same way, the human soul is a universal certainty. It is different from the angels, who represent the laws of nature, rather it has the freedom and capacity to develop and change as the soul exists and is active in directing the human body. However, the human soul is considered an embodiment of the universe and possesses a mysterious potential to affect all the certainties of the universe.

The human soul has potential and can acquire qualities that, with divine permission, can overcome the obstacles of natural laws. This ability is to the degree, as in the example of the Prophet Abraham (PBUH)[3], who was not burned by the fire, that a deeply sincere prayer can neutralize even laws of nature. Such events are noted in the life of Prophet Jesus (peace upon him). "And behold, there was a woman who had the heart of infirmity eighteen years and was bowed together and could in no way lift up herself. And when Jesus saw her, he called her to him and said unto her 'Woman thou art loosed from thine infirmity. And he laid his hands on her and immediately she was made straight and glorified God."[4]

The Almighty Creator granted an important aid to the prophets by way of miracles. He showed His kindness to holy persons and ordinary people alike via lesser acts of grace. In this section, our purpose is to attempt to direct this spiritual energy in such a way as to help us to achieve our goals. In doing so, we will learn how to trust wisdom, justice, timing, and the divine will of the All-Merciful Creator. Once this trust is gained, we can then reinforce our belief that we can and shall succeed. The success of this effort is not an automatic result; it is a divine reward for your labor.

Strong beliefs must not be confused with weak expectations. One is a tree that has put forth sprouts: the other is only a seed. Do you believe that the universe has a creator? Are you truly certain?

---

3 PBUH means, "peace be upon him"; PBUT means "peace be upon them." We use this phrase for all messengers, prophets, and angels of Almighty Creator when we mention their names.

4 The Bible, Luke 13:11-13

If the seed of belief in us could turn into "true" belief, then the explosion of feeling the recollection of the All-Powerful Creator would be inspired in our hearts and **would burst our bosoms asunder.** Remember, when the verses from the Quran were recited during the worship service, the companions of the Prophet Mohammad (PBUH) could not bear it and he fell into a faint.

The potential results of the mighty force of verified belief may be seen in this tradition: "**If you knew the Almighty Creator properly, mountains would move with your prayers.**"[5] There is a similar approach in the Gospel, "The Lord said, 'If ye had belief as a grain of mustard seed, ye might say unto this sycamine tree, Be thou plucked up by the root, and be thou planted in the sea; and it should obey you.[6]

There are three levels of belief: the level of knowledge, the level of witness, and the level of internalization, which is also the level of certainty. The level of knowledge refers to learning that the fire burns from someone else; the level of witness refers to feeling the terror of the burning fire beside you; and the level of internalization refers to being caught in the fire and burning oneself. Belief of certainty, or internalization, is the most powerful level of belief.

When your belief has reached the level of certainty, no one can stop your efforts or destroy your morale and you will progress on the road in which you believe with all your force. Those who work diligently toward their goals will develop, for themselves, clear, living, and powerful beliefs.

b) From Knowledge to Certainty

The human soul was created from different forms of belief. To speak of behavior, regarding the soul is to speak of a form of belief. When your beliefs change, the way in which you conduct your spiritual life also changes.

5 Prophet Mohammad (PBUH), Jami'us-Saghir 5:319, Tradition no. 7448. The success of man shall increase in the measure in which he shall use two values together: working with foresight and sincere desire/prayer. All results in your life are the answers given by destiny to this pair. You may see in our book called Mysteries of Wishing the subtleties of converting our prayers to the roles that have been accepted in the book of destiny.

6 The Bible, Luke, 17/6

When you strengthen your beliefs, you increase the power of control you have over your life. A very strong belief is effective enough to give direction both to its possessor and to those in close contact.

Trusting in the Almighty Creator, believing in your success, and hoping in the future will nourish you through knowledge and intensify your passage through its definite steps. **Thought is a seed trying to bud, whereas verified belief is a tree that continually gives fruit.** You can cultivate the seed of defeat or victory with a single thought. Here is the journey:

a) You absorb **knowledge**, learn it, use it, and repeat it. After a while, this knowledge brings forth an inclusive **thought.**

b) If you continue to nourish the thought by repetition, it will **produce various opinions** (weak beliefs). This is how you begin to produce your own truths.[7]

c) If you nurture an opinion, **it will turn into a belief.** This belief can be destroyed from an attack of a very strong belief. If you nourish the belief by defending and experiencing it, it will reach the level of **high certainty** (verified belief).

Knowledge and thought express the level of belief through information and enlightened knowledge; opinions and beliefs express the level of the witness and belief of high certainty expresses the level of internalization.

The condition of verified belief cannot be destroyed by direct attack; it does not accept intelligence, thought, or reason. Rather, it is the essence of the soul. It is everywhere: in your arteries, in your genetic makeup. **You cannot attack something that has taken hold of every one of your cells.** A verified belief is so deeply embedded in yourself that you are not aware of it. Its boundaries are so encircled around your own boundaries that you cannot define it. It has become automatic and it appears to act of itself. It is ridiculous to question it as it does what it will within your sub-consciousness.

---

7 We derive 'the separation of right from wrong," factually, from birth. What is later learned is in the form of a definition of these differentiations. Right and wrong are different for everyone, yet, "there exists" right and wrong for everyone.

c) The Mirror of Limitlessness

Belief of certainty is the only resource that we can use to turn the explosion of feeling that the recollection of the Creator inspired in our hearts like **a mirror of the limitlessness of the Lord of the Universe.** The source of this spiritual strength in some people lies in their well-defined and specific beliefs.[8] [5] Man receives and the Creator gives. Man is limited and the Almighty Creator is without limit.

The source of all we have acquired, the life that surrounds enlightened knowledge, our family, morals, beauty, intelligence, wealth, and us is the work of the All-Powerful Creator of the universe. However, as much the attributes of Limitless Power may shine upon you, you will be that much more nourished by the eternity of God Almighty.

Believing that you can do something is followed by praying that you will be sustained by the Limitless Power. The help of the Almighty Creator opens the way that is suitable to your beliefs. In whatever way you might struggle to walk on, He makes that road easy for you. The strength of a soldier is derived from the strength of the army behind him. If we were to depend on only ourselves, we would decay and perish, but we are born and you developed with the Creator's strength. The power that appears to belong to us as we look from the outside, in fact, belongs to the Creator in its nature and essence. Let us take a lesson from the Mawlana Rumi **"How could God, who nourishes wheat with the Sun, not reward your reliance on Him?"**[9] **Therefore, on our journey to success, it is not on our own imaginations that you rely, but on the true divine power that causes us to exist.**

These words invite us to trust in the Almighty Creator: **"Pray to God, firmly believing that He will give you your reward. Know that Almighty Creator does not accept the prayer of a heart unmindful of Him and busy with other things."**[10]

8 If we can believe in the Creator as we see Him, this divine power will enlighten our life. If the source of our self-confidence is not the Almighty Creator, rather our own personal self, we may be strengthened for the purpose of our trial; however, when our appointed time is over, we will be taken from the world in the sin of giving a partner to God.

9 *Mawlana* Rumi , Masnavi, vol.3, p.34

10 Prophet Mohammad (PBUH), Tirmizi, Daavat: 65; Musned, 2:77

d) Belief Comes First

I watched a news program that highlighted four out of hundreds of newly graduated youth who applied to take a civil servant selection test in Istanbul. What each applicant said was, "Even if I just had one chance in a million, I would take this test. I don't think I am going to pass at all. Whatever we do, the ones who are going to pass are the ones with influential connections. It is luck, maybe I will pass after all."

They understood that some seemed to be successful, not because of their studies, but because of the strings that are pulled for them. Those who did not have such influential connections did not believe that they could succeed if they studied hard. Rather, they tried to do what they did not believe in.

If you hope to succeed in something that you do not believe in, you will be in conflict with yourself. **It is better to do something small with belief and hope than to attempt something big with hesitation.** When you have belief and hope, you will find success.

Yet, some prayers and wishes are extraordinary. For example, the prayer of Jim Dornan who greatly needed money to treat his child; the prayer of Einstein who vowed to shame those who denigrated his intelligence. Jim Dornan developed an international marketing network, and Einstein laid the foundations of quantum physics.

Everyone who has left a great mark on our lives and who has left behind great works has had such prayers...they believed and the Master of Destiny gave them permission to experience what they believed. **If one day you complete an unforgettable work, you will be in debt to your prayers.**

Now, I think I hear an objection, "Good enough, I believe I will succeed, but I still can't. I can't succeed in spite of believing."

Let's make this clear, belief does not create results, rather it supports us in many ways on the road to the results. However, we cannot change the destiny of human beings. Even if our belief affects the free will of others, it cannot control them. As you will read in the final section of this book, our interpretation of the plan of destiny encircles our life.

It is narrated that an imam (which is a Muslim preacher) said during a Friday sermon, "If you walk pronouncing 'In God's name,' you can pass over the water without sinking." A villager, who heard these words, began walking toward the river and continued to walk over the water instead of over the bridge. One day he invited the imam to his house and while he was going along with the imam, they came to a river and the man walked over the water to the other side, yet the imam did not dare to go into the water. The surprised villager called him and said "Imam, wasn't this the thing you said to do? Come on over." The imam answered him, saying, "It was my tongue that said it, but it was your heart that believed it."

As another example, a day before my doctoral examination, three of the four questions seemed to come into my mind; I later learned that they were the exact questions of this examination. We may experience such extreme events; however, such extraordinary occurrences are rare, difficult and have very specific emotional conditions.

The villager was well intentioned, innocent; had strong beliefs, but he had not learned shrewdness and hypocrisy. He was not given to pleasure and was far-removed from pride. Because of the first qualities mentioned, he believed he could walk on water before he even began crossing over. **For this reason, you need to strengthen your belief that you will reach your goals before you begin on your way.**

Belief is controlled by the right hemisphere of the brain and reason by the left hemisphere. Additionally, Belief lies within the spiritual universe and reason within the **boundaries** of the material universe. Belief is nurtured by the power of the spiritual environment, reason by the power of the physical universe. The road for nurturing your spiritual energy passes from what you believe to what you do. Therefore, one must use reason to arrive at a decision; however, if you want to succeed after having made a decision, you need to concentrate on the power of belief.

Our reason is related to what is known. One who has never experienced a spiritual surrounding cannot imagine anything other than the material. This is why inventors who discover the unknown generally succeed with feelings of belief, trust and belief in Almighty Creator, which they have reinforced after repressing their reason. Rather than by a reasonable solution to what they are searching for, they reach it by an intuition, by a divine direction, which appears to be chance, or by inspiration.

Even as ridiculous as the idea of going to the moon may have seemed to ancient man, the idea of doing something we don't know how to do seems to us. So when we are thinking, let us use both our belief and our reason. After we make up our minds to do something, let us silence the reason that says, "You can't succeed!" and change it to a cry of belief, saying, "You can succeed!"

The famous Muslim thinker Said Nursi said, "**He who has obtained belief of certainty can defy the universe.**" I would like to share with you the secret of overcoming obstacles: **No commander ever experienced defeat until he succumbed to the fear that he would suffer defeat.** Moreover, as Sultan Yildirim Beyazit said, "He who fears defeat will always be defeated."

Before every success, there was first the belief of success and success relied on the support of this belief. Christopher Columbus, before he reached North American, believed that there was a road to India from the other side of the world. Edison, before discovering the incandescent light, believed he would discover it. **Those who succeed believed first and then did it. Those who do not succeed, try to do it first and then tried believing.**

2. BELIEF MAKES THINGS EASIER

However strong your trust, belief, and hope, your energy, enthusiasm, spiritual, and material support must be just as strong. With this combination, your troubles will decrease accordingly. Here is exactly what can happen:

a) Awareness

Heightened belief is like an automatic proficiency; a skill you need to learn that you did not know before. After learning this skill, you develop it through conscious exercises until it becomes automatic and resides within your subconscious. At this point, you do not consciously attend to every detail for driving a car, typing with ten fingers, singing a song, or walking. Similarly, if you want to do something, you simply start doing it, and your actions will be created.

In the same way, when you work on something that you believe in, all your resources focus on your service toward this goal. Your memory, recollections, intelligence, heart, conscience, whatever you possess, all come to your aid. However, if you allow your anxiety to overwhelm you, neither your memory nor your reason nor your conscience can work as they ought to.

Unbelief in success is a barrier to success. If a baby believes it could not succeed in walking, it would neither try nor succeed at learning how to walk. Likewise, you cannot make a sick person cling to life if he or she has lost all hope of living. It will seem a torture for him or her to struggle to live if he or she does not believe in living. In this type of situation, you would have to work that much more in relation to however little you believe in something.

In other words, while a student who is not afraid of not passing can get high grades by studying 30 minutes a day, a student who studies in the fear of not passing his exams must study 5 hours a day to achieve the same results.

Those who use their belief in their daily life are protected by the light of the Master of the Universe. Those who use only their reason are limited to only their own enlightenment. Further, your personal light will be weaker than the light of a flashlight in the pitch darkness when you rely on your reason alone and you may think that the shades of darkness hide monsters ready to tear you to pieces. The road you know is the only road you see. However, if you walk in the light of the Master of the Universe, you will see that you can hold a map of the universe in the palm of your hand. It is your belief in Him that allows you walk to on the right road.

b) Through Intuition

The stronger your belief is, the more intuitive you will be. Your feelings, estimations, and chance choices will be as accurate as you are trustworthy, hopeful, and believing. You can increase your intuition and receive revelations in the form of support for your goals. The channel of intuition certainly does not work through slyness, hypocrisy, or internal compromise; rather demands the internal purity of a baby who needs milk.

In particular periods of my life, when I was innocent, patient, trusting, and full of hope, I experienced a great deal of support via intuition and direction. For example, I was exhausted, tired with unstoppable headaches. Then, I once read that garlic oil was useful for general health. I went looking for garlic oil wherever that I thought it might be for sale. I looked for weeks for this oil without giving up. When I had finally exhausted myself from looking for three months, I stopped looking.

Several days later, I had the intuition to visit one of my old friends at his office. I went there and there was another visitor, a teacher who was visiting my friend and who mentioned, during the course of the conversation, that he had imported garlic oil to sell.

It would appear that I had gone to my friend's office by chance. Someone who might look at this story superficially would have thought that that teacher was also there by chance. Whereas, it was a hidden Limitless Power that brought us together at that exact moment to realize both our goals.

A similar situation can happen to you. Suppose you are walking along without a plan and the one you are going to marry appears that the house you are looking for attracts your attention when you stop at a street corner. Ideas, which will change your life, come into your mind through associations with the people and things you come in contact with every day. If you want this kind of support, you need to work very hard and your heart must be filled with belief, hope, and trust in God.

c) Through Information

If you work with belief, you may obtain secret support via inspired knowledge from the Master of Destiny. In this way, **you may be doing something without awareness and suddenly you understand that your actions were given to you as revelations for the resolution of the issues you have sought for years to answer.** For example, I was about to take my doctoral exam on political science. There was just one exam in Ankara and it was very important that I passed. My responsibility was to work with all my power to desire success passionately and then to resign myself to the will of God. **I carried out my duty in accordance with the strategy of this book "Think and Succeed."**

I reasoned in this way: "I am weak in political science. To pass a course like this, I would have to read a least one hundred books for a month. But, unfortunately, I did not have enough time to study all of the related books."

Although I thought so, I tried to carry out my duties in accordance with the strategy of this book "Think and Succeed." I had only one month to prepare. Yet, I sincerely performed my responsibilities as I wanted to pass the test so much that I even studied when I was stopped at a red light in my car.

I will point out the support I received in the final days of my intensive studies on my doctoral exam. I had not known about the practice of democracy in Greek city-states. This subject obsessed my thoughts in an odd way. However, I learned this topic after hours of asking questions of a friend who was completing his master's at Ankara University. That evening, I studied one section each of two books for two hours and. I surrendered to the sensations and promptings that flowed through me.

The next day, four questions were asked on the exam concerning this topic. I could never have known what questions were going to be asked; however, I had learned the answer to one question from the discussion with my friend and the answers to the other two questions were from the books I had studied the evening before. General concepts in literature were the last question.

Certainly, it cannot be this simple every time as your intuition will not always work in your service. What you need is to work as hard as you can and sincerely believe in the Creator of the universe.

d) Through Surroundings

If we do not believe in our goals, neither the men nor the angels around us will believe in us. This is the law: **People who believe in what they are doing will receive support. Those who believe a lot will receive a lot of support and those who believe little will receive little.** Further, whoever performs evil will be supported with evil and whoever performs with goodness will be supported with goodness.

Suppose we have a heart filled with desire that exists in complete trust. If our body is powerful, we will only be supported by ourselves; if our body is needy, we will also be supported by the aid of others. For example, the Almighty Creator supports a weak baby with the service of his mother and a strong eagle by giving it powerful claws.

See how the Almighty Creator supports His needy creatures: let's say you slip, the bread in your hand falls on the ground, and you throw it in the garbage. You cannot know that the piece of bread was taken from you by the Limitless Mercy who has been observing you ignore the hungry kitten that was waiting in the corner for hours. You walk away and the cat that has to feed itself and its kittens come and eat the bread. I have seen many sights of that kind.

I observed this example: Once, I was driving on the highway with my wife. It looked as though the city was made of concrete from one end to the other. I wondered how the birds in the sky could feed themselves. Then a truck passed us filled to its tailgate with grain. The pigeons landed on the bed of the truck and when they had eaten their fill, they flew away. When I looked at the horizon, I saw pigeons flying towards the truck from kilometers away. It was as though they had received a revelation that they would be fed from this truck that appeared like a dot in the distance.

The Master of Destiny may send you external supports in an unexpected way: For example, think of the rescue of the Prophet Joseph (peace upon him) who was thrown into a well in the desert by his jealous brothers. He was a good, sincere, and virtuous child. What happened then? A convoy found him, took him as their slave, sold him to an administrator of the king of Egypt, and later, after he grew up, he became the administrator for the treasury of Egypt.

If you try your best and believe sincerely in the Creator of the universe, divine help will be sent to you even if it seems like you have fallen into a silent well in an uninhabited desert.

As you can see, most of the time people may not know why or how they help; but the Master of Destiny charges them. Sometimes a person will not even be aware that they have been sent to help us. Our Creator knows our beliefs and our needs and even if we cannot express our troubles, He can send us human support.

I was looking for an illustration that I could use in a seminar on the uses of hypnosis and I tried in vain to get several friends to participate. While I was thinking about how I could offer the audience a demonstration, a friend sent me related software over the internet, saying, "I know you are interested in this sort of knowledge."

In short, your sincere and certain belief is an effective prayer and invitation for the supports of others. Believe in what you do and observe your supports. What I mean here it is that simple: If I knock on your door and convince you that you can earn ten times your investment in a year, wouldn't you become my partner with your all of your assets? As such, the most effective way to influence people is to convince them to believe in themselves.

3. BELIEF CAUSES CHANGES

Your belief changes your health, physique, habits, feelings, and behaviors, without your awareness. The basis of the different characteristics that people show on the outside is their different beliefs. **Every belief you change starts to change you from the inside out.**

a) On Health

The relation between epidemics, bacteria, and viruses in the cycle of sickness and health cannot be denied. However, the effect of your feelings and behaviors that arise from your beliefs about your sickness or health is very great.

The feelings of people who believe in the divine wisdom of getting up early, being active, full of confidence, content, patient, and tolerant will be calm, patient, and confident. They will know that sickness is an angel sent to earn to give humans thankfulness, loyalty, love of life, and the moral values that will prepare them for heaven. Additionally, because they will learn their lessons quickly from this visitor, they will recover faster and the burden of their illness will pass away more easily.

If a human internalizes negative values such as jealousy, haste, arrogance, selfishness, anxiety, fear, and impatience, he or she will become sicker and be sick more frequently. Additionally, untrusting, suspicious, pessimistic, and hopeless people are fundamentally encircled with these unhealthy values. Conversely, belief, trust, and hope always bring about positive values. **True powerlessness is spiritual and a helpless person cannot be successful.**

b) On Feelings

Let us think about these beliefs: The Almighty Creator is merciful, I can earn eternal heaven in this world, the angels love us, life is beautiful, I am important, I am capable, I will develop a lot, my father, mother, spouse, children are very valuable, humans are very beautiful, I am entranced by nature, I take pleasure in work.

You have read that beliefs are in a chain from the universe to the individual. Can someone who believes have the same rich emotions as someone who does not believe? For example, saying “The Almighty Creator is cruel” closes most doors in general – all the doors to happiness even- while saying “I am ugly” only closes the specific door to happiness.

Therefore, when we cannot determine our own beliefs, we find trouble and give in to the negative suggestions of our surroundings or our own negative experiences. We begin to generalize negative events.

Happiness is not material in nature and it cannot be measured by something material. It is also not related to obtaining capital, rather it is related to the accumulated meaning of life.

We once visited Bosnia and, while we were dodging Serbian bullets, the children of war were playing; completely unaware of what was going on around them. While their mothers and fathers wept with the pain and challenge of rebuilding their lives, again beside their ruined buildings, the innocent children carried on their old games in the mud. **While a child can be happy in the mud, a king can be unhappy on this throne.**

c) On Behaviors

Our established beliefs determine our automatic behaviors and our prejudices and construct our personalities and our images. Our beliefs form our preferences, our preferences form our habits, and our habits form our lives.

Let's think about these beliefs: Happiness comes from earning by the sweat of the brow. Honesty leads to victory. Everybody has an interior beauty worthy of respect. I am a benevolent person. I like doing meaningful things. I don't waste a second of my time.

Our beliefs can go astray at any time or place. For example, someone who believes that he or she knows the value of time, might sit in a park, read a book, and think. Someone who believes life is meaningless might wait lazily wherever he or she happens to be. One who believes in the value of humans might greet every new face with a smile, while someone who hates humanity will not want to see anybody.

In this way, we must be able to develop our supportive beliefs that are related to our goals. For example, I feel happy working; I give importance to knowledge related to this topic; I am always doing this or that.

Years ago, we were giving effective communication seminars. In these seminars, when we were working with body language, we said to our friends, "smile continually." We agreed to this and starting to work, and shortly after, we saw that some participants were no longer smiling. Why? Because they were not first smiling inside their heart. In other words, the feelings you have inside your heart will reflect on your body.

As you see, if we cannot profoundly determine healthy and supportive beliefs, we cannot move on. If we try to move forward by forcing ourselves intellectually, we bear up a little but then we will lose concentration and retune to our previous state.

Here is the greatest secret: Our true face is our face when we are not concentrating. For example, if our face is like a rock and we smile when we see you but, when you leave, our face returns to its old appearance. **A truly happy face is a face that can smile even when it is absent-minded. If you have enough good beliefs, you can do this. So think:** What is it that your beliefs do to you when you are not aware?

d) On the Physical Body

I would like to make a startling assertion, which is not a scientific one, but relies on my own observations; there is a connection between a person's belief, the spiritual world, and their physical appearance. What is interesting is when two people share the same world of belief and soul; they begin to resemble one another physically.

You can observe a light, a cleanliness, a shine, and a joy in the face of one who thinks about holy, noble, clean, virtuous values whereas you will observe an unpleasant darkness in the faces of pessimistic, ill-intentioned, and selfish people.

Furthermore, the lines of a person's hands and face, the general posture of their body, their gestures, and mimicries express their personalities. When we change our personalities based on our beliefs, our physiques participate in this change as well. For instance, **someone who believes in ugliness grows uglier and someone who believes in beauty grows more beautiful.**

According to the legend, a hunchbacked king was very grieved by his hump and he dreamed of eliminating his problem. Therefore, he set up a statue of a figure that did not have a hump in the entrance of his palace. Early every morning he would go to that statue and imagine himself as having a straight back and, slowly, his hump disappeared. Life is sometimes like this legend. You may notice that people, who have lived together for many years in intellectual and behavioral harmony, they begin to resemble their partners.

When you look at somebody's face, you see the soul rather than only his or her physical body. The human body acts in harmony with the soul that it represents. Therefore, to speak of beautiful, superior, lofty beliefs and moral values is to speak of a strong, harmonious, lovable physical appearance.

4. ANXIETY IS DESTRUCTIVE

Belief is the seed of productivity, while anxiety is the seed of destruction. You cannot achieve a goal that you do not believe you can reach. Even if everybody else encourages you, your anxiety will pull you down and you will become an obstacle to yourself. **Anxiety holds us back from thinking, from enterprise, from action.**

Let us have a look at the causes of anxiety:

a) Lack of Confidence in the Creator

The universe is under the rule of the All-Powerful Creator. Therefore, it is reasonable to stay away from a known fire, yet it is unreasonable to live in fear that a meteorite will fall from the skies.

This life is a divine plan. If the Creator smites us, there is no one who can save us and if He protects us, no one can harm us. **There is thus no reason for us to fear suffering of negative** occurrences. As such, it is senseless to say, "What if he or she abandons me, if I can't get out of poverty, if I don't pass this exam, if this illness lasts my whole life..." Because of thoughts such as these, many people are unnecessarily the victims of their fears. A famous Turkish comedian used to refer to his fear of dying in a plane and died the day he first flew.

The Almighty Creator allows us to develop by suffering. Nevertheless, He does not oppressively mistreat us. While, He might not give us everything we ask for, exactly how we ask, there may be a thousand acts of divine wisdom in His activities. What we have to do is to desire, work, and trust that we will receive a satisfying reward of divine justice in the right place and at the right time.

Sometimes we know the power of our Creator but we are impatient and fearful that He will not give attention to our wishes. When we think like this, it means that we do not know the Endless Mercy. He leaves shelters under small branches covered by the winter's snow. The little sparrows who could not escape from the winter stay warm and fill themselves with the small fruits of the branches of those shrubs. Moreover, it is He who creates what happens in your vision and in your hearts at this moment.

b) Claiming the Power of Creativity

At times, people forget the Creator's rule over everything and some do not even believe in His existence. Rather, they think that the universe has come about by chance or they believe that they are in full control of their own lives. This is a very great error.

Premise and provision of the real powerful belief is the thrust in the Limitless Creator, not your small, created, and poor ego. Believe in Creator first, and then believe in His merciful supports that He will send you in any way He wishes.

Think of that scene from Anatolian ancient history: The powerful king Nimrod who claimed he was God and in the end was punished by the Almighty Creator who sent an insect to him, which burrowed through his nose into his brain and killed him.

A poor man who revolts the Almighty Creator and imagines he is a powerful creator will suffer every disease, every sort of loneliness, and he will be deceived in every sort of treachery and will experience disappointment. Man's body was created from an egg and was destined to become earth. Man is a weak, profoundly sensitive, divine work of art in need of compassion.

When everything goes well, people will be very pleased and shout, "Yes, I did it!" When they become exhausted or crushed by betrayals, they will say, "I was wrong. I can't do it." Is it we who create our own activities? We can't even create our own chewing actions. We can only want to chew, and then God Almighty creates thousands of chemical reactions in our brains and bodies to create that action. No one other than Almighty Creator is the creator of anything. To create an event, one would have to be in complete control of "knowledge, will, and power" of all the quantum fields. For this reason, we must rely on the power of the Judge of the Universe.

Of what are you afraid? Not being able to sow the wheat or that the ears of wheat will not ripen? **We will cast the seed, we will reap the harvest, but our strength will never suffice to cause the harvest to be.** Centuries have gone by since man knew the soil, but man has not been able to create a single grain of wheat. Are we afraid of not doing our schoolwork or are we afraid that we will not be able to pass the exam? Our duty is not to pass the exam; it is to accumulate enough knowledge and experience to make us worthy of passing. If we succeed, it will not be we who gain the result. People who say "I did that," should be careful of what they say. If they claim results for which they were not responsible, their beliefs will be thrown out of balance.

c) Negative Generalizations

Anxiety and mistrust might cause negative experiences via generalized attitudes toward the present and the future. Analyze the words, "I can't drive, so I am condemned to failure in driving." If you can't drive a car now, it does not mean that you will not learn to drive in the future or develop another skill. A friend once said, "I cannot be a poet," but if you had asked him when he was a baby, would he have said, "I can't learn to walk." **Whoever is afraid that he cannot do something today, is building the foundation of not being able to do it tomorrow.**

In other words, one could say, "Now I simply can't do it but one day I will be able to do this and other things as well." **Your life will be imprisoned by the belief that you cannot do something. You will not be able to break out of your imaginary boundaries.** You may feel like you are not sufficient now, but if you say "I can't be intelligent," your intelligence will stop developing. If you say to yourself everyday "I am intelligent," you will be amazed at how much your intelligence will develop.

There was a time when every skilled person was unskilled. There were years when every rich man was poor; look at Bill Gates's past. **There was a time when the intelligent person is doubtful of his or her intelligence;** think about Einstein's youth. Those who generalize their current limitations should not hope for success in the future.

Mawlana Rumi said, "If you have loaded your goods on the ship, you need to rely on God. Will you be drowned during the voyage? Will you safely reach the place you wanted to go in good health? If you say, 'I will not chase after a vain hope as others do and go out on a journey,' you will never participate in any kind of commerce."[11]

5. EXPLANATORY EXPERIENCES

By observing examples of experiments of the effects of the power of belief, you may clarify this topic in your minds.

11 *Mawlana* Rumi , Masnavi, vol.3, p. 251

a) Scientific Experiments

I would like to offer some examples of experiments recognized by Professor Robert E. Ornstein from the University of California.[12] In a study funded by the Menninger Foundation, a Yoga master, by means of suggestion, was able to cause a difference in the temperature of each hand of up to 11 degrees. Additionally, some Tibetans can raise their body temperatures high enough to melt ice.

A level of belief exists that can change even the order of natural laws. It is difficult to consciously achieve and replicate things; however, with divine permission, it can be done. The Prophet Jesus' (be peace upon him) animated the figures of birds and raised the dead with the permission and power of the Almighty Creator. These are extreme examples of this permission.

Ornstein, who compared Eastern and Western psychology, to achieve synthesis for data that science does not accept said:[13] "In recent times, although there are some adverse studies, certain studies confirm the idea that esoteric traditions and secret environmental powers affect us."[14]

Are there profoundly effective environmental powers in ordinary life? We need to understand this in the correct way. In addition to natural laws, there are various powers that we can control with our spirits with the permission of God. All these powers ultimately arise from echoing of the name of the one and only, Limitless Creator.

12 These experimental examples were taken from The Psychology of Consciousness by Prof. Robert Ornstein, a synthesis of Western and Eastern psychology. Ornstein's work is a scientific study that invites materialistic thinkers to take the existence of spiritual realities seriously.

13 The philosophy of science is materialistic. These include discoveries that can be repeated in a laboratory environment and develop materialistic explanations. We are speaking of a dimension previously unstudied by science, unseen by the materialistic eye that can only be perceived by means of the conscience, feeling and the eye of the heart because it is subjected to divine providence and cannot be repeated by the will of man in an experimental environment.

14 See, Robert Ornstein. The Psychology of Consciousness (p. 185). asserts that one can completely comprehend the universe based on objective observation alone is like saying one can identify the elephant with one's eyes closed. According to contemporary scientific discoveries, 90% of the universe consists of dark matter. The billions of galaxies, which we see in space through our telescopes, consist of only 10% of the visible universe. Science that, as yet, cannot comprehend dark matter, also cannot assert the nonexistence of a spiritual universe. At most, science can only say that it does not know.

b) Chemical Substances

Let's look at an experiment conducted in the United States using university students. The students were divided into two groups. One group was given a stimulant and was told that it was a sedative. The other group was given a sedative and told that it was a stimulant. The students were then requested to complete surveys about the effects of these drugs.

The result showed that those who took the stimulant, relaxed because they thought it was a sedative. The other group also experienced what they had believed they had taken (stimulant). Please note: the medicines taken were not placebos, they were real medications. Belief defies matter.

c) Healers

You all have heard amazing stories of recovery from illness from people who have gone to healers. I knew such a female healer. People crowded into her garden and among the crowd, certain people were telling other how they were saved from various troubles by the healer's prayers and her breathing on them. In this way, the new arrivals prepared to believe in her through these perhaps made-up stories.

We express our thoughts on this subject in a seminar where we discussed the effect of the power of belief. A teacher once supported our approach by relating an experience he had had in his childhood.

His mother suffered from frequent headaches. One day, his mother gave him some money and said, "My child, go to that person. Have him write out a charm for a headache and give him this money." When the child took the money, he ran to the grocery store and spent it all. When he did not have any money left for the charm, he decided to make up his own charm. He scribbled on a piece of paper and folded it over in a triangular shape. He then wrapped it up in a strip of plastic and gave it to his mother. A few minutes after she used the fake charm, the mother was freed from her headaches.

What can be derived from this story is that instead of believing in healers who have no power at all and, sinning by so doing, if we believe and trust properly in the Ruler and Creator of all things, the Beloved God, we can be freed from our troubles in the true sense.

II. HOW CAN WE USE THE POWER OF BELIEF POSSIBLE?

1. REMOVING OBSTACLES

In order to nourish our beliefs of courage and success, we must first take away the destructive beliefs we maintain of ourselves that hold us back from inside. For this purpose, let's focus on the four sources of belief, which include external suggestion, observation, internal suggestion, and personal experience.

For this purpose you need to (1) determine what your destructive beliefs are, (b) discover their foundations from the variety of sources of belief, (c) shake these foundations by interrogating them from the aspects of logical consistency and specificity-generality, (d)take note and determine the sources of constructive belief that are the exact opposite of your destructive beliefs.

We can acquire all types of negative beliefs. For instance, a number of these words can be spoken within the subconscious: "I am weak, I am lazy, I am a coward, I am stingy, I am cruel, I am heartless, I am unfaithful, I have no support, I lack intelligence, I am unlovable, and I am irresponsible."

Let us say, for instance, you hold the destructive belief that "I am irresponsible." Write this belief at the top of the left page. Separate the left hand page into two columns. Name the first column "determination" and the second column "destruction." Then write the constructive belief, "I am responsible," at the top of the right page.

Work on the left column of the left page. Determine the sources and references of destructive beliefs that are external suggestions, observations, internal suggestions, and personal experiences that made you think that you were irresponsible and write them down there on separate lines.

Go to the right column of the left page. This time, destruct each reference by criticizing it: For instance, say, "That generalization is wrong. That experience was only in the past. This was the word of an unjust person. That was a misunderstanding," and so on. Write these ideas on the corresponding lines.

Go on the right page, read the constructive belief "I am responsible." Think of it and ask, why? Try to find constructive references, observations, suggestions, and experiences in your life that show that you are responsible rather than irresponsible and write them down. Find just opposite; if you can't think of any, think about what you need to do to become responsible and write down these ideas.

Now let us take away the negative beliefs by means of the four sources of belief.

a) External Suggestions

Obstructing negative suggestions: To uncover the obstacles that are negative suggestions, consider what negative suggestions have been made about you. Which ones made you sorry and to which did you react? For instance, my mother says that I am disorganized. My father says that I will never amount to anything. My friends accuse me of being scared. My teacher asserts that I am lazy and my brother accuses me of being jealous and selfish.

Destroying negative suggestions: Destroy these negative suggestions by thinking of times when you demonstrate the opposite. For example, you might say to yourself, "Alright, sometimes I do clean my room. Yesterday I made my bed...I don't have to do what my father says because I have learned to walk and talk. I have reached such and such a grade in school and that means I can do better things. My father does not criticize me all the time. He only does this when he's angry or perhaps he does not really believe what he says.

You can make up new thoughts each month to overcome upsets. You need to search your agenda for information to destroy these negative beliefs.

There are several dimensions to destroying negative suggestions:

1) The first is related to your negative opinions about yourself at a given moment. Never make a generalization of all of your personality or of your whole future solely based on these negative suggestions. If people call you lazy, this may be only with reference to your schoolwork or to your situation at a given moment.

2) You may not have sufficient substantiation about yourself to make a negative judgment. If people call you a coward, you may question your own courage. Understand that these thoughts might come from anger, prejudice, and ignorance at a given moment.

3) An important way to cope with upsets is to take steps to destroy negative judgments about you and develop positive expressions. For example, if others call you disorganized, reject disorganization in your mind and straighten up your belongings.

Responsibility for your life lies in you, not in someone else. Therefore, we should not condemn ourselves to stay within the limits that others impose on us. If you can find people who appreciate and encourage you and not be jealous of you, do not abandon them.

b) Observations

Obstructing negative suggestions: Most people lead their social lives in the psychological environment; for this reason, the decline and rise of society is collective. The collective masses influence each other. For example, most people imitate the same fashions, the same music, and the same values. If the atmosphere is rising, it pulls the majority upwards; however, if it is declining, then things are typically going very badly.

Even if we do not behave like a herd, we will definitely make judgments about ourselves based on our observations. "A business owner went bankrupt in spite of all his experience, I too will go bankrupt. Everybody out in the world is without mercy so I have to be merciless too. Everybody lazes around so that is the reason why I am lazy."

Destroying negative suggestions: We generate limiting beliefs about ourselves by making generalizations from the negative things we see in the media and by our observations on the streets. Being needlessly involved or excessively centered on negative things nourishes our negative beliefs. However, **those who are losing together with the rest are those who copy everybody else. Everybody's life is different.** Therefore, exceptional success demands originality; do not imitate negativity.

Maybe you observe others who are unsuccessful. You might try to compare them with your life and label yourself with the same qualities. Do not do this because you and your life are unique.

The same medicine will not benefit everybody. A negative event may be caused by thousands of historic, psychological, and physiological reasons. The same conditions do not cause the same results in every time and place. The conditions for every situation differ every time. Even the worst conditions can be opportunities for people. The master of life is the Almighty Creator and He is not constrained to any situation in any absolute way. In the end, people will receive the rewards of their intentions and efforts. So, something that seems bad to you can be good for you.

In addition, if you observe unchangeable obstacles in your life, do not be pessimistic. Spending your life struggling with unchangeable conditions is like swimming against the tide; wasting your life for no purpose and suffering for nothing. We must seek to harmonize with such things as we will live and we will die. Our biological gender is something we were born with and we cannot deny the existence of biological and physical limitations. It is true that an 80-year-old cannot run as fast as a 20-year-old can.

Lastly, observe and focus on the good and positive aspects of your life. Note that people who are self-confident and those who have achieved success in life, though they came from a poor village, people who are happy, in spite of every difficulty, people who were educated, who get ahead, and are influential in society are those who founded good families and had good relations with their surroundings.

c) Internal Dialogues

Another way to turn a thought into a belief is to make internal dialogues. One form of this is direct mental impressions and the other form is questions about the grounds of the idea.

The impression is a direct and clear judgment of what you are. The judgments that you repeat over and over about who yourself turn into beliefs and shape your behavior. If a man says to himself every day for forty days, "I am crazy," signs of madness will appear. In this case, write down the beliefs you want to reinforce and include them in the list of impressions that you will call on: "I am industrious, intelligent, responsible, and clean, I love to do good deeds, and I keep my word."

The second and more rapid internal conversation method is to think about the following questions: "What are the three most important pieces of evidence that show I am a charitable person?" With this question, your conscience will try to find at least three good deeds you have done by searching your life. You will reinforce your belief about current activities, your situation, and your behavior. Also, ask yourself, what is the most important indication that I am hard working? From what aspect am I intelligent? What are three signs of my intelligence?

For the internal conversations, you need to be able to change your life; you need to clearly understand the behavior that belief requires. To increase your courage for the belief "I am brave" you need to learn what behavior signifies bravery. Your belief is a magnet that draws values from its own essence. Your belief in your courage invites courageous behavior and your belief in fear invites fear.

Let me mention one limitation I made by my own internal conversations: I cannot draw a good picture. Why? I drew good pictures in elementary school. A teacher who came to our school as a substitute hung my friends' pictures on the wall, but not mine. I thought to myself that she had done this on purpose. In time, I became sore at both the teacher and the drawing and, in the end, I came to not being able to draw a picture.

In cases such as this, set aside time for constructive internal conversations such as questions and plain impressions. Write down your belief inspirations and questions. Read these sentences aloud and position the sounds in your mind. Hear you own voice from near and far in your imagination. Speak your words to nature. **Let them speak from the mountains and from the clouds. Let humankind, flowers, insects, and fish speak.** Let them speak until you say "Yes, this is true. I know. Thank Almighty Creator that this is the way I am." If strong belief and trust come together with your positive intentions, you can build a foundation for above average change. So, get ready to discover the amazing power of intentions in the next chapter.

d) Personal Experiences

Determining negative beliefs: "I didn't pass my exam. I never will pass it. My nose is very big. People don't like my face. I am generally ignored, so I am not a pleasant person."

Overcoming disillusionments: The most important factor in our belief is our own past. The effect of our past on our future is a great one; however, if our past experiences are negative, we must break this effect mechanism. By leaving the past in the past, we can turn a new page. This road is reached by stopping our production of negative beliefs about our future, what is caused by our negative past.

A runner who has fallen down repeatedly might end up believing that he or she will never be able to get up again. **By accustoming ourselves for years to the things we have done, we determine what we are going to do in the years to come.** If we do not change our mentality, we will continue to live this way and will die in the same way we lived. **If we abandon ourself to the flow of a bad past, it will lead to a bad future and a good past to a good future.** If the past was good, it's fine, but if it was bad, we have to break with the past immediately.

We can close the past off right now and start life over on a blank page. We envy some people. "They were lucky. They had a good upbringing. We are the children of a merciless father and an indifferent mother. We were poor. We didn't get an education." **Let us leave the past behind with pardon and repentance and tomorrow morning let us be like a newborn baby and make ourselves a pure future.**

Every one of our negative personal experiences should remain in the past. These experiences left us their lessons and went away. If they had not occurred, we would not have these experiences from which to learn. On the other hand, we have had many positive experiences. We should remember and note down all our positive experiences to leave even to our children. They will give us strength, courage, and confidence and will destroy the negative opinions we have about ourselves.

Little problems lie hidden under many attacks of depression. Humans think of one, small problem in their lives over and over and they become stressed, which frays their nervous systems, and uses up their energy. Drop by drop they make an ocean. If we look at life in such a negative light, we might kill ourselves over a pimple on the end of our nose. Most people are victims of the imaginary pain that they make up for themselves. These people could not live two days if you sent them to the country of the children who laugh and enjoy themselves in the uninhabited, waterless, burning desert lacking entertainment or a home. My advice to people who want to be happy is this: "When a problem comes, live through it one time. If there is something you can do about it, do it, and then just forget about it."

Do you see the tragedies that happen because of ignorance? A man killed his wife because she would not turn on the TV channel he wanted to watch. A villager killed a child because it was chasing a rooster. In the feud that resulted, four people from the two families were killed. A young girl committed suicide just because she had gotten bad grades in one course in school. Don't let us turn problem drops into a problem ocean.

2. DEVELOPING ACTIONS

The most important source of our beliefs is our activities. The activities that we repeat the most often become our habits and our habits shape our values. Our values become our personal beliefs. Our personal beliefs spur us on to the same similar activities in a circle. In this way, a person falls into a behavioral circle.

a) Affirmation of Belief

Which negative beliefs shall we change and which positive beliefs shall we substitute for them? Which activities shall we perform in order to develop the positive beliefs we have determined on? The first step is to be aware of the beliefs on which we are going to work.

Examples; I can/can't succeed, I can/can't work-, I am afraid-I am brave, I can/can't bear it, I can/can't persuade people, I can/can't control my temper, I can/can't stay in this marriage, I am weak/ strong, I am bad/ good, I am cruel/ compassionate, I can/can't get along...

Beliefs are fixed automatically by repetition of activities. If a young man, for instance, gets up very late, watches TV for hours, his mother caters to him, he avoids social activities, and he doesn't study. A young man like that will get used to laziness in a few weeks and in a few months; he will believe he is lazy. When he believes he is lazy, he will be forced to laziness.

If a behavior does not turn into a habit, you can immediately change or stop it. If it has become a habit, you can change it with a few weeks effort. However, if it has become a belief, you will have to work for five or six months insistently. Our bodies, our cells, our souls have memories. Information, which has attained the level of belief, is the most difficult knowledge to eradicate.

Let's look at the beliefs, "I am lazy,-I am hard working." If someone has nurtured the belief that he or she is hard working, he or she will not sit around idle. He or she will be bombarded by continual commands telling him or her: you work hard; you can't be idle, you should be sorry for every idle second that you spend; you should hate useless and unneeded sleep, get up and work, read, write, explain, and listen to something. Those who are convinced of their laziness hear these commands: "Don't tire yourself out, you can't save the world, it is stupid to serve the nation, there is nothing more pleasant than sleep, forget selfish people, enjoy yourself."

To destroy their belief in laziness or to develop their belief in industriousness they must determine the activities that will potentially facilitate it and then they must work to apply these things by repeating these activities until they become habits.

b) Affirmation of Actions

We can find a series of activities to nurture every belief we want to develop. These activities may appear different according to the country, city, culture, and socio-economic environment in which we live. We shall examine one by one the beliefs given in the section above and we will determine potential activities that will nurture each belief.

Let's look at the example "I can't get along with my spouse:" My thinking that I can't get on with him or her may be based on my past mistakes. We fought, we argued, we blamed each other, and now this belief, having developed, pushes me to continual contentiousness. Very well, what do I have to do to get along with him or her?

I have to be generous toward my spouse (when I get up in the morning, when I go to the kitchen, when I come home, when I am talking on the telephone). I have to ask how he or she is feeling (while talking on the phone, when we get together in the evening, while eating together). I must thank her (when she brings me water, when I am called to dinner, when the garbage is taken out). I must not react immediately to her anger (to my coming home late, to my not taking the garbage out, to my leaving socks in the hall, to my not putting salt in the meal, when she gets angry for my having made her wait).

What are you going to do and when, where and in between what other activities? It is not easy to answer these questions.

While, you may have determined your goal, you may not know what activities will nurture your belief to achieve this goal. For instance, which behaviors should be repeated for those who want to strengthen their courage: 1) ask those who know, 2) read the relevant books, 3) and the most important is to be a careful and acute observer.

Since you are reading this book, you are already doing the first two. Concerning the third, you need to pay attention to the people in your surroundings. In particular, you ought to be mindful of the people who serve your goals, as well as those who act as your models. Why are they that way? What do they wear, how do they walk, how do they look and, possibly, how do they feel?

c) Carrying on Activities

You have already written your activities down and you know what activities you need to repeat to develop your reinforcing beliefs.

Good morning, have a nice day! You jumped out of bed, rejoicing that another wonderful new day had dawned and you go out onto the balcony, you nourish you lungs deeply with the life of the air. You sent forth a smile to everything that envelops you and serves you: the air, the sky, your environment. You prepare to experience uninterrupted beautiful adventures all today. The beauty of today will be the result of your decisiveness. Until you are use to your new lifestyle, you will carry your agenda with you like a compass.

In the morning, you have a routine; you wash your hands and face, straighten up your room and belongings, iron your clothes, make breakfast, go out of the house. Today, you will do all these things with a different mind and according to a new belief system.

The adventure begins. Before you start the important business of the day, you open your agenda and determine what you are going to do relate to your new beliefs. What can be done that is appropriate to today's surroundings and conditions?

How are you going to treat yourself? If you look at your clothes and your body, what will your reaction to your face be? What are you going to say to the people you meet? What activities are you going to choose especially for today for the purpose of development?

Nothing can persuade people more than the personal experience of success. Your will power will grow stronger when you see that you can keep your word and carry out the decisions you have made in a timely manner. Passing your exams nourishes the belief that you will pass future exams.

Do you want to be a writer? Write one sentence today and write a paragraph tomorrow and the next day. Increase the amount you write every week. Be aware of what you can do from the minute you begin up to each level you reach. In a short time, you will see that you have developed your belief that "I can write." Some people have developed into writers by continually writing letters to their friends.

At the base of problems, such as incompetence, inability, helplessness, insufficiency, and depression, there is one single error: laziness, not doing one's duty, neglect of responsibility. You need to look for the opportunity to take action. In physical, verbal, intellectual, individual, or social forms, every kind of action should be directed toward education, culture, tourism, religion blessing, intelligence, excitement, happiness, and success.

3. MENTAL EFFORTS

Please note that what you think has the potential to turn you into what you live. People force into being what they think is going to happen. We direct whatever we repeat in our minds to knowledge, to being, to speculation, to belief; and our belief governs our behaviors. So, let us use this progression in our own behalf.

a) Successful Models

Thomas J. Stanly researched the richest 1,300 people who make up 1% of the population of the USA and wrote about common characteristics of these people in his book *The Billionaire Mind*. In the book, it appeared that these elite were not super geniuses but were stable in their family and social relations and chose well-adjusted life styles.[15] Therefore, we see that the road to prosperity passes, not through cleverness, but through stability, harmony, work and, most importantly, dedication to our beliefs.

What is the purpose of the lifestyle that we have shaped for ourselves in the world? Have you decided to serve religion, politics, art, science, or commerce? Read the life stories of the people who were leaders in the fields you have chosen and learn what they did. See how and in what they succeeded. Try to see them, feel them, and experience them. Just knowing that they were there will encourage you and inspire you to action.

If you have no model of success, you have no example to inspire you. The real loneliness on the road to success is not finding a successful model. When you see the success of your models, it will nourish your belief in your own success. People who belittle success stories are forced to remain little. For example, thinking of Einstein motivates an aspiring scientist; thinking about the lives of the Prophet Muhammad (peace on him) for a Muslim, Jesus (peace on him) for a Christian and Moses (peace on him), for a Jew, is inspirational. There is a model, a guide, a pathfinder for every profession, art, business, philosophy, and these pathfinders are innovators.

Have you decided your rank and place in life? Have you read the rank and place of the lives of the innovators? If so, go from time to time into your imagination and let these innovators move you. In this way, let your soul inspire your body to action.

15 Radikal Newspaper, Feb. 8, 2000

b) Imaginary Speculations

Watching the motion of a ship from the shore resembles the impression we get of the same from the movie screen in our minds. Thanks to this, we can use images of the things we have not experienced to produce realistic effects. For example, if we bring to life what we want with all of the details, we can reinforce our ability to do something. We may call this rehearsing the ideal plan in our imaginations.

If you have a weak imagination and mental invention, you can begin by speculative thinking. For example, you can wander like a butterfly from flower to flower and like a bee, from valley to valley. Become a tree in your imagination. Let the leaves dance in the wind and listen to the chirping of the birds amongst the branches. Be a drop of rain falling to earth or a river flowing to the sea. When you sink deeply about these images, you will perceive how inspiring they are from different aspects of the universe.

What sort of person do you want to be? What do you want to feel? Where and how do you want to behave? Who do you want to affect? What sort of adventures do you want to experience? Let your wishes be sufficiently reasonable and achievable. In addition, you need to read a lot, observe, and know, very well, that you want to make these wishes happen. A child pilot coming out of a cave is not imaginable.

Sit still or walk around, experience your "model life" to which you aspire by simulating it in your mind. Observe the colors, the dimensions, the things around you. See what you say to who, what you hear from who, what you feel, how you act and with what speed. What sort of people are your friends? Where do they go? What do they wear? Whom do they talk with? Where and how do they work?

As your film grows clearer, its effect will increase and will draw you closer to reality. **Your dreams are like architectural plans you have drawn of what you will see in the future.**

I am not referring to dreams directed by uncontrolled, unconnected random associations. I am talking about mental stimulation and you will determine how long it lasts without swerving from your target. **An un-**

controlled and vague aspiration is the mortal enemy of the mind. It blinds thought and analytical powers. Nevertheless, when you direct your dream in a conscious way, your abilities find a foundation. The dream that Einstein called "more important than science" is the controlled, intentional, clear, and conscious dream.

c) Internal Voices

Another way to convert an idea to a belief is to repeat it as a voice in your mind over a long period of time. If a human tells himself 100 times, "I am crazy," he or she will truly develop the symptoms of insanity. The characteristic that makes us believe in the suggestion is not the suggestion itself, rather the things we do with the suggestion.

It is not enough for us to believe in an idea; for example, that we are attractive, for us to be attractive but it is enough to keep us from holding back the attractiveness we have developed. Believing in the suggestion that we are brave will not give us more bravery; rather it will prevent us from repressing the bravery we already have. The purpose of internal voices and suggestions is to open the way for our development in this direction and to remove obstacles, brakes, and pitfalls from our paths.

If humans believe they is brave, they will line up activities one after the other that will develop their courage. In addition, if they believe they are coward, they will be unable to avoid actions that will further develop their cowardice.

Our suggestion is this: Write memorable sentences of no more than 4 to 8 words that express your relation to your goals. Settle the sounds in your mind by reading these sentences aloud then listen to these sounds in your mind. Say them in high and low tones with various positive feelings. Then listen to your own voice from near and from far. Let them speak to you. Let them speak from the mountains. Let them speak from the clouds. Imagine that the flower, insects, and fish speak. Imagine that they say to you, "Yes, I know I am certain I am this way. I thank God, I am this way."

CHAPTER TWO:

THE POWER OF INTENTION

I. WHY WE NEED THE POWER OF INTENTION?

INTRODUCTION

Now it is time to discover the power of intentions, the secret of an elixir that very few people are aware. Go back to your car. Your intention is "How to get somewhere in your automobile." Are you heading for the desert or for a city at the top of a mountain? The cities you will visit will be listed according to the criterion of your purpose.

Intention is the purpose, the rationale depending on the goal hidden behind behavior, the thing you actually did is the intention with which you did it.

The Master of Fate gives rewards not according to the goodness of your work but according to the nobility of your intentions. This is the real secret! The secret of why two entrepreneurs doing the same thing can obtain different results is concealed in their intentions. Readers will realize different results, even from this book, according to their intentions.

Are you aware of the purpose hidden in your heart? Why do you send somebody a present? Is it because you love them? What do you love about them? Is it because you expect something in return? What reward do you expect? The most import point is how sincere are you in the intention you chose. Is your intention good or bad from a divine moral point of view? Is it little or big? Is it from the heart or is it false? Your destiny will be shaped according to the answers to these types of questions.

When you finish this section, you need to look at the envied rise or the amazing fall of certain persons. You will be able to see the deep meaning of events with this understanding.

Behind every effort are (1) the whole of the goals and (2) the package of intentions. The whole of goals explains how we aim to achieve what is visible and the package of intentions tells us with what level of sincerity we want to reach these goals.

The Master of Destiny gives every person who labors a definite opportunity to get ahead; He brings everyone's affairs to an end according to their intentions. In the last analysis, y**our results are shaped, not according to "the perfection of your actions" but according to "the sincerity of your intentions."**

1. INTENTION AND PROFUNDITY

Our intentions are the secret purposes concealed in the depths of our hearts. We may not be able to discern the intentions that are hidden in the depths of our consciousness and that concern our every behavior. A lack of awareness of an intention does not free us from the effect of that intention. So, let us discover the intention first:

a) The Nature of Intention

The first step in feeling the magnificent power of intentions (bases) is the ability to discover the intention. Our intention is the result that is most closely connected with our personality, which we hope to obtain by our actions; this is our objective. It is what reveals why we do something, which is the reason for a hidden feeling. If we do not reveal it, it cannot be easily understood, but we can feel it through the language of our bodies. Together, with the Almighty Creator, we can listen to the essence of our hearts.

Let's learn the three golden words: **'What, how, why?"** What do you want? How are you going to get it? Why do you want it?

The "what" word asks us about our goals; to be a poet or an artist; these are all goals. The "how" word asks about our activities; what strategies are we going to use to reach our goals? The word "why" asks about the emotional and spiritual meaning of a goal: Why do you wipe away your brother's tears?

If you have an answer to the why of your action, then you have an intention to that action. In other words, your heart is really alive; you take responsibility and deserve good or bad results for your action.

With the same unique action, you may have good or bad intentions and your intentions will change the meaning and result of your actions. For example, you can feed the birds with the intention of helping them or with the intention of dropping them to your traps. In each case, the results are different.

How great your intention is, that is how great your results will be. If you have a brilliant answer to the question "why" then you may expect to have a brilliant result from your efforts.

You can feel hidden intentions of any action, even of the plants in your environment. A seed is not sown in the soil without intention. At the heart of every flowering seed sprinkled in the spring garden, there lay hidden the wish to father another flower. In fact, the heart that has no intent is a sealed one.

Not having intentions means stopping the heart. If your heart is not functioning, the results of your efforts cannot achieve even the beauty of the desert. If spirituality of your intentions spreads out of your heart, the four seasons will live every day in the lush valleys of your personal world.

Those who do not invest in their hearts with sincere intention cannot intensify their lives.

Our minds, when focused on experimental science, relate to the questions of "what and how" but cannot develop the capacity to find an answer to the question "why." The secular philosophy of science sees the universe as the result of coincidence and does not believe that the universe has a heart. Those who content themselves in looking at life and the universe through the window of science cannot become acquainted with the spirituality of the universe.

Thousands of students lose hundreds of chances to attend university. Many people pass their lives drably and ineffectively in spite of their capabilities and on account of their lack of intention. They can catch many opportunities if they deeply understand the effect of sincere intentions in their future.

For example, think of a pregnant woman called Hanna who intended and prayed to give her unborn child to God's service. See how her sincere intentions affected all humanity. As a result of the acceptance of her sincere prayer, she became the mother of Mary, who was the mother of the Prophet Jesus (PBUH). A word, accompanied by a few tears from the eyes of a lone woman when she was all alone fundamentally affected the history of the world.[16]

Everything we do that is not connected to our intentions will be stolen by intentions wandering here and there: A person who does not belong to himself will fall into someone else's hands. One part of a day that you spend without intention, you allow another part to be seized by idle talkers, a part by scroungers, and a part by lottery ticket salesmen.

Not everything done has a conscious intention; rather it might have a minimal purpose. Why does a shopkeeper open his shop early? This may depend on many purposes at the same time: to earn more money, to increase business, to support more people, to raise the economic level of his family to get more money to feed more poor people.

16 Qur'an: 3; 35

Very well, with what emotional purposes (with what intentions) does he want these and similar goals? Why does he want more prosperity for his family? Why does he want to give more help to the needy? What does he hope to obtain by all these things?

Humans work and the Creator elevates them in respect to their intentions. There are particular and different roads to achieve success in every field, every business, and every capacity of life. Concepts that sustain one sector may not aid another sector. Knowing how to drive does not help you become an eloquent speaker. Being a good businessman does not help you become a good artist. It is the opposite in the case of intention. A good intention has a good effect on all aspects of life. The light of a good intention illuminates all the fields of ability.

What will the merchant in our example do with a lot of money and greater business space? Will he increase his reputation, does he hope for respect from people, does he do this to achieve satisfaction by realizing himself. Or does he do it with the purpose of a divine intention or does he nourish dreams of satisfaction with lots of money? Good or bad, great or small, countless intentions may emerge according to the person's place in life.

b) The Life of Intention

True-life essence is the life essence that comes from the spiritual body that includes a spiritual heart and soul. If the life essence of the heart leaves the body, the life belonging to the flesh has no value. The life essence of the soul influences behavior by means of intentions. It is intention that animates behavior and it is sincerity that animates intention. If sincerity dies, there is no intention and, if there is no intention, behavior becomes meaningless. Why did you smile at him? Why did you give her that present? Why are you educating that child? Why are you going to school? If you do not have an intention, what you do is meaningless. If your intention is not sincere, its value will not endure.

Action without intention is lifeless, somewhat like dough waiting to be prepared. Behavior without intention or purpose is a mechanical behavior, like the rolling of a stone. No specific meaning or value comes from its essence.

Those people on the street who lack intention are like schools of fish or, more correctly, they are people who have never lived intensely. They appear to be alive but their essence is closer to lifelessness. They merely conform to their surroundings, unconsciously, and blow here and there like the dust is blown by the wind. Because they do not think about why they do what they do, they do not know it. They only do what everybody else does and that is it. Modern capitalism produces plenty of robot humans and works to use them as consumer and filler material.

The life essence of the soul affects activities by spreading the means of sincere intentions like the odor of flowers. The true-life essence is not the cellular life; it is the life that cannot be made in a laboratory. The true-life essence is not from the material of the body, but is the meaning of the soul and shines in the behavior of our body. Vital, and thus very effective behavior, is behavior that depends on sincere intentions and is felt with genuine belief. A human being gains secret powers to the degree with which he or she believes with a sincere belief.[17]

Ignorance is a weakness in the first degree and slyness is a weakness in the second degree. The ignorant will always remain weak and the sly will fail in the end. If people are well intentioned, they reach the end victoriously even if they sometimes appear to fail.

Let us look at life as a race in stages that leads to a happy eternity. The runner who collapses immediately is the one without knowledge. Those who know lead the race may be those who know but later on lost because they only were able to apply their knowledge. On a higher level you will see even those who applied their knowledge were eliminated. However, only those who experience their knowledge "with purity and with sincerity" can pass on from this stage. These individuals are at the peak, but the danger of losing their genuine natures lies in wait for them.

17 This concept is viable for good ways as well as bad. Evil spiritual powers coming from his or her belief may be reflected from a person who has sincerely dedicated himself to the devil. Spiritual beings may be created from a type of angels from the spirits of good people. The spiritual beings of evil devils may be created from the spirits of evil people.

The formula for success that we will derive from this is the following: **Knowledge, action relying on knowledge, action relying on good intentions/purposes, and intention must be very sincere and sincerity must be carefully protected.**

Purity is spirit; it gives life to the intention. Intention is spirit; it gives life to action. The living action spreads its effect by deeply affecting the world as spirit.

Action without intention is worthless and intention without sincerity is without spirit. Our results depend not on our false intentions but on our true intentions. It is not what we say to other people; we can even conceal it from our own mortal natures. Only our pure conscience can experience it. Our morality keeps our conscience pure; therefore, we can only approach purity by pursuing the road of "high morality."

If intention is not sincere, it reduces the effectiveness of the intention of our efforts. The intention of a hypocrite is not an intention; it inevitably retreats backwards and actually causes the opposite effect. Let us ask ourselves these questions: "Am I deceiving myself? Do I really want this result? Am I being hypocritical? Do I hope to deceive by doing this?"

People can be hypocritical toward others; however, the worst thing is when we are hypocritical toward ourselves. It is easy to be honest with others; however, to be honest with ourselves demands ability. *Mawlana* Rumi advises that those seeking a goal do so in this way: "**Make little use of trickery. This is the business of good fortune and of fate. Wealthy Almighty Creator guides the trickster little.**"[18]

Whatever is within us will always overflow to the outside. "We think" our intentions are what we surmise them to be but sometime they are not. The Master of Destiny knows the truth that we have hidden even from ourselves. While we are praying for something from the depths of our spirits, He looks, not at what we are saying, but at what we are secretly whispering to ourselves.

---

18 *Mawlana* Rumi , Masnavi, vol.5, p.42

c) The Spiritual Goal

The goal of the hungry man is to feed himself, but how can he do it? The wish of a lonely person is to find a partner; however, how and whom will he or she find? Our need may be one but there may be thousands of ways to satisfy it. Our intention brings out our goals from our deepest being and searches all of the possibilities of life to satisfy itself. Our mind may cause us to target road A but destiny may cause us to attain the goal to which our intentions aspire through door B.

The goal of our heart is not the goal of our mind, rather is the intention of our goal. Seyfi's goal of studying at the university was to convince everyone that he was an exceptional child. He passed the university entrance exam. His heart was entirely involved with getting high grades and showing off and his family heard about it. If his family ignored Seyfi's success, Seyfi would continue for a long time from one success to another. Nevertheless, because his intention was a negative one, after the allotted time, destiny said "this far and no farther" and blocked Seyfi's progress. Even if his family had applauded Seyfi, Seyfi's success would still have ended because his intention would have been realized. He had no other spiritual goal left.

On the other hand, Leyla's intention was to attend university to gain capacities that could spread love. She tried hard but she did not pass her exam. Her intention to control her life continued and she sought ways to realize her spiritual goal even outside of the university. She learned the art of marbling paper, designed works encoding love, and succeeded in making them into books and selling them over the internet.

There are limits to material goals in this life and, sometimes, some of these roads close. If somebody has occupied one position, all other candidates will have to wait their turn. Not all students can enter the university. There is a limit to the quota in every field. Not everyone can do the same job, even if he or she has the ability to do it. Life is a plan. However, there is no such limit to intention. Everybody can achieve the same spiritual goal, the same intention. For instance, everybody can take his or her place in history as a symbol of love or hate.

How can this happen? By any way, by the most unexpected ways, perhaps by ways that were considered impossible...Frozen water can breaks iron to pieces. Some people, once being poor, have become rich. Some commanders can realize victory even though they lack weapons. If you have a noble intention, reveal it. Hear its cry, make Limitless Mercy who is now watching over you hear it now.

The goal that makes the real revolution in the life of a man is not an intellectual goal but a spiritual goal. The intellectual goal considers a time years from now. It is inclined to overlook what needs to be done now. The spiritual goal, however, fills every second. It seeks means to realize itself in every environment. The result that would be achieved in twenty years by those who do not have a spiritual goal is attained in a few years by those who do have a spiritual goal. Your spiritual goals are your intentions, your very deep purposes.

Your mind is continually scanning through millions of pieces of information to find a solution to your purpose. It searches through the contents that come from your five senses, revelations that come from angels, telepathic messages from human beings, associations in your brain, your dreams, your illusions, and even the temptation of Satan.

You need to have heard of the USA's Echelon monitoring system, which is used throughout the world. According to reports, Echelon is able to listen to all telephones and is capable of searching through all telex, fax, and internet communications. The system records keywords into the Echelon word list and computers put these words in order to form billions of messages. Supposedly, this amazing technology consists of ten centers and hundreds of satellites that revolve around the planet. This seems frightening to people, whereas, the search of our deeper mind makes is much more wonderful.

The purposes for Elias Howe's discovery of the second needle in the sewing machine came in a dream or of Archimedes finding the power of water to raise things while he was taking a bath were both spiritual goals. They wanted something for another intention and wanted it very sincerely. Knowledge is like molecules of air flying around in front of you. **If you do**

not listen with or by means of your spirit, the pieces of information that permeate the spiritual world will not flow into your mind.

If your heart is not concerned with information that is not related to your intention, you will lose the discoveries that enlarge the meaning of your life. Do not be afraid to have great intentions. The Creator does not care about your ancestors, your intelligence, or your wealth when He gives rewards to you. Indeed, He created them all Himself. He looks at the profundity of your heart and the humility of your intentions. Here is the secret of why people from among the poor, shepherds, people lacking friends or relatives, and marginalized people have profoundly influenced history.

Your heart goes carefully over all of the information it has obtained to find a solution for your intention. If it finds data to support your intentions, it brings it to your attention, and observes your reaction to it. If you do not pay attention to it, it discards that data that could have been the key to a discovery. If you do pay attention, it holds on to it. If you pay a lot of attention to it, it retains very strongly. It remembers it continually. It uses it continually and produces various connotations of it.

This is the reason why a cancer patient can suddenly overhear somebody mentioning cancer in a crowd. This is why, when you are looking at hundreds of books, you will suddenly be guided to a particular one on the shelves. Once, when I was working hard at my computer, I did not hear the neighbors around me. Suddenly I heard the phrase "the evil eye." When I turned around and asked "Did you say the evil eye?" they laughed heartily. I heard this word because a section of my book was related to the evil eye and I wanted to obtain every piece of information on the topic that I could.

2. RESULTS OF INTENTION

When you link your activities to high intentions, you will experience strong support. **The more sincere your intention is, the greater your power to defy obstacles will be.** Following are the probable results of intentions:

a) Intentions Elevate Values

The value of your activities is as great as the intentions that lay behind them. "Deeds are in accord with intentions. People are rewarded for their intentions."[19]

You see the inequities of life: One person worships and suffers great losses, another neglects his or her worship and is credited with piety and you wonder; "Where is justice?" If you could add in the intention that lay behind those activities, you would see that it balances most of the inequities.

Every action is a seed. You ought to search for its genetic plan not in the brilliance of its appearance but in the intention in its essence. Therefore you need to not be deceived by appearances.

To clarify what I mean, think on the following phrases: A great tree grows out of a tiny fig seed, but only a handful of greenery sprouts from a large potato. You will see real results come out of, not the material body, but the genetic plan deep inside.

Another example: The tears of a tiny ant reach to the God Almighty and are enough to send clouds to a waterless valley. But the entire Pharaoh's might was not able to stand in the way of a little baby who was Moses, (PBUH) and who was destined to overthrow his throne. As you see, the powerless but sincere ant can achieve bigger results than the arrogant Pharaoh.

How great will the results of our activities be? They will be as much as our intentions, as much as our purposes, as much as our sincerity, as much as what we want to do, as much as our spirit, as much as we can desire. Don't you want as much as the whole universe?

Suppose you wanted to protect orphan children, but you have the means to protect only two children. While you are caring for these two orphan children, you can shape your intention in two ways: "I truly want to protect these two children," and "I want to protect all the orphan children." You will receive the result of the first intention. Nobody

19 Prophet Mohammad (PBUH), Al-Bukhari, İman:41; Muslim, İmare: 155

but you knows what you have done and only the two orphan children benefit from your actions. When you conceive your intention in the second way, you will affect your spirit, your feelings, and your wishes in a different way. You will be an example to people in your circle and hundreds of people may be influenced by you and will want to help orphan children.

The limits of your intention draw the boundaries of the results to which you are the means. **If you start out with universal intentions, you will be surrounded with universal support.** A person who works for the good of humanity rises to the level of a representative of humanity.

Even under the limited conditions of this world, greater intentions produce greater results. In the next world, people will receive the exact rewards of their intentions. This is a magnificent possibility, a wonderful potential. One, who has only helped one orphan, if his or her intention was to help all orphans, is accepted as having helped all orphans. Look at these words again: **"Your deeds are according to your intentions. A person is only rewarded for his or her intentions."**[20]

If you intend to do a good deed, make all of humanity your goal. What you have done will be passed from hand to hand and from tongue to tongue.

One evening, when he was eating his dinner, a man became obsessed by the wretchedness of the hungry children in Africa. At last, he could no longer eat and he burst into sobs. He thought of those children as his own children. He sighed with great sincerity, "If I could only feed those children." If he had done something within his possibilities, he would have gained a great treasure. Indeed, this prayer later materialized in the form of a foundation dedicated to building water wells, agricultural projects, and educational activities.

What he did, what passed through his heart, is inscribed in his life's book. **The hungry children's helplessness opened the doors of heaven for some people.** Some people, considering their great successes, will be shocked when they see the records of their activities and will cry,

20 Prophet Mohammad (PBUH), Al-Bukhari, İman:41; Muslim, İmare: 155

"Where are the good deeds I have done?" Their arrogant and self-serving expectations have erased those good deeds. Their malicious criticisms of others have exhausted their capital. They are bankrupt and do not know it.

Someone else may have cultivated good intentions through repentance for her mistakes. She may have struggled many times with the evil into which her soul fell. In the end, when she expected Hell to burst out from among the pages of the book of her deeds, Heaven, which encircles the skies, emerged for her. Perhaps she did little that was good but she did it with great sincerity. In addition, she succeeded in avoiding slander, which wipes out goodness.

The sublimity of the role you will play is connected to the greatness of the ideals to which you will dedicate yourself. Those who consider only their relatives are as great as their relatives. Those who consider humanity are as great as humanity.

b) Intentions Effect the Results

Your intentions change the meanings, perceptions, and outcomes of what you do. You receive bad outcomes when your intentions are bad and good outcomes when your intentions are good. Think about the following examples:

A person desires praise, so he or she talks about his or her accomplishments. Others observe his arrogance from his attitude and they admonish him. Another person speaks about his accomplishments with the intention of being a good example for the youth; he or she gains the love and respect of his audience.

A person who drops a bottle of water while trying to serve his spouse will be treated kindly. If the same person does drop the bottle with the intention of punishing his or her spouse, he or she will gain hate and anger.

A person goes to college to become a beneficial member of her society and her degree will help her do good things. Another person goes to college to show the greatness of his race. If he becomes the leader of a country, he will take his nation to war.[21]

We need to learn lessons from these people who earn evil from good deeds because of their intentions. Bad intentions will produce evil from good deeds, treachery from helpfulness, and hatred from respect.

On the other hand, the intensity of the intention multiplies the results of the work. Just as millions of different plants can come out of the same soil, hundreds of different results can emerge from the same action.

Possible intentions when planting a tree: Trees can be used for birds' nests; food for animals who eat their leaves; to cool animals in the shade, listening to the rustling of the branches; prevent erosion; stoke boiling water; contribute to preventing climate change; produce relaxing greenery and oxygen; be a souvenir for me; cause new trees to sprout; or add value to a rural piece of property.

Omission: When you enlarge the purposes of your actions, your heart shakes with excitement; it draws your body to that plot of ground and plants that tree.

Do you want to achieve great results from brushing your teeth? Do you want to turn those seconds into worship by thinking how you are imitating the Prophet Mohammad (PBUH) and nourishing the love of your spouse by getting rid of your mouth odor? An ordinary activity but with so many results.

We see that the Limitless Power, which created various plants using the same materials from a handful of earth, has exalted thousands of various purposes to the one piece of soil He created. We too can obtain thousands of different results from a single action by imitating what He has done in the universe.

21 Please note that our intentions affect and change the outcome of our efforts in this world as well as in the hereafter.

c) Intentions Determine Advancement

Some people advance quickly and then stop where they are until the end of their lives. The place where they stop in their journey to success is the place where their purpose gives out. **A human cannot succeed in an endeavor higher than that of the life intention that he has chosen.**

For example, a salesperson might work only to get by. For that reason, he does not advance from being a shop salesperson for ten years. However, my friend used to sell trousers in the streets. Every time he sold a pair of trousers, he thought about saving up the necessary amount to become the owner of a shop of his own in the future. Fifteen years later, he is the owner of a big store.

An athlete, who plans to run only a hundred meters, cannot run in a marathon. We have to find such a great intentions for our lives that we can spend all our lives pursuing these efforts. It must be so sublime that the moment we have achieved our goals we will have nothing left to do in the world; this is the moment when we are satisfied to leave this world.

Very few university students–in our country- plan what and how they are going to do when they graduate and enter the world of work. However, doing so will only elevate their view of the world.

If we start out without knowing where and why we are going somewhere, we will wander aimlessly through the streets. **Purposeless action is like a rootless tree. It will stay a bare trunk in spite of what we do.** The reason so many romances end so quickly is that they do not have a sound purpose underling them.

In 1987, I was passing through one of the streets on my way to the school bus. The street recalled the images of Texas in old American movies and was filled with coffee houses. Everybody drank tea and watched old Turkish movies in these packed coffeehouses. On some of the streets, people were playing the lottery. I asked why they were waiting around and was told that they were looking for work. When employers came, they would choose people and the ones who were chosen for that day's labor would be among the lucky few. Soon, a little truck pulled up.

A husky man gestured, saying, "You and you" and the ones who were chosen climbed into the truck. Some of them would grab on to the tailgate of the truck and say, "Mister, let me come too."

They would find work on an average of once every ten days. On the other days, they wasted their time sitting around. Some of the men had loveable wives and children waiting for them in their homes on the mountain. How can a man expect to overcome his problems without investing in his own capacities, without dedicating himself to developing his knowledge and experience?

These men stood around not knowing what they could do to have a better life. I tried to show some the way, yet they did not even listen to me. **You are not permitted to help someone who does not want to be helped.**

Those who live without purpose are as valueless as stones just used for filling, in this world that is surrounded with wisdom. Even a bee earns value by working to serve the purpose of the Almighty Creator for the nourishment of humanity. If you want respect in the universe, you need to have a purpose for living. If you want a place in the council of the universe, hold on to the love, which is in the language of nature. Then hold fast to a sharing lifestyle and help others.

Will people reject you if you live according to high intentions? Yes, but only those who do not have purpose in their hearts. These worthless people love to ridicule. However, the day will come when the brilliance of your life will blind them and they won't even know to say, "Just think, we had a genius in our midst." They will say, "Those were simple things, even we knew them."

3. ANALYSIS OF INTENTION

Is our intention sound, does it contain intentions that are consistent, is it inclusive, can we make changes if we need to?

a) Soundness

A sound intention answers the question "why." It is separate from an action and goal**. The action** means going to the speed-reading course. **The goal** means learning to read quickly. Nevertheless, the **intention** is to collect, quickly, "the knowledge to be used in doing good deeds."

Some students only think about passing their exams when they are studying their lessons. They are focused, not on the intention, but on the goal. However, **studying one's lessons is laying a foundation for success in life.**

When studying can be connected to such a great intention, why do we associate all efforts on passing an exam in two months? Is an exam worth this much trouble? On the other hand, if you tell your mind that this is for the intention of success in life, your mind will cause you to work without tiring and with pleasure. **If you say the same thing every day to your mind, it will do the same thing for you every day.**

The words of my mathematics teacher, Mr. Cuma, still ring in my ears, "Children, don't study to get good grades, study to learn." If you study just for the exam, perhaps you will pass, but you will gain nothing but sweat. If you study to learn and to use that knowledge, you will both pass the exam and be able to use that knowledge in hundreds of various fields.

b) Harmony

Contradictory intentions make efforts ineffective. The Almighty created our universe with a harmony between various intentions. Therefore, you need to make harmony between your intentions and the intentions of others that mutually interact with yours.

Harmony/disagreement of intentions with that of others: My heart wants to spread love with this book. If I succeed in this purpose, people who want to spread hate will not read this book. In addition, if they want to they may even hinder it being read. If someone wants to spread love and he or she needs a book to do this, he or she will be offered either this or another.

Harmony/conflict between the purposes/activities of others: A young man loves his freedom (purpose) and he needs a job (goal). He tries to find a job in which he will feel free (action), to be a public official. All his efforts go in vain because the drudgery, the limits imposed on one's life by a job as a public official conflict with his lifestyle purpose. He changes his mind and, two years later, he opens his own shop.

Purpose/action harmony/conflict with oneself: A young woman wanted a pure marriage with the young man whom she loved. However, the young man secretly committed serious crimes in the past and would commit bigger ones in the future. The Almighty knows his bad past and probable bad future. To protect the good intentioned woman, the Almighty hindered the marriage since she did not deserve to become the spouse of that good looking but bad intentioned man.

On the other hand, for the same case, interference from destiny may be observed another way: The Almighty, instead of hindering the marriage directly, rather directs the woman to a correct decision by making her know the real hidden dangerous identity of that young man. How? Maybe she was warned in a dream. Perhaps a Khidr[22] like guide appeared to her in the guise of an old man and advised her.

However, she would not listen to warnings. She closed her mind. She abandoned her sincere spirit. She grew angry and changed her good intentions. She said, "I am going to marry, even if I die for it, even if he is a murderer." She withdrew into her ivory tower. Since she insistently lost her sincere intentions, this time, she deserved the dangerous marriage. Then, the Almighty lifted the obstacles and they married Two years later, she understood that she had run off to marry a killer and it was too late to protect her life.

22 Hidr, in Islamic belief, is a hidden personage who journeyed with the Prophet Moses (PBUH), has been informed of the secret causes of events, has been given secret responsibilities, and is believed to be still alive.

We are weak humans. **We walk with our eyes closed toward a future we cannot see.** We do not know whether the soil on which we walk is a trap or a hole. We do not know whether the passenger who is getting into our taxi will hold a weapon to our heads. Will our child, whom we raise, destroy our home? We don't know. How can we protect ourselves? With good purpose, we can.

The rope that we take in our hand may be a snake; however, it does not matter. **If our intentions are completely pure and we hold firm to our sincerity and our 'Noble Morality" we will be protected in the end.** How? Sometimes, it can be by failing the exam, sometimes by suffering depression, sometimes by being betrayed, sometimes by rejoicing and being appreciated.

c) Honesty

We need to know our true intentions very well. But, let us not confuse our purposes with our wishes.

I asked some students in a seminar, "Who wants to be rich?" Nobody raised his or her hand. How can you not want to get rich? The Owner of the Universe is rich and He wants to show grace to humans. Would living an ordinary life make you any stronger?

I changed my question. "Who wants to be rich to help the needy, the helpless, and the friendless?" Now, everybody raised their hands. I understood that they identified wealth with what rich people who misused it did. They thought, "It would be better for me to remain poor than to act in degrading ways like to be rich and stingy, safeguard my property, imagine myself superior to ordinary people by thrusting my riches." Their intentions were correct but they formed these intentions incorrectly. Wealth does not force a man to be stingy. Stinginess is a personal choice. Neither is wealth happiness. We often confuse means with ends.

d) Inclusiveness

Our intentions ought to include our entire future. What we want tomorrow may not be what we want the next day. The goal may change, but the purpose must remain the same. When we evaluate our activities, we must pay attention to the whole of life, **because, whoever who laughs last, laughs best. Real success is the success that ends in success. A successful life, if it has ended in suicide, has ended in failure.**

When we determines our purpose, we are only aware of our own situation and current conditions. **Whereas the life we lead is intertwined with the lives of others and will lead to an endless future.** The Master of the Universe plans life by taking into account all of one's life, from the past to the future, all intentions from what is known to what is hidden, and all existence from that of one person to that of all people.

You cannot know the future, but the Almighty knows. Let's say that you want to plant a tree in a specific place. But that place will be under the water of a recently breached dam. If you could know the future, you would plant the tree in a different place.

This means that you want to do something now with good intentions. But the Almighty does not allow you to succeed because of an obstacle waiting in your future. Further, what you want to do now for yourself may be against you in the future. So, instead of what you want, the Almighty opens the door of another solution for your benefit.

You need to shape how you will act in dimensions that you cannot envision or know by your intentions. The goal you desire now may appear suitable to your purposes, but years later, it may be contrary to your purposes. The Eternal Judge, who knows the future, may not create the answer to your wishes in this world based on this wisdom, but He may change your reward or leave it for the life to come.

A friend of mine wanted to get into a certain profession. He failed his first job test and was very upset. A year later, he took a test for a job that offered better possibilities and passed it. The unhappiness he had suffered during that year disappeared. He said, 'It was a good thing that I failed the first test because it allowed me to get a better job."

What is more interesting is this: Five years later, the people who had passed the test tried to find ways to get out of their jobs because, while the company had good conditions in the beginning, with time broke down completely. Specifically, the administration broke up the trained staff for ideological reasons. Some people resigned and those who could, found jobs at other firms.

If you truly want to help a deserving person succeed, would you encourage him to take a job that you know had a gloomy future? You are responsible for the results of your help. So, **if you are going to help a person, you need to consider how that person is going to use that help in the future.**

Think carefully, suppose a mountain suddenly blocks your path in some place or if a mighty bridge is built before you when you arrive at the edge of a precipice. When a problem appears, I think, "Where did I make a mistake?" I examine not only my activities but also my intentions and what I feel in my heart. The current results of our activities should not deceive us. The results we obtain when we wanted to obtain good results connect to our sincere intentions and may look bad at this time. We need to wait. The real results will come soon and we will be shown how correct what we did was.

e) Correction

The first step to resolving a problem is to correct one's intentions. Even if we do solve a problem caused by an unknown intention, it will explode again from some other direction.

Consider this example: When I was a high school student, I was crazy about a ballpoint pen. One day, I lost the pen and I was unhappy all year. One day I thought, "The Creator has punished me because I was too fond of the pen." I asked for His pardon and asked for the pen for the last time as I made up my mind that I would not be sorry anymore. The next day, I found the pen at school, next to the maps. It had not been used since I lost it and I thought it had been kept waiting for me.

Another example: I picked up our first car and drove it to our house that first day with a childlike pleasure. On the way, the car broke down and I was stranded and struggled with it until one o'clock in the morning when the car ran and broke down again. I accused the car dealer saying, "They sold me a defective automobile!" The help I received from cab drivers and gas station attendants didn't help the situation. I couldn't just leave the car in the middle of the road and I felt badly because my children must have been worried about me. In a silent side lane, tearful from my troubles, I started to think. Why did this happen to me? My intention to love the world for its own sake conflicted with my beliefs. I immediately changed my intention and I felt sorry for my faults.

After trying one more time, I left my car and decided to head home. The car ran and didn't breakdown and finally I got home. I never experienced any more trouble for years afterward with the car that put me through that terrible experience on the first day. **If intentions suddenly but sincerely change, results can also change in that moment.**

4. EXPLANATORY EXPERIENCES

I shall relate two experiences that show the effects of intention on activities:

a) Job Changes

In the first years of my government job, my desire to produce my works was strong enough to make me explode. My dream of writing books conflicted with my working conditions. I finally gave up and got used to the atmosphere of the government administrative office I worked in.

With a sudden decision, at a moment that I didn't expect, my work office changed. I departed from my office and from my work friends. At first, I felt as though I had been exiled as an unwanted government employee. I was miserable for several days. Then, I suddenly realized that my new office, free atmosphere, and new surroundings gave me a wonderful chance to write my desired books. I understood that, which was the acceptance of my prayers and I gave thanks to the Almighty for this change.

Again, in the same job, years went by and I wrote several books. But, at the same time, I began to see my not having been promoted to some high level of personnel, where I would have acquired great experience and a serious career, as an injustice and insensitivity. It was as though I had been deprived of a position to which I was entitled. Even though I did not see, it befitted me to ask for intervention and every day passed with the tension of the thought that I had been neglected.

In fact, I was passionate for an official position by not thrusting in destiny's plan of the Almighty. Then I was appointed to an administrative job by a sudden decision, without having been asked. However, the excitement and happiness of the first days were followed by great regret. This time, I longed for my writing and my readers and, although I desired destiny to give me this position, at this stage, it was an imprisonment for which I did not avidly wish.

Fortunately, my job changed again and, now, I work in an atmosphere where I can focus on my new projects. What I understand from these experiences is this: Something seemingly bad in the beginning can be good in the end and something seemingly good in the beginning can be bad in the end. Good intention is the key.

b) The Present of Butter

I learned an interesting tactic necessary to our affairs from a politician with whom I was working closely, which is to offer presents as a way to obtain political or administrative support from important persons.

One day, I too wanted to influence some politicians and officials. On a journey to my native city of Trabzon, I bought ten half-kilo packages of the famed Trabzon butter. When I got back to Ankara, I offered the gifts, visiting the persons whom I had selected one by one. They all thanked me for the gifts. I went home filled with tremendous pleasure at having caused important people to fall into my foxy trap, knowing that I would be able to ask a favor of them in the future.

The next morning I wanted to cook an omelet with some of the butter I had set aside for myself. I put a half a teaspoon into the pan and turned the burner on. This is when I realized that the butter had spoiled. I went into shock in a minute later. I can't describe my shame. I flushed, I turned pale, I turned purple, and I sweated. How could I ever show my face again to those important people? I am a very sensitive person. What a shame! What had happened to me?

For minutes, I repeatedly talked about whatever came into my head about the grocer who sold me the spoiled butter. I blamed myself: If I had given them a carcass, it would not have smelled this badly when they cooked it. Now, all the apartments of those important people would smell just as mine did when their wives melted the butter in their houses. They would have a disgusting day because of me. They would throw my present in the garbage. In their minds, my reputation would stink.

Exchanging gifts is a wholesome practice. Nevertheless, behind my pure-appearing behavior, there was a disgusting, self-serving intention. My intention caused me to fall into a trap and destiny gave me a humiliating reward for my good actions.

c) The Voters for the Deputies

I visited a friend of mine who is a Member of Parliament and he told an interesting recollection about the voters.

He formed a plan to increase his support in a district of a city where he had collected few votes. He decided to pay special attention to voters who came from that district, who were also especially talkative and influential people. When they called him, he immediately answered the telephone and when they wanted something done, he carried it out, acting as an intermediary. In this way, he came to know many voters by helping them.

After he worked like this for a while, he wanted to go to the district, contact the people, talk face-to-face with them, and get an impression of his image within this district. He visited the district and, contrary to his hopes, he was not very respected; in fact, respect for him had decreased. The voters, whose problems he had solved, spoke against him when he returned to the district. They complained of his arrogance and they attributed his good favors in solving their problems to other people. He went home amazed and abandoned this plan.

I asked him his intention of doing this work since I felt he had made a mistake in intention. In fact, he did not make these efforts sincerely or with good intentions or affection for the voters, rather, he had looked down on them. He pleasantly helped them on the one hand and, on the other, his heart was self-serving and hypocritical. He acted in this way hoping to make positive propaganda for him and, thus, influence the voters. As a result, his mistaken intentions quickly left all his hard work empty and fruitless.

II. HOW CAN WE USE THE POWER OF INTENTION?

1. DEVELOPING INTENTIONS

As the abilities, desires, and goals that we wish to possess increase, our intentions also multiply. Therefore, we must develop a consciousness of awareness and desire for these abilities to base and improve the potential of good intentions. Let us explain:

a) Search for Abilities

If people search for something, they also develop reasons for the search. A heart filled with intentions supports a mind filled with goals. **If you have**

an intention for living, you direct yourself toward life. If you have some things to do in the universe, some things will be done in the universe for you. If you have plans to serve the universe, the universe will prepare plans to serve you. Therefore, you need to equip yourself with superior wishes.

An excellent memory: To record information when you learn it. This is the ability to retain every important information. For example, to easily learn the names of the people whom you have met. This is the ability to seize very important information floating around your environment and which has escaped you because you did not feel any interest in it.

An excellent reasoning ability: To perform very complicated mathematical operations without using a pen, a keen comprehension that allows you to instantly distinguish true from false, the ability to distinguish the goal of newspaper items and political speeches. This is the ability to see the hands of skilled deceivers who pull their puppets strings behind curtains.

Collection of knowledge: To use a computer effectively, to speak a foreign language well, to be an expert in any field of science.

Collection of abilities: To drive a car, to perform music, to draw and paint pictures, to make repairs, to organize.

Success goals: To pass an exam, to educate a group, to found or administer institutions, to produce artistic or literary works, to discharge a responsibility, to go abroad.

Now take each of these wishes one by one and ask "why?" If you obtain the wishes we have listed, what is the meaning and value for your spirituality?

b) Study of Human Beings

If your imagination cannot discover the sea, you will not want to learn to swim without seeing the sea. Open your eyes to the world around you and you will see that every human has developed some characteristic that is worthy of praise. I love to talk to everybody I meet about the subjects that interest them. It is exciting to hear about a different practice or methods of philosophy when I meet these people. Every human adds a different meaning and intention to my life. **People are happy to explain what they do to those who appreciate them. If you ask them things attentively, they will give you an attentive answer.** For example, I was interested in alternative medicine, hypnotism, acupuncture, and psychology. I wanted to debate physics with physicists, chemistry with chemists, and sociology with sociologists. I do not have to limit myself to my own profession. People who want to get ahead must live filled with a desire to attain the exciting contents of the universe. Science and knowledge are the wealth of humanity and everyone has the right to wander in the mysterious pages of the universe, to gain knowledge on every subject. We ought not to forget that the majority of extraordinary successes have not depended on diplomas. Our lives are certainly not long enough to discover ever subtlety of the universe. Everything in the basic profession we have chosen will enable us to possess a sufficiently rich interior world to know, at least, the main outlines of other subjects.

If we become experts on one subject but remain ignorant of everything else, we will not be able to govern our lives effectively. To become a leader in life requires that one have a general background along general lines. The road to this goal passes through maintaining broad interests and giving importance to the study of people from different worlds.

Let us use this idea; let us learn everything from one thing we select and one thing from everything else. Never mind that a chef has learned to prepare all types of foods as his profession demands, but let him give us one good dish. No matter whether a performer has learned all the songs, just let her give us a song we know. It is fine for a physicist to extend his knowledge of quantum theory, but let us also know something about physics.

c) Focusing on Needs

Wealth and prosperity, in the hands of thoughtless and ungrateful people, lead to ruin. Being unaware of the value of your benefits also leads to ruin. The thoughtlessness of such persons is terrible. When the Almighty

Creator bestows poverty on them, they scold and say, "Where is justice?" and complain of their destiny to everyone. The Almighty Creator gives them fortune and wealth and they turn into atheists and say, "I didn't need Him. What prayers? From whom was I going to ask anything? To beseech the Almighty Creator is the comfort of the poor." This is a disgrace. Such people can only arrive in the other world used up and with empty hands.

The sense of need is the most effective prayer. People ask into their life the thing they feel that they need. They rejoices for them and they are thankful. Love is not offered to the one who does not want love. Someone who does not want heaven cannot progress on the road to heaven. You cannot increase your knowledge without a desire for knowledge.

It is need that calls everything from nothing into existence. Requesting things from humans brings scarcity, but asking something from the Creator causes a person to achieve treasures.

If our family meets all of our needs, then we do not give importance to individual abilities. A child, whose every need is instantly met by his family cannot learn to want something and work to achieve it. Someone who does not deeply feel economic, social, or cultural needs can only learn to spend his energy on his own selfish personal needs.

When we think back on our past in which we did not experience any need, it is very likely that we will not see any profound wishes there. We will want justice for them when we see innocent people who have been wronged. The first benefit we will receive when we take interest in the needy is for ourselves. **People who do not suffer, or are unaware of those who suffer, do not attempt to find ways to relieve suffering.**

However, you need to determine your needs concretely and in detail. I was explaining "Success Strategies" to some friends studying at the College of Law during a seminar organized by a foundation in Ankara. I asked who had prayed in the last ten years. Everybody raised their hands. I asked, "Who wants something very much?" Again, everybody raised their hands. "Who wanted everything good and prayed for it?" I asked. Everybody raised their hands. I was suspicious of their answers, so I made my questions more concrete:

"Who wants to have a superior memory and keep everything he or she has learned and the name of every person he or she has met in his or her memory five times a day? Who wants to use a computer with complete proficiency, to write successful articles, and to speak a foreign language? Who think about these wishes at least five times a day?" When my questions became concrete, the hands raised decreased one by one. I began to watch them; one person raised her hand and said, "We never thought of prayer in this way."

2. PROTECTION FROM EVIL INTENTIONS

In our lives and relations, we must protect ourselves both from our own evil intentions and from the evil intentions of those with who we are in relationships.

a) Our Intentions

Our intentions directed toward selfishness, self-service, self-aggrandizement, and smugness are bad and harmful. Our intentions directed toward sharing, humility, self-realization, and kindness are good and beneficial. Both the harmful and beneficial examples are shown in the box below:

BENEFICIAL INTENTIONS	HARMFUL INTENTIONS
My work is to be worthy of respect.	I want people to respect what I do.
I do it out of goodness.	I do it for a reward.
I'll do it as my duty.	I'll do it to get rid of the job.
For my honor and humanity.	To get my leader's attention.
To be useful to everybody.	To be useful to myself alone.
To surpass myself.	To be superior to others.
Because I think it is the right thing.	Because others find it right.

A woman once said, "I tried to make my husband pleased with me through self-sacrifice. In spite of every kindness and service I did for him, he left and abandoned me. What mistake did I make to deserve this infidelity? Although I only behaved kindly to my husband, why has the Master of Destiny punished me in this way?"

I asked her what the intention behind her kindness to her husband was and she said, "I wanted him to be attached to me."

Focus on her intention. Her intention was wrong. **The reward of kindness concealed the selfishness within it is abandonment.** Her intention to attach him to her had destroyed her efforts to develop herself and her spirituality over the years. Her behavior turned into an oppressive, uncomfortable lack of trust felt by her husband. Some people go to fortunetellers with corrupt intentions and lose the peace they had as a punishment from destiny.

The woman in this example should have tried to possess a loveable purity and a beauty of nature. She should have resolved to have such an outstanding personality that it would have overwhelmed unfaithfulness. She should not have forgotten that a human could not show faithfulness if not by the grace of God.

You love the rose because of its sweet smell. However, the rose does not smell sweet because you love it. **The way that the rose succeeds in being loved is its wish to smell sweetly to be worthy of love.** However, those who choose the disgusting over the pure can gain nothing.

The rose, if it wants to be loved, tries "to change those with whom it comes in contact." Whereas "if it wants to smell worthy of love" it must resolve to develop itself. Who does not love a lovable person? An intelligent rose does not seek out an insect whose nose is accustomed to the smell of carrion.

b) The intentions of others

The results of our intention will return as rewards to us and the rewards of other people will come back to them. However, when we are in a relationship, influence of the negative reward of one person's bad intentions on another person is unavoidable.

You entered into a partnership with good intentions, but your partner has bad intentions. The misfortunes of the company, which your bad intentioned partner brought about, affect you as well. You are prepared to feel badly if your partner, whom you approached with good intentions but did not investigate, had bad intentions.

If your intentions are truly good, you will find these bad intentions through intuition. You will be warned through revelation. In general, promises of material and spiritual advantages corrupt our intentions and we fall into the traps of bad people. If you are offered an opportunity, if a business promises you a large sum of money or some item is on sale at a very cheap price, will you let the chance go? Be very careful if you are involved in a bargaining process. Have you been smitten by an attractive body? Did you fall in love? This is how the hook is baited. This is how traps are set.

Here is the story of an employee of mine. A man sat down beside him and was making phone calls to this and that person and my employee overheard him. It seemed he was a contractor and was building magnificent country homes in the vicinity of Bolu and selling them to members of Parliament at bargain prices. A few houses were left and they were very cheap. The employee was taken in by the outward appearances of the pictures, the phone conversations, and the fake documents. He paid the money as he asked for one of the homes for himself, thinking that he shouldn't let the deal slip through his fingers. Months later, it occurred to him to go and see the house. Once at the address, he found an empty lot on a mountaintop.

Can someone be so stupid as to fall into such a transparent ruse? The author of these words has fallen for many such tricks. You cannot believe how many people have been duped thinking they had bought busses, houses, or lots. There are even people who have used other men's identity papers to marry young girls who thought they had found a handsome bachelor. Where is the law to prevent such criminality in this country?

One who lays homicidal traps for an innocent person ought to be ready to meet mortal misfortune himself. We cannot accuse anybody when we fall into a trap while pursuing our own selfish interests. The justice of destiny will intervene in the end, but the person who is victimized will suffer as well.

We ought to hold on to this ideal: We should think positively about people, yet not regard anyone as a pure angel. Everyone can make a mistake; therefore, what we have to do, even though we mustn't be as timid as birds, is to act carefully and cautiously.

Someone may be lying. Look into their eyes. Do they avoid your glance and tense up tight? It is true that many people are masters of role-playing. Pay attention to your conscience and your feelings. Can you read a total sincerity and honesty in a person's face?

This is not enough. Look at their relationships. Their past is the mirror to their future. You should pay attention to deeds and not to promises. **The best indication of what someone is going to do is what he or she has already done.** Is he or she greedy? Is he or she mad for money, position, and fame? He or she will get into trouble and it will rub off on you.

If you think you have found an honesty that you can trust in every way. I would still advise you to draw up business documents, even with you brother. You need to support your marriage with an official ceremony and sales and purchases with documentation from a notary in order to protect you.

On the other hand, if we are afraid of every relationship and avoid every enterprise, we will get nothing out of life. A risk-free life is a life without success. If we want to get ahead in life, we must take risks, certainly, but we have to assess our risks. Let us not behave like a young gazelle, prancing in a jungle filled with lions. It is enough if we act alertly and cautiously against possible pitfalls that surround us like experienced parents and leaders.

3. STRENGTHENING SINCERE INTENTIONS

One aspect concerns the routines and commonplace experiences of our lives, while the other aspect is of your efforts related to goals that, when accomplished, we reap the rewards. If we nourish both aspects with strong intentions, our level of life energy will rise and its tempo will increase.

a) In Daily Life

Let us start by examining what our daily life is made up of: You wake up early, wash, perform your devotions, exercise, eat breakfast, greet the members of your family, get ready, leave the house, go to school or work, finish your work, go home, read, relax, be involved, and share. Every day our bodies perform hundreds of activities and our minds think thousands of thoughts. Why? So many people have left this question unanswered that it is unbelievable that they can live.

Just as we attach every action in our lives to good intentions, we can furnish our lives entirely with good intentions. The general intentions, which we determine, can spread to all of our activities.

I have this sort of life and I do this and that because I want to be a good person. I want to make my loved ones content, I want to be helpful and add to the happiness of the world. I want to increase my spiritual pleasure in life and leave a positive mark in the world. I also want to prepare for a peaceful departure from this world, to discover divine secrets, and to increase my personal honor.

Imagine that you took a visually impaired person by the hand and helped him. Suppose that when you saw a child in your apartment building, you told him that you liked his diligence. Think about how you choose to sit on the balcony this evening. Now, ask yourself about your intentions of these actions. Why do you do them?

Try to elevate great and positive intentions from time-to-time to these types of momentary actions. I helped someone because she is a human whom the angels love very much. I sat on the balcony because I wanted to observe and enjoy the clouds that are shaped by the hidden brush strokes of the Creator. This new life style will reconstruct your interior world.

You can connect other purposes to your actions through good intentions: I am smiling and, thanks to the comfort that smiling brings, my strengthened immune system destroys my illnesses. Through the contribution of the development of my courage, which I achieve by holding my head high, I become stronger in defending my rights. **We can connect everything we do to great purposes and every act serves the purpose to which we connect it.**

No act is condemned to be petty. Giving a drink of water to a dog that is tortured by thirst earned a woman entrance to heaven. What made a young man the killer of thousands of animals was the thoughtless tossing out a cigarette butt in a forest.

b) Important Goals

Everyone knows that raising a tree is a long-term job that starts by planting a sprout, but very few people govern their lives according to this knowledge. Unfortunately, since the development of the movies, many people live with the magical illusion that they can achieve their goals instantly.

Permanent important achievements do not result from our daily-varied jobs. Achievements are the result of work that we have performed in an orderly way. There can be not result from things that exist one day and are gone the next. What are you bring up like a child every day? What buildings are you adding new bricks to every day? I am speaking of your goals. I believe that the readers of my book "Think and Succeed," have long ago made a written list of their goals. You should have these possible goals: A happy family, superior quality children, a good academic career, and a lucrative professional life.

Why? Why do you want this? You need to make these things happen so that you do not easily lose out on the benefits of life. Someone who wants a family only for his or her pleasure will abandon that family if he or she finds more pleasure outside of the family. There is no road for a person to be successful other than pursuing a goal with insistence and steadiness. There is no satisfaction in everyday results; however, the road of stable continuation to reach long-term results is achieved by holding to a strong purpose. You need to find the right number of reasons to have that family and to be attached to it.

On the other hand, a student who does not find sufficient intention to enable him to keep an academic career will not finish. He will tire, he will become stressed, his memory will weaken, he will find his status to be low, and he will be overwhelmed and run away from the situation.

Consider this: How many young people are filled with ideals? They go to unknown countries of the world to receive and give education. Many of them do this with indescribable sacrifices and only on survival income. They are deprived of their countries, their loved ones, their pleasures, goods, and status. If they did not hold great intentions, which promised them such a great reward, they would surely be overwhelmed. The pleasure they derive from the greatness of their intentions suppresses the pain of the difficulties they encounter. Heaven has entered their bosoms and Almighty Creator had filled their hearts. For this reason, the palaces that they erect cover the world each day more and more.

c) Developing Sincerity

Intentions leave their mark on every act, more or less. However, supernatural and unexpected, very great results may come to being from the acts that are performed with extremely sincere intentions.

If your intentions are good, to be a very sincere person is to be something like a divine light or an angel. The spiritual energy of a very sincere person can be felt from a definite distance. There is a sort of energy that is like vitality or a feeling of importance that envelopes the body.

Some current prevailing diseases destroy sincerity: Moral deficiencies, such as the increase of hypocrites, the spread of opportunists, pride, ridicule, selfishness destroy the strength of our sincerity. **People who talk**

without serious intent and, in particularly, who speak sarcastically, in time, lose all of their sincerity.

Are you sufficiently sincere? Do you consider the intentions that are concealed behind your behaviors in the various fields of your life?

Do you bring a golden gift to a wedding you attend so as not to be embarrassed before society or because you sincerely want to do it? Do you invite your friend to be your guest just because it is a social custom or because you truly want to entertain him?

When you say, "I love you" to your wife, is it to smooth over some tension or is it truly because you do love her? Is the reason you praise a speaker because you liked his speech or to get his attention and gain his good will.

My advice to anyone who wants to develop their sincerity is this: Do not tell lies, do not be hypocritical. If you cannot contradict something contrary to what you believe, at least remain noncommittal. Do not mock people, do not belittle them, do not be proud, do not let you sense of honor depend on other people's approval or praise. In the end, the greatest source of sincerity is to make your choices rely on the friendship of the Creator alone and avoid expectations of material profits.

CHAPTER THREE:
THE POWER OF EMOTION

I. WHY WE NEED THE POWER OF EMOTION?

INTRODUCTION

Have you thought about how much stronger an effect comes from feeling than from thought? Until today, you could not resist certain entreaties. Certain troubles have kept you awake at night. How many sacrifices have you made? Millions of people have endangered their lives for love, spouses, children, friends, religion, or art. Why?

Feeling is the excitement that runs the motor of your automobile. Nobody can hear a whisper, but a cry will wake everyone. Your dulled feelings are like a whisper, while your strong feelings resound to the skies. We are talking about an exciting channel of power. You are about to discover that living without feeling is lifelessness.

Man has been granted one of the smallest bodies of the material universe; however, one of the largest of the spiritual universe. Humankind is like an atom with respect to physical space, but the physical space is as dust compared to man's spirituality. Humans are the most highly endowed living beings on God's earth. Humans have a heart that can hold all the material meaning of the universe. **"The heart is such a thing that, if you place in it seven hundred of the seven skies, it would disappear and fade away."**[23]

What achieves this immensity for man is not his physique. Concerning the human body, it is nothingness, it is ready to decay. Further, man's intelligence is no more valuable than an intelligent robot. The key to what elevates humankind is something else: When human intelligence is united with positive feelings, a being more valuable than the galaxy comes into existence. Even the enormous universe cannot be compared to the divine love hidden within the heart.

Someone who has used up the power of his feeling grows smaller, becomes lazy, and drowsy. **Feelings are the fuel for enthusiasm in your work.** People who lack feelings experience a constriction of their interior universe and their happiness is limited. Even though people do sometimes use their intelligence, they always pursue their feelings. Intelligence cannot silence feeling and feelings lead humans both to death and to life. It is feeling that shapes all pains and pleasures.

The life that inhabits matter actually begins where matter ends. Life without feeling is a vegetal life, a mechanical life. Feeling is the essence of the substance that elevates vegetal life to the level of spiritual life. Life with feeling is a life of the soul. Just as the odor of flowers spreads, so does the energy of life spread with feeling. **All of the irresistible temptations of society are the work of thought that contains deep feelings.** As such, whoever does not include feeling in his life lives relatively without life.

In this section, we are going to speak about a spiritual profundity that experimental science maintains as outside of its field of research. We shall discover the subtleties of a dimension that profoundly influences the universe.

1. FROM EMOTION TO MATTER

The path between feeling, spiritual body, and matter is one of the most mysterious roads in the universe. We think that matter is more real and

23 *Mawlana* Rumi , Masnavi, vol. 5, p.73

the soul is more imaginary; however, it is the spiritual body that is closer to reality, not matter. Matter is like a bubble relative to the spiritual body that is behind it.

Man, with his lazy body, groans under the weight of a hundred kilos, but the spiritual strength a mother gains the instant she sees her baby about to be run over by a car can overturn an automobile. **This occurs because feeling is the essence of meaning and meaning can influence matter through metaphysical dimensions.**

a) From Nothing to Existence

As physics develops, philosophies change. Newton's solid matter theory collapsed with the development of particle physics that resulted in the discovery of subatomic matter. When electromagnetic theories were developed, scientists proposed that matter was not composed of particles, rather was composed of energy waves.

Quantum theories destroyed the concept of the continuity of waves. In fact, material is made up of little packages of energy. Further, unified field theories have claimed that energy waves, which make up matter, flow continually from materially non-existent form to material form.

It has also been understood that matter flows from material nothingness to material existence at the speed of light just as though it were a bubbling froth, continuously nourished from below, disintegrates into particles, and then is united into atoms and molecules at the top. Just as the Sun continually emits light, matter is sent from a limitless, unobservable dimension. **The universal river that emerges from its hidden source flows like a waterfall over the river bed of time.** At this instant, you, as well as the book in your hand, are continually flowing along together.

Where does matter come from and where does it go? Science has attempted to understand the state of emptiness from which matter arises and to which it returns. Today "Unified Field Theories," which have brought the whole universe together in one point, are filled with mathematical formula that function in the continuity of the development of matter from nothingness and the return of matter to nothingness.[24]

The source from which matter is derived is deified by some spiritualist philosophies as "The zero of probability where causality ceases to exist, the endless field of knowledge and power where all knowledge, rules and laws are born and from which they are controlled. It is the limitless field of energy where what is going to occur on the surface of things is determined before it comes to be. At the same time, the field of nothingness is the field "of nothing at all" according to materialistic criteria."

The creator of everything cannot be both limitless and nothingness. To reduce the one and incomparable Creator to the universe and to attribute His qualities to an unknown nothingness behind matter is illogical, unjust, and misleading.[25]

The Eternal Judge refreshes the matter of the universe in the cycle of being-nonbeing. We experience cycles in seconds, days, weeks, years, and centuries and the annual cycle is a journey to the nothingness of winter and the existence of spring. The most rapid of cycles is experienced in the deepest of all of them. Further, one could compare the universal system to countless wheels turning together at different speeds.

The book you hold in your hand AT THIS MOMENT is not the same material as it was a second ago. It is the light coming into your eyes right now that allows you to see, not the light that existed a second ago. Light goes away the instant that it comes to you, yet it fills the space so quickly that we are given a feeling of "continuity." If we are 30 years old, our spiritual body may be only 30 years of age; however, if we consider our nerve cells, our continually renewed physical bodies are only one year of

24 See Paul Davies and John Gribbin, The Matter Myth, Simon and Schuster, New York, 1992.

25 The Creator, who brings forth this emptiness/mirror from Himself, the source of the universe that reflects His names through this emptiness/mirror is Almighty Creator who is present in every point of the universe with His attributes and His power but is outside of the universe in His person. The logic of His presence outside of the universe resembles the logic of the Sun being outside of the Earth. His being in every point of the universe is like the presence of the Sun in every part of the Earth. Just as He sent His message from the first human up to the present by the means of prophets, so to He speaks with every human being by means of their consciences.

age, at most. On a quantum level, the age of the material of our physical bodies is not even one second old.

For example, the cells that make up our eyes and tongues are renewed without our awareness. Moreover, our tongue does not resemble our eyes and our eyes do not resemble our tongue.

As the years go by, we can look at our friends with the same pair of beautiful eyes whose color has not changed. No one can destroy and renovate such an exceptional skyscraper without anyone being aware of it, except God.

In ancient times, the smallest structure was thought to be an atom that was indestructible because it was thought to be indivisible. However, today we do not know how far we can go in dividing the smallest structure of matter. There are no longer building blocks of matter; rather, packages of energy, which are the smallest structures we can attain, make up the basis of energy that flows continually through the material body.

The universe flows from a secret ocean to material existence that arises on its banks like rivers. It flashes like a light for a moment then empties into another ocean and dissolves like a bubble. In the depths of everything that appears permanent around you, there lay a mighty journey. **Creation is like an hourglass and the universe represents the flow from one chamber to the other. As an explanation to this,** the Quran best states it "And there is not a thing but its (sources and) treasures (inexhaustible) are with Us; but We only send down thereof in due and ascertainable measures."[26]

b) The Meaning of Matter

While all different everything comes from similarities, just as every building is made from the same grains of sand, so too is every piece of matter created from the same homogeneous packages of energy. The differences arise, not from the essence of matter, but from the forms of its organization and the reason for these differences in the organization are art, knowledge, and feeling.

26 Qur'an, 15:21

In the superficial dimension, one piece of matter appears as a human being and another as a piece of wood; however, when they are looked at from the profound aspect of the quantum, both are the same. What distinguishes the two materials is not their material essence but the difference in the planning and organization of the two.

The meaning of matter determines, not the content of the particles of which it consists, but the form and arrangement of those particles. For example, an artist produces different pictures from the same paint. The plan you impose on matter tells your thoughts, your aims, and your feelings. In this way, millions of names come into being from the Artist who organizes matter. The origin of meaning lies not in the paint applied on the canvas but in the brush stroke.

All the appearances, sounds, odors, and tastes reflect beauty and are spiritual. A butterfly tells you about its Master. The birds sing songs of the greatest Performer. **You see the plans of the greatest Painter in the colorful gardens in the spring.**

If someone criticizes your work, you will become offended. What appreciation can you feel for someone who does not admire your outstanding poetry or who is not moved by your compassion? Anyone who is unmoved by genius is ungrateful. What about us? Think of the Sun in the morning and the stars in the night. Even animals are not indifferent and unmoved by the wonderful beauties of nature. The bees hover around the flowers and insects come together with the flowers. How many flowers on all sides of the road await a smile from the passersby, yet no one sees them because someone crushes them and they disappear from sight.

Is this universe not the work of someone? Who is the most ungrateful? Mawlana Rumi refers to the Creator when he says, "This universe is like a bit of straw in the Hand of the hidden wind of the universe/ the Hand is hidden, behold the Writer/ for even in the gathering place of souls, the Soul of souls does not appear."[27]

The material essences of a painting that decorate walls consist of the

27 *Mawlana* Rumi , Masnavi, vol. 2, p. 99-100.

canvases, the frames, and the paint. However, the heart of the painter gives a painting its magnificent profundity and value.

The soil is precisely the same thing: the seeds are poor little grains, without awareness, prepared to decay. Nevertheless, from the seeds that are scattered over the "same thing," living things and plants with different colors, shapes, odors, and flavors sprout.

Thus, humans may be distinguished according to their feelings. Human beings have feelings that may make them both angels and murderers. Humans can arouse hatred and admiration with their feelings. The insensitive person will resemble a stone, the bad intentioned person a scorpion, and the well-meaning ones, birds.

Your hair is the same hair as that of others but we attribute a meaning to the way you cut and comb it. Your face and eyes are more or less the same as theirs but you are distinguished according to the way you glance. Your body resembles ours very closely but we respect you according to the degree with which you care for it. In short, if we are insensitive, we are like copies of one another, like cats of Van. If we are sensitive, the development of vast differences between us is inevitable.

c) Spirituality and Material

The 20th century was born with materialism and the discovery of matter. It placed heart on the margins of matter. In my opinion in the 21st century, individuals will research the heart and spiritual bodies. From this research, they will discover spirituality to a degree that will supersede all the old forms of knowledge.[28]

Modern physics does not recognize a body more luminous than light.[29] However, doctor of physics, Prof. Lijun Wang of the Princeton NEC In-

28 In my view the approach set out in Prof. Robert Ornstein's "A New Psychology" is a pioneer work of the development in the modern world.

29 The limits of physics has been drawn by the formula E=MC2. The problem is the nature of the field we encounter when we pass beyond this limit. Some philosophies with limited horizons think this field, which is described with such terms as "virtual" and "imaginary," to be the Creator Himself. As believers we reject this theory that a field of mirror-empty space- nothingness that does not have a body of its own and displays a virtual Sun within it, has a creative power.

stitute in the USA, proposed that the speed of light could be 300 times faster than what the speed previously suggested by researchers. The scientists, although they demonstrated this discovery, pointed out that it would invalidate the Law of Cause and Effect and that the concept of time, as it is known, would "collapse."[30] According to a theory, actually, "The speed of light in the first instant of the creation of the universe with the Big Bang was endless. Light decreased to its present level as measured by Einstein through slowing down with time and with the expansion of the universe."

These new approaches are destroying the traditional flat, geometrical, and mechanical theories of the universe. In fact, the truth of the legendary explanations is coming out. That a material body could be in more than one place at the same time is a new discovery for science but an ancient one for Sufi mysticism.

Are we coming to understand the secrets of the miracles of the prophets? I think of the Prophet Mohammed (PBUH) from whose ten fingers water gush like flowing from ten fountain and it is reported 70 people were fed by him with a handful food. There are similar sayings concerning the life of the Prophet Jesus (PBUH). The feelings are here. They wait for sincerity and profundity right here.

When the divine command comes, matter created from light in its essence will serve the desire of humans who have sublime enlightenment.

d) Creator and Created

Only a small portion of humankind is atheistic. They are drowning in their own garrulity. They envision a secular religion and their gods are "money, woman, and the philosophy of science" or they worship religions derived from "the founders of the ideologies." Their temples become secular places such as monuments, statues, fancy shopping malls, and cinemas.

The rest of the people think that the artistic profundities everywhere in the universe cannot spring from nothingness or by themselves or by

30 Zaman Newspaper, June 5, 2000.

means of natural causes, rather they believe in creation of everything by the Almighty. On the other hand, some people only imitate the beliefs of those around them while some people are polytheistic. Additionally, a large group of people believe the oneness of the Creator by understanding that the universe is a single unit of energy in which exists a common inspiration in everything and these individuals believe that there is one Lord of knowledge who observes everything closely enough to distinguish one thing from another.

On the other hand, according to the beliefs of the spiritualists, that creator is the profundity of the universe; it is its spirit. It is the universe itself. At this point, a philosophy emerges presenting as its objective the divinization of humankind: human as a part of Almighty Creator or human deified. They say to humans, "You are the masters of the universe. You have endless strength. Power lies in your essence. You can create." This philosophy is a terrible error that prepares an indescribable distress.

In the face of such pretensions, the wise people see that they were created from a miserable egg and that they were destined to die as a sickly being in need of compassion. They sense that they have no power in their own essences and that they live under the control of a hidden Power. They do not rebel against the Creator, imagining they are gods. They bow before His majesty. They humbly open their hearts entirely to friendship with their Master. They know that the heart that loves the Creator is like the king of the universe. The universe is ready to serve every heart that submits to the Creator.

We believe that the Creator is one that He is not of the nature of created things. He is without compare. He is absolute and His nature cannot even be imagined. Everything comes from Him but nothing in the universe is Him. Nothing that we perceive can be Him or a part of Him. Everything is His creation.[31]

31 You may analyze our views on what sort of a system creation took place in my book entitles "The Journey of Eternity" [Sonsuzluk Yolculuğu]. I recommend the discovery of the Creator to atheists because the eternity in which they do not believe and which they do not wish for shall not be given to people who have not heard the message of the ambassadors of the Creator and do not believe in the Creator. Is it worth it to lose the chance to exist forever in the palaces of heaven for the sake of the ordinary short lived pleasures of the world?

The creation of Almighty Creator is like the Sun sending forth its light. The source of being of matter is God's name of Nour [The Divine Light]. Created matter is the manifestation of the Divine Light as shadow. True being is The Divine Light; true nothingness is matter. We see and observe not true being but true nothingness. The miracle is described thus by Mawlana Rumi, **"True being is concealed in nothingness."**[32]

The Almighty Creator has given the form of nothingness to true being and of being form to nothingness. The shadow of God's name of The Divine Light is perceived as matter. Matter is the dimmest form of the corporal degrees. Intensiveness and inclusiveness of existence decreases when it descends little by little from the Light of the Limitless Power to matter and increases as it moves upwards. The most inclusive-spiritually intense being is the being of Almighty Creator who is the source of all corporal beings. An intensively lightened existence can cover a less lightened existence.[33] Just as the energy breaking away from the Sun decreases and diminishes coming to earth, so the energy manifestation from the Creator is that much veiled and overshadowed as it manifested down to matter.

Just as whatever approaches the Sun will be influenced by its energy, who or whatever approaches the Creator will be nourished by His Nour, the Light. To approach the Creator, is possible by approaching the heart by means of a moral life. The manner that reflects this behavior is the overflowing tears with worship people experience at nights. When a person is experiencing sublime feelings and those sensations want to burst forth like a dam, the heart of that person is very close to the heavens. The poor body is imprisoned in the cage of this earth; however, his or her eyes are on the horizon, gazing longingly at the skies he or she wants to fly.

---

32 *Mawlana* Rumi , Masnavi, vol. 6, p. 282

33 To understand the theory you may take as an example the density of matter. A teaspoon of matter in some stars is as heavy as a thousand tons of matter on other stars. You know the difference in mass between a handful of lead and a handful of sponge. Quantum physics has demonstrated that the universe, which was created from a zero volume, can be reduced to a drop. With a similar reasoning, a tiny spark of a spiritual existence can grow so dense that huge planets can shelter inside of it.

2. THE EFFECT OF EMOTION

Your strong thoughts, which are reinforced by your feelings, will reinforce your wishes and facilitate the opening of your potentials.

a) Spiritual Energy

One of the sources of spiritual energy is profundity of feeling. Dervish order uses methods to neutralize material feelings and experience deep feelings: Don't sleep much, don't speak much, shut yourself in a dark cell, repeat the name of the Almighty Creator, concentrate on an image, count your breaths, listen to special rhythms, or whirl like the Mawlavi Dervishes. The intention is to tear the consciousness away as much as possible, from the five senses and to experience the emptiness filling with the enthusiasm of the transmissions that originate from the spiritual depths.

The intention of the ancient dervishes in performing these sorts of exercises was not to show off their miraculous powers but to achieve spiritual purity. The intention of people nowadays is to put on a show and it has taken on the atmosphere of a quack medicine show.

If you walk on fire and glass, and demonstrate that you can raise peoples' hair with your spiritual power, what will it gain you and your audience? Is it worth spending years doing? We should not have time to waste on such petty shows as this.

Some religious brotherhoods eat glass and razor blades, cut their bodies, pierce them and then make a show of making the wound disappear by spitting on it. There is no practical use in such displays. If we aim to do this, it will rob us of years. It would be better if we avoided sharp substances but spend our lives trying to develop useful abilities.

The poverty of the Oriental societies, which aspire to spirituality, and the wealth of Western societies, which are focused on materialism, is obvious. However, they call the Western society, which has embraced technology since 1950 the "Depression Belt." Today Orientals are happy in their poverty and Westerners are unhappy in their wealth. We want to live a rich and happy life. This middle way is possible.

If what is important for you is to fly mystically in the polluted skies of the world without waiting for heaven and to travel through the Hawaiian Islands and to the Poles, you can dedicate all your life to mystical ways. Let me remind you that just when you think you have succeeded your life will be over. If you intend face eternal life full of peace and tranquility, do not waste your time like this. Almighty Creator grants miracles only to the prophets. The spiritual power which people like us can gain with such effort will only be things to help in putting on shows as simple as blowing a feather in the air.

So enlarge your goals, focus on them, hurry, leave a trace behind you, and leave a creation. Let what you do be in harmony with the universe and its Master. You will not be able to use it to put on a show. It will not be noticed like a flash of lightening. Nevertheless, the energy of the deep feelings will always be with you.

b) Motivation

One cannot speak of inspiration and excitement without feeling. If you are without feeling, you do not want to move, a speaker without feeling does not influence anybody. If a child screams in a street where people are walking in silence, everybody goes into action. **Feelings can increase the power of one wish a million times. It is feeling that changes the voice to a cry.** The difference in power between a chemical and an atomic bomb is not derived from the size of the bomb; it derives from the intensity, the content, and the techniques.

If you want spiritual beings that will support you until the end of the world to be created from the words you speak, pray and ask for them with your heart, with all your sincerity and with your feelings. Every prayer formed by your tears will spread into the universe in the shape of thousands of angels formed from the substance of your spirit.

The spiritual and material things of value you have bestowed on humankind produce beautiful feelings in their hearts. Material things of value are limited but spiritual things of value are limitless. If you give away all your wealth, perhaps you may make a few people happy. In fact, contrary to what you hope for, your children may quarrel with one another over the inheritance you leave them. On the other hand, it costs nothing to spread love and the treasure of divine love within you is sufficient to make hundreds of thousands of hearts happy.

The Gospel says, "Ask and it shall be given you, seek and ye shall find. Knock and it shall be opened unto you."[34] The Koran says, "Call on your Lord with humility and in private: for Allah loveth not those who trespass beyond bounds."[35] Why when your feelings are hurt, why begging and beseeching? It is because delicacy of feeling is more spiritual. As the spiritual level increases, so does the level of vitality. The Prophet Mohammad (**PBUH**) said, "These three prayers will be answered without a doubt: the prayer of the oppressed, the prayer of one in a strange place [a traveler], and the prayer of a father for his children." Beware of the curse of someone even if he or she is an unbeliever because there is no obstacle to keep it from reaching God. "Even if that person is a great sinner, the prayer of a person who has been oppressed will be answered."[36]

Please note the common themes of all of these sayings: suffering humans, the sick, the oppressed and the innocent, orphans, those who have no one, mothers and fathers...these are all people with deep and sincere feelings. The words and meanings of these people come not from their lips, but from their hearts. The strength of these people lay not in their hands or tongues, but in their spirits.

You will understand then that the secret of success is not in brandishing your fist left and right and bawling "I am a powerful giant." **The secret of success is to desire it with sincerity and to achieve a profound feeling of need for the Limitless Power.**

A neighbor phones you and tells you, "Your enemy's house is on fire." Anybody with a conscience would be a little sorry. If he says, "The trash in your garden is on fire," you would be worried. If he says, "Your house is on

34 Matthew, 7:7
35 Qur'an, 7:55
36 The Prophet Mohammad (PBUH), Cami'us-Saghir 3:300, No. 3454; 3:127, No. 2915; 3:526, No. 4204

fire" you will be frightened. If he says, "Your child who is locked in your house is burning up," you would go into shock. You understand that when information changes, the feelings change, the strongest feelings beget the most effective actions.

The invincible person is the human who confronts the situation with the strongest feelings. Excitement is contagious. Whoever can control his feelings[37] can direct the feelings of others. The leader we follow is the leader whom we think possesses the keenest feelings for the path he is following. The thing that moves us is not the word games of orators but the feelings with which they invest their words. We are talking about "deep feelings" not "emotionalism." When your feelings control you, you are smashed against your surroundings like a piece of straw blown about by storms of emotion. When you are in control of your feelings, you destroy the obstacles before you and turn them into passing storms. **If you are without feeling, you are abandoned and silent like a dark winter night.** Just as fire and water harden steel, feeling strengthens a person.

c) Internal Riches

We can use our feelings to increase our internal riches. Every feeling can be expanded until it includes the universe. Love can grow until it encompasses everything. Anger can turn into a massacre. Compassion can grow until it takes in all children. **You can distribute your money to a few people, your smile to a few thousand people but your love to billions of people.** Positive feelings are like light. They are copied on every screen. They come in at every window. Just one of them goes out from one heart but millions of them enter through other hearts.

You are not wealthy enough to buy a whole neighborhood but just by wishing it, the whole universe can be yours. If someone who cares for me says, "You are MY brother or sister," they are telling the truth. When I look at a flower that I like, I feel as if it said, "I belong to you." **I am lost in**

37 To control your feelings, to conceal grief, sorrow, anger and similar feelings and not show them is not success. Success is, on the contrary, to experience the right feelings at the right time and place and to get rid of unsuitable feelings.

admiration at the generosity of the Master of the Universe: He has bestowed upon the poorest human being a seed of love enormous enough to encompass the whole universe. The Moon belongs to those who love it and the Sun and the mountains to those who adore them. Whoever uses his or her heart is free in loving as a lover with the rain.

Millions of people have died without using this innate potential wealth because humankind is the only creature, which has the liberty to hate, and, regrettably, is the only one that generally chooses to hate.

We cannot achieve spiritual profundity by thoughts that cannot produce feeling. The world of thought is a narrow one; the world of feeling is wide. When the intelligence says, "There is no more food left on the plate to nourish me," the feeling will say, "Sense the flavor of each morsel of food." **Feeling can fit the lives of a thousand people into the life of one person.**

Thousands of thoughts give rise to every feeling. For instance, the word "beauty" is an abstract expression. Under this abstraction, you bring together thousands of concrete beautiful things: flowers, butterflies, spring, and winter. The concrete natural aesthetic produces an abstract thought: "beauty." As the fact of "beauty" increases, the energy with which it is charged and the thought produce appropriate feelings: joy, happiness, enthusiasm.

The fact of beauty, which is composed of thousands of beautiful things, is the source of joy and happiness. At this stage, you produce your feelings and your feelings shape first your actions and your choices and afterwards your beliefs and personality.

3. EXPLANATORY EXPERIENCES

Let us try to see the effects of feelings on a series of concrete experiments:

a) Sudden Change

Suppose you make a sudden decision under the pressure of feelings and your whole life changes after that decision. Strong anger will lead to the death of a man in a fight. Strong compassion will lead to saving a human life, in spite of mortal danger. Strong love will cause one to dig a tunnel through a mountain, if necessary. Feelings are so powerful that if they envelope one's body, no one can have the power to block them.

In the beginning of 1999, I was wandering around a book fair in Ankara. I looked with envy without malice at the thousands of books and writers who were signing their books. With the desire to share with others the messages and principles that had been keeping me awake at night, I suddenly said, "I have to write something. I want to be one of the writers who are signing their books at the next book fair." In that instant, my feelings were as strong as that of a mother who has had her child stolen away from her. I felt all the cells of my body quiver. After this prayer, I completed writing my book, "Think and Succeed," within two months, as if I were in a race with my own shadow. However, at the next book fair, I wandered sadly through for days because I could not have a signing for my book since my publisher could not participate in the fair.

Two days before the end of the book fair, my publisher phoned me and said: "Tomorrow is your day to sign. We will wait for you at our booth at 1pm. We have advertised it." This sudden development was a surprise birthday present given me at the New Year by Limitless Compassion.

Certainly, we have to act for our prayers to come true. However, what happened to me, time after time was that, although I could not do anything other than wish, my wishes were made true through the actions of others. If you can sincerely wish for something even as much as a baby does, officials who take orders will hasten to serve you. **However much you intensify the feeling with which you charge your wishes, the effort you need to expend to achieve that goal will decrease by that much.**

b) Silent Change

Do you know the story of Yusuf Islam, formerly known as Cat Stevens, who was once at the top of the European music charts? While he was swimming along a pleasant beach, a killer wave swept him away from the shore and brought him face-to-face with death. At the instant when he sincerely thought he was going to die, he turned sincerely to the Master of the Universe and said, "My God! If you save me, I will devote my whole life to your cause." Immediately after this, a great wave took him up and brought him to a calm shore. Because of the shock he had experienced, Cat Stevens forgot the prayer he had uttered that had saved him, but soon he became interested in religions and, years later, he came to know the Creator whom he had searched for in the depths of his spirit.

There is also the story of the great dervish Bishri Hafi. There was no way that he could free himself from the drinking that had enslaved him. He repented of it many times but, because he could not resist the insistence of his friends, he would fall back into his habit. One rainy night, when returning home drunk, he saw a sign on which was written the name of "Allah" in the muddy waters under his feet. He was startled and shocked to see the name of the Eternal Judge before whom he was ashamed dragged on the ground, so he sorrowfully took the sign from the ground and took it home where he cleaned it and hung it on the wall. He knew he was doing things that did not please Almighty Creator; however, he was grateful for the Almighty Creator. He loved God.

The next day, Hafi was shocked by the message that was excitedly brought to him by a great dervish. His desire to be freed from drunkenness was accepted and this divine message was conveyed to Bishri Hafi by means of the dream of a dervish. Such a sudden feeling was a present given him as the help of the Creator. You must be able to feel the violence of that sensation that caused Hafi, who could not free himself from his habit for years, to change in an instant and, in a short time, join the ranks of the unforgettable great ones of the age.

c) External Supports

When I completed middle school, I used to shut myself up in my room beside the books I had lined up by my bedside and read the poetry I had written. I was grieved that I did not have the possibility to continue my education. People I did not know would come from the neighboring village to see my family and continually insist that they send me to school. Why me?

I would explain every night until late to the hidden Power whom I deeply believed heard me how much I wanted to study. I could only tell Him. Years later, I was to discover the One who would never tire of listening to my troubles and who sent His messengers to support me.

You might have a useful goal, but you might think that laws are preventing you from achieving. This is not a problem, if need be, they will change. Even if they do not change, we have to work for what we believe to be good.

The seed that falls from a tree on the dry soil has no tongue; however, it wants to live and push up a new tree. A blind rat takes the seed and plants it in the earth. The seeds do not have hands and feet to travel as far as the forests of the Amazon and they cannot wander off to look for water. While they wait, day and night tons of dead planktons on top of the oceans[38] are carried to the skies by the winds. From there, they are loaded onto the clouds and brought down on the roots of the trees that are waiting for water from that sky, kilometers away. The One who does this without fail will not leave your heart alone and helpless either, if you want it, because He has not created any work of art more beautiful or valuable than a human being.

38 Planktons are microscopic creatures that increase by eating dead life forms in the oceans and collect on the surfaces of the water when they die. When the air bubbles submerged into the water explode under the pressure of the wind, the plankton on the surface fly into the air and rise to the clouds with the suction of the wind. In this way the ocean is cleansed of tons of dead planktons and the rain nourishes the forests.

II. HOW CAN WE USE THE POWER OF EMOTION?

Nourish your perceptions of value to reinforce positive feelings, use your opportunities for feeling by shaping them with your wishes, and expand your capacities for feeling by cleansing your body.

1. PERCEIVED VALUES

You can give your life meaning within the limits of values that (1) you have achieved and (2) those you can achieve. You can also define the values that you have already achieved as the field of satisfaction and the values you can achieve as the field of hope. Your values can be specific or general, within you or outside of you, acquired or yet to be acquired, and material or intellectual.

Your intensity of feeling reinforces the reflection of energy of feeling you have in yourself, such as joy, exuberance, envy, excitement, trust, self-satisfaction, importance, being liked, acceptance, desire, longing, approval, thankfulness, participation, mixing in, and satiety. Conversely, feelings, such as sorrow, shame, mistrust, worry, dissatisfaction, disrespect for yourself, and disgust, confine your heart in an ever-narrowing cage, which make you want to escape from yourself, from life, and from everything. We will now come to understand the two tasks that will help us develop in the first direction:

a) Existing values

A positive and reinforcing feeling nourishes you by focusing on the positive values which envelope your life. Feeling peace arises from thinking about the things that give peace and thinking of peace comes from realizing the sources of peace.

If you made an inventory of your being, what would you find? What are you composed of, as a being? What would emerge if you wrote a list of your material and spiritual values?

A thoughtless person is only aware of the values he or she has after he or she loses them. Likewise, many people, who are surrounded by values, are in a state of crisis because of their thoughtlessness.

It makes no sense for you to cry at the death of somebody whom you did not appreciate when they were alive. **You have no right to grieve in the absence of something at whose existence you did not rejoice.** Further, there is no need for you to comprehend the value of your warm home after it has been destroyed by an earthquake or by war. Similarly, we should not wait for a meteorite to fall on the city where we live to appreciate what a great happiness it is to walk in safety under the roof of the sky.

If you cannot imagine the absence of the blessings you do have, you need to try to deprive yourself of them for a little while. In the old days, certain dervishes would dig a grave in their gardens, lie in it, and imagine being dead in order to understand how valuable the divine gift of life was. **Someone who never thinks about death only experiences a false and deceitful joy in living.** Specifically, no one can embrace life until he or she knows death. Those who hasten to engage in good deeds for eternity are those who do not forget death.

If you cannot imagine the value of water, do not drink water for one day. If you do not appreciate your home, spend the night outdoors. If you do not place value on your eyes, blindfold yourself and try to go on with your work for an hour.

Look at the general values you have: I can see the Sun. I can hear the birds. I can touch my hair. I can walk with my feet. My face is not paralyzed; I can smile. My lungs are not congested; I can inhale the pure air of the spring. I am sane, I am aware of myself and my life. I am a living being and not a rock. My brain is working, I am not like the animals, and I can learn and develop.

I have a country; I am not stateless. I am not something scary like a scorpion. One can feel honor because of a great many of the things of value I have. They are beautiful and honorable. I can eat food; I can drink water. I can write with my fingers. I can take care of my needs. You can count thousands of general things of value in this same way.

Look at the personal things of value you have: My mother and father were very valuable people; yet they could have been murderers and immoral people. I have brothers, sisters, and relations. We have a house and a car. I am literate. I completed educational courses and I have earned diplomas. I have made friends.

What is there that is useful to you in your life? For example, if your eyes are of no use to you, throw them away; if they are of use, be grateful for them. I recommend that you begin your day with five minutes that you set aside when you step out onto your balcony in the morning before breakfast. If you spend those five minutes of every day thinking about the positive values in your life, in time, all your tensions will pass away.

b) Anticipated Values

The second most important means for the perception of values is the profundity of hope and expectation. Few people hold on to life based on their possessions; however, most of them survive through hope. Everyone who has food to eat and can survive honorably may be considered to be greatly blessed as opposed to being poor. Yet, we know there are many people who suffer misery.

The capitalist philosophy pools wealth in the hands of the minority. However, nearly a billion people in the world live on the verge of starvation. Further, every day, tens of thousands of children die from lack of adequate nutrition. In many regions of the world, blood is shed and tears flow and some people struggle to live, in spite of physical obstacles and, others, despite social disasters.

The One who sent us into the world planned the compassion in a mother's heart and the milk in her breasts before we were born. We reduce the world that was created with love to injustice and torment with our own hands, while the Creator warns us, "Despair not of the Mercy of God."[39] Because helplessness, abandonment, defeat, ruin, collapse, feebleness, come entirely from pessimism and hopelessness, when we lose our expectations, we have nothing left to activate us and we abandon ourself to oblivion.

We confront every sacrifice in this life with hope. For example, people go through years of difficult studies with the hope of a profession and personal gain. They marry in hopes of happiness and sow their grain in hopes of a harvest. It is the hope of healing that makes every patient rush to the doctor.

How hopeful are you? Are you conscious of your hopes for the future? What do you expect of your capacities, your personality, your relationships, your labors, your wealth, your culture, your family, your friends? The heart that gives the force of life to humans, suffers under so many indescribable tortures of the world, is the hope of going to the Creator, heaven, and eternity. How many people put up with the brief sufferings in the prison of this world because of their longing for the world to come?

Hope cannot be experienced unless you try to feel it. You need to want it and this wish will make you work to achieve it and keep your heart alive. Further, you need to pray and beseech for this. In doing so, your trust in the Creator will be nourished and you will know that a grace from heaven will be given to your heart. Like someone in a foreign country who is waiting for a letter from his family, you will live in the hope of every moment that a letter will come to you from the beyond.

Even if your hopes do not come true in this world, at least they will cause your life to be filled with effort and trust. Know that there is no one who is more lazy or sorrowful than one who is hopeless.

When our desires and hopes are exhausted, our efforts to develop will cease. Place high expectations on your needs so that they will be so far away that you will strive to reach them all of your life. Let the day that you achieve them be the day that you feel ready to fly beyond the world.

39 Qur'an, 39:53

2. POSITIVE EMOTIONALITY

At the base of our illnesses is the hidden misdirection of our lives, or the exaggeration of our negative feelings. It is not possible to protect the spiritual and physical health of someone who lives with feelings such as fear, grief, pessimism, jealousy, vengefulness, hate, and disgust for long periods of time. Medicine is useless for a person who is submerged in such feelings.

Additionally, life is not a rose garden. Certainly, negative events and pain will find us. We will experience injustice, disrespect, and faithlessness. However, to drown in negative feelings is an individual's choice.

To be governed by positive feelings is also a choice. Yet, it is not enough for things to go very well for us to continue with our stable sense of happiness. Rather, we must identify and choose the positive feelings that will strengthen our energy and we must enter into a real or imaginary environment that will allow us to experience these feelings.

The rule is this: (1) Negative feeling exhausts our energy. If these feelings continue for too long, the damage to our bodies cannot be repaired and sickness will begins. (2) If positive feelings are contaminated with selfishness, they will cause damage, just like negative feeling. For instance, just as hate causes damage, loving for selfish motives is equally damaging. Our goal must be to experience positive feelings with conscious efforts.

We cannot systematically live in a supportive environment as news of immoral behavior, embezzlement, and robberies are thrust into our living rooms by the news media. Therefore, if we do not control what we see and hear, our resistance to negativity will be destroyed. You need to take precautions.

Let us imitate the language of the universe and use positive-strengthening feelings. Let us also examine a few feelings such as e**xcitement, love, tenderness, self-sacrifice, friendship, sincerity, appreciation, forgiveness, and respect.**

a) Compassion and Love

You will come across people in your environment that cannot see, cannot walk, or are helplessly in the grips of poverty. Try to enter their world. The enthusiasm and patience they have, in spite of everything, will touch your heart and you must not shut yourself up in your home, office, or store.

You will see the children living in tents within disaster zones and look into your eyes with love. After the icy nights in which they shiver, they still expect to feel that they are tenderly loved by someone.[40] Ask the local authorities who the poor people of the neighborhood are. When you learn that a mother in the next apartment building is feeding her four orphan children flour soup, the cake you are eating will stick in your throat. Experience compassion and stop sitting nailed to front of the television that is trying to harden your heart.

A honeybee flies enthusiastically through the mountains and no bird sits motionless on its branch for 24 hours. Even the wind moves about the earth. Love was not created to shut a human up within four walls.

People love what is beautiful and the reason why people forget to love is that they do not pay attention to what is beautiful. You discern joy in the chirpings among the branches of the trees on spring mornings. If you watch the ants and butterflies in the grass, you will smile to yourself. If you are wetted by the rain drops that carry spiritual forms of life, your cells will quiver from a sense of peacefulness.

Life is not just the ugliness of a bunch of gangs who are busy robbing each other. **You should long to smile as you see the sun rising.** The coming of the morning light, which the world greets with festivity, should not find you sleeping in your bed like a corpse with the curtains drawn. Do not frown at nature that smiles **with gladness at the repetition of the Divine Name.** The honor of walking under the stars and beholding the skies was not given only to the inhabitants of the mountains.

40 We went to Düzce, one of the cities destroyed in the earthquake. The earthquake victims greeted us like family members. When a neighborhood living in tents assembled their families to say good-by to us, it was as though they were bidding farewell to brothers and sisters going to a foreign land they would never see again.

Saying "I love you" does not increase feelings of love. As stated in our book "Love Intelligence," the ability to love is not dependent on a decision. It depends on the existence of the reasons for loving and on the ability to recognize those reasons. As the reasons to love that you discern in a being increase, the intensity of your love increases as well.

For example, a soldier was separated from his wife and two children and was left face-to-face with nature. He felt as though the trunk of the tree he embraced was a beloved, a child, or a flower. If even a tree can give you such deep feelings, you will long to return to that tree once again, even years later, and hug its trunk. This is not poverty of love; it is the wealth of love.

You rejoice when you love and to be loved is to love. I recall the words of the Caliph Ali (May mercy be upon him), "**Treat others so well that, when you die, even your enemies will cry.**"

b) Excitement

A drab and grey existence is a life that is shut away from nature and imprisoned by the house and television. City life imprisons us in piles of concrete and tears us away from life, whereas, our Creator wants us to experience, in our hearts, the thousand and one arts that spread over the four seasons. The lawful excitement that protects honor and elevates a human being is the feeling that comes from the pursuit of sacred values.

There is no excitement in the prison of television. Rather, excitement lay within the games of children and the joking back and forth between a husband and wife. Excitement lay in nature and in the smell of a grill at a picnic. It is in watching the stars at nighttime, listening to the chirping of birds at dawn, wandering through cities, and traveling to different cultures. Th**e life that succeeds by continually renewing itself and giving itself variety is enveloped by excitement.**

I have spent hours talking with one of my neighbors about the amazing characteristics of the Van cat. I listened for days about the family life of domestic pigeons as discussed by one of my army friends. I have discussed the sociology in Germany for days with another army friend. A person's interest in the things that he or she does not know is an attitude that opens the horizons of the world as material for thought. Every different world carries within it an amazing excitement.

Excitement lay in action and it is concealed in walking, looking around and observation, and trying to discover different cities, mountains, and countries. You will suffocate in drabness if you sit waiting for something to happen. However, if you wish get up and sit down right now, take a deep breath, flex your muscles quickly, or quickly return to your surroundings and look at them carefully. These little activities may be enough to fire up your excitement.

Excitement produces greater movement; new and different things from greater wishes. If you express admiration for a beautiful piece of poetry or a fine painting what happens? What happens if you share your pleasure for a tasty meal with the chef, telephone a journalist who has written something truthful, or go in person to congratulate a mayor who has performed a good service for the city? If you do not appreciate those who work for you, you will not be able to find anyone to work for you.

If people look for spiritual enjoyment and you cannot give it to them, they will turn away and find someone else. **There is no excitement in laziness and indifference and enthusiasm cannot exist in the same place. Therefore, we must live pessimistically, in the comfort of laziness, or enthusiastically, in the tiredness of labor.** There is no third option.

3. OPPORTUNITIES FOR FEELING

Let us examine the three areas that can contribute to the arousal of vitality of feeling: special events, special places, and special dates.

a) Events

Taking an exam, receiving your diploma, feeling love for a child or a flower, setting out for a picnic, going to bed tired, getting wet by the rain, experiencing a severe headache or toothache, meeting and an old friend, putting on new clothes, receiving a present, hearing your child says his first word, hugging your child for the first time, rejoicing when your child brings home his first report card or when you receive a promotion. Do your senses fill with excitement and feel more alive than usual when you experience things like these?

You can eat an apple in two ways: you can bite it, chew, and swallow it while you are busy thinking about the soccer game that evening or about the bills you have to pay tomorrow. Your body has eaten, but your heart has not been able to experience it. Look at what you have done and be aware that it is a packaged present that your Creator has given you. Concentrate carefully on the taste on your tongue. This is like a glass of water that your beloved offers you. **The pleasure of drinking the water is overshadowed by the joy that the existence of your beloved, who offered it, gives you.** Feel the taste in every part of your mouth. The joy you will feel, which will cause your cells to quiver as it grows, will overshadow all your loves.

The soul of a madman is not that of a saint; there is a chasm between souls. Some souls are as dry as a rock and some are as pure as the wind. Someone who lives in unawareness should not be considered to have a soul because there are so many things that they do not participate in with their souls that they live like corpses. These individuals eat the apple with their mouths, yet they watch TV with their hearts. Their eyes are open but their hearts are asleep. Let us make our spirits live the beautiful life that our bodies live. If we do this, a drop of honey we taste will make us wander at the mountains and valleys among the buzzing of the bees.

b) Places

The intense feelings that people experience in certain places is derived from the collective memories of those places experienced in a spiritual dimension. Everybody who passes through such places is affected by the general intensity of feelings in those place, good or bad, according to their own dispositions.

Temples, battlefields, places where the most important events of history have occurred, cemeteries, regions where there has been a recent earthquake or disaster, and ruins of cities are places where collections of energy are experienced.

From time-to-time, our lives will become dull and monotonous. By planning our holidays and our free time, we can arrange visits to these types of emotionally moving places and refresh our spirits.

c) Dates

What makes dates different from one another is the meaning people give them and, thanks to the meaning, the change in the spiritual environment of commonly shared feelings. Because of events that took place on those dates, those common feelings are activated when their anniversaries recur.

Religious holidays and the month of Ramadan for Muslims, Sundays for Christians, May 1 for Socialists, Thanksgiving for Americans, birthdays, the anniversary of a death or a marriage for everyone, the times when one experiences the first days of spring, the last days of autumn, or the first snowfall of winter...

What makes special dates powerful is the intensity of feelings that people experience on those dates. As such, dates are the most effective opportunities for nations to purify themselves of their diseases. The sincere prayers made by nations on the same day on such dates are much more effective than scattered prayers.

4. CLEANSING THE BODY

Positive affectivity is possible and easy with bodily and psychic internal cleanliness. We need to do things to activate the body that is torpid with harmful hormones and the toxic matter it has accumulated. The brain, which struggles to administer the body in which waste has accumulated, does not have any energy left to devote to intellectual and feeling activities.

If our bodies have become clumsy, we can make them work again with ten exercises that others can accomplished with one exercise.

In fact, if waste accumulates in our bodies, a noise comes from every organ. You drag your body like a block of wood. You feel as heavy as a truck. You feel a tension inside you and a pain in every cell. The intensity level of this pain is critical.

Think of your body as a skyscraper with trillions of cells made up of independent souls. What is holding this skyscraper together are the orderly mechanisms that allow it to function? What happens to you when your arteries narrow, you suffer damage to your kidneys, your stomach malfunctions, you lose your elasticity on account of the waste that has accumulated in your cellular environment is similar to what happens to an automobile when it breaks down.

The one who moves forward the fastest is the person who succeeds in putting his body under easy control. For example, some people carry their bodies on their backs like the weight of a truck. They lose their breath when they climb the stairs, they cannot get out of bed, and their knees will not allow them to walk for an hour.

Do not think that these people take pleasure in living and laughing. Just as they cannot laugh with enthusiasm, they cannot weep with joy.

What we call exhaustion of the intellect and the brain is our inability to expend the surplus energy of the body because it is so clumsy and, thus, not able to devote enough energy to other activities. People who do not keep their brains active might not be aware of such problems until they receive warning signals.

You can avoid accumulating harmful hormones if you stay away from negative feelings. However, you need to take balanced care of your body and pay attention to your nourishment, conditioning, and level of your respiration and sleep. Your bodily cleanliness will bring with it a control of the intellect and feelings.

a) Nourishment

*Leave your stomach one third empty after every meal. Excess food collects waste, which, for the most part, cannot be cleansed from the body. The waste collects and the body will one day rebel. Drink plenty of water, an average of two liters a day or eat food that contains a lot of water. Decrease red meats and even poultry. You may eat as much fish as you like and one egg a day is enough for your protein needs.

*Fast for one month each year or go hungry from time-to-time. Eat vegetables and fruits that contain a lot of liquid. Your food should be raw and living. Over a few months, you should slowly stop eating bread, dough, and processed foods. Take breakfast seriously, but in the evenings do not eat late and eat as little as possible. Finally, stop snacking between meals except for in season fruits.

*Do not drink more than ten cups of tea and avoid overly salty foods and sweets. Chew so that you do not swallow large amounts of food. Manage to eat slowly and take small bites and chew them well, in a leisurely way.

*You should become accustomed to eating honey, black cumin, spinach salad olive oil, fresh squeezed orange or grapefruit juice and seasonal fruits.

b) Breathing

Engage in deep breathing exercises from the diaphragm each morning and evening; at least twice a day and if you are more committed, several times a day. Take a deep breath through your nose for a unit of time and hold it in your lungs for four times as long as it took to inhale, then exhale through your mouth for two times as long as it took to inhale. For example, if you breathed in for one second, hold it for four seconds and then let it out for two seconds. If you inhaled for two seconds the period is: 2/8/4 seconds, respectively. You ought to do this a maximum of 25 times at each session.

When you have the chance, go to the valleys, mountains, rivers, or seaside where there is a lot of oxygen. Air your room out.

c) Conditioning

*Take a walk or engage in similar light physical activity three times a week. Divide your physical activity into three parts. The first 15 minutes use as a warm up, the following 20 minutes engage in a more forceful walk or exercise, and the last 10 minutes set aside to cool down with slow movements to restore balance to your body and balance to the blood that has collected in the tissues you have used.

*Physical activities that do not last 45 minutes are not active enough to cleanse the body. It is very dangerous for your heart to work out intensely, suddenly, and without warming up. If you do not have enough breath left to talk when you are engaged in physical activity, then you have gone beyond the capacity of your body. Therefore, you need to increase your timing slowly. You can increase your speed every week as your blood vessels expand and in, 6 months, you will be able to fly like the wind.

*Move your body faster than average. Walking fast is like a quick cleansing. If you do not have a problem with time, you can choose to do your work with physical movements rather than use electronic equipment.

*A stressful life will cause you to lose excessive energy by tensing your muscles and, over time, will destroy your nervous system. Therefore, relax your muscles frequently.

d) Sleep

*Scientific studies have demonstrated that we have two different sleep waves. These waves comprise two different periods: 11 PM to 6 AM at night and 12 PM to 1 PM in the day. In addition to your nightly sleep, try to find the opportunity to sleep 30 minutes around noon. If you don't have the time, 15 minutes of rest will still benefit you.

*Sleep that exceeds eight or less than six hours a day or irregular sleep continued after you wake up in the morning damages your brain and body. If you sleep more than you need, if you don't get up early in the morning (before sunrise), if you sleep before noon, or in a noisy surrounding, and, especially, if you go to sleep immediately after you have eaten, all the problems you have accumulated will explode at some point and will take their revenge all at once. Mistakes in sleeping can cause weakening of the memory, dissatisfaction, chronic tiredness, lack of productivity, and even depression.

CHAPTER FOUR:

THE POWER OF PERSISTENCE

I. WHY WE NEED THE POWER OF PERSISTENCE?

INTRODUCTION

Could you eat an elephant? Could you take a tour around the world? If you know the technique of patient persistence yes, you can do these things; if not, you can't! During your life, you will walk as much as if you had taken three tours around the earth. You will drink more than fifty tons of water. The answer to the question, "Will you make some work of art or literature?" conceals the answer to the question, "Will you patiently persist in doing an original artistic work?"

Your form of persistence is like using the gas and brake pedals of an automobile. Great success is the fruit of patient persistence that is directed to a defined goal. The greatest secret of human of learning, rich people, and geniuses, in short, of those who have won out, produced, and affected things, is their persistence. Take this seriously! If this ability were as easy and simple as it might appear at first, everybody would succeed.

When you direct yourself toward the road to advancement, the Owner of Destiny will test your seriousness by placing obstacles in your path. However, through persistence, many paths that will look as if they were closed will yield to your persistence and be opened by the Creator.

Persistence is like a seed that wants to be a tree and bear fruit. **Those who persist in thinking and believing are resilient in their behaviors.** Persistence insures that what is small will increase and speed up production and advancement.

This is the formula: **Success Level = Persistence x Action.** Your capacity for action can only be as big as the limits of your current physical power; but your persistence capacity can be as big as your life and the life of the universe. Divine Wisdom created everything in a slow, calm, orderly, continuous, uninterrupted, and restful manner. Let us mimic this divine wisdom.

If you persist in thinking in the same way, you will move ahead in that direction. Attitude and behavior reflect persistence, which begins with thought. Life is the "thought-feeling-behavior" cycle. Persistence in thoughts and feelings repeats behavior, develops habits, and makes the road to success automatic. As long as you don't give up, your heart will learn to persist on your behalf day and night.

You can plant your sapling tree right now; the moment for you to start working is right now. If a tree is planted, it will grow, but if one does not feed it, it will decay. Persistence means planting the tree and nourishing it regularly; it does not mean to wear out its life by eating all of the fruit.

1. THE MEANING OF PERSISTENCE

What is the relationship between purpose, repetition, and resting, the three elements that make up persistence? Why is persistent patience possible within the triangle of thought, feeling, and action?

a) The Element of Purpose

The most important element of persistent patience is purpose. To what purpose does your persistence hope to gain?

As you know, living is conforming to changes in a very difficult surrounding. You go forward, struggling with a difficult climate, such as in an airplane. Whatever stops and does not change collapses and decays. Every living thing, business, and work of the imagination is born, is developed, and comes to an end.

Your life is the greatest work that you have administered and you administer your life by patiently protecting it from threats, staying faithful to your responsibilities and working on your goals. You need to extract from the management of your life and bring out the elements of persistence that you will practice.

You will persist in four different goals: 1) being patient in misfortune, 2) opposing your destructive desires, 3) moving toward your goals, and 4) retaining your spiritual devotion. If you fail in one of these goals, you will be unsuccessful for the rest of your life.

How can we overcome difficulties? What should our models of behavior be in such situations as illnesses, accidents, disasters, betrayals, loss of jobs, and the like? If we do not know the answer to these questions, we will almost certainly stumble and collapse on our road to success.

How can you sustain yourself on the level of superior morality? The tranquility of this world and the hereafter is related to retaining one's awareness of the duty to the Almighty Creator along with one's ethicalness. If we cannot establish the values of honesty, justice, respect, virtue, modesty, peace, belief, worship, prayer, and the like, our skyscraper of success will fall at a certain stage. We must take precautions against evil from without and from within as many people have become victims of evil and have failed at the height of their fame and success because of their moral weakness.

In the area of productivity, what are you going to produce? Where are you going to work, what profession are you going to discharge, where are you going to travel in the world, how are you going to entertain yourself, what is going to become of your property?

You need to decide these things as soon as possible. The pages of life have been planned out. Not everybody can be president. One person must sell while the other buys. One must teach while the other must learn. If the tickets run out, you will have to wait for the next bus. **If you delay for a short time, you may be condemned to wait for a long time.**

This means that the earlier you begin developing your future, the farther you will advance. The road is long but life is short. Additionally, the road is the same for everyone and not all of us continue the race with the same persistence. If nobody encouraged us to aspire to great goals when we were young, then, today is the day that we can begin to do this for ourselves.

b) Cycles of Repetition

Every seminal design has a reasonable, intelligent period for getting things done. If we can determine this intelligent period correctly, we will have neither too little nor too much, we will not destroy the relations we have built, and we will not perish in our endeavors.

Making this happen is bound to our shaping the situation in an orderly, but adequate, way. Your child wants to hear, regularly, that you trust him or her. Your spouse wants to feel, at definite intervals via your behavior, that you love him or her.

It is beneficial to drink water, but it is destructive to drink water continually. It is beneficial to think but to think about the same subject continually damages the brain. Worship, work, and sleep all have their definite times and limits.

Excessive selfish ambition leads us to depression, fearfulness, and failure. **Selfish ambition exhausts our patience and we want to have everything now.** In this way, we strain our nervous systems and, in doing this, the next day we might suffer a nervous collapse and we have to give up.

Persistence is like a two-directional arrow. Persistence with intervals for rest will destroy obstacles; however, unremitting persistence will destroy the persistent person. The heart has a short resting period after it beats. For example, if it beats 100 thousand times a day, it also rests 100 thousand times.

You can persist throughout your lifetime if you take periodic breaks. For example, a student who takes rest brakes can read 200 books a year, but if one reads continuously for 48 hours, one will collapse and become unable to read anything. Therefore, repetition must be periodical and you need to take breaks in between your work and activities to replenish your energy and strength. The technique of "divide, take pieces, and swallow" can only work through persistence. **Success demands a lot of work, but the first reason for failure is working without a break.**

We can repeat what we do five or ten times. In fact, we can fill our whole day with these activities if we work in blocks of 50 to 60 minutes, which is enough. If we have breaks for relaxation and entertainment of around 10 minutes each, this will allow us to start over again. Finally, a good night's sleep at the end of every day will permit us to bear the same load the following day.

Persistence is not just the continuation of one days' work; rather, it is the effort of a lifetime. Persistence develops all of our abilities, just as a tree growing normally.

If we work away at a thought process or at an activity without taking a break, we will shortly suffocate with stress and explode. Therefore, if you want to succeed, try to do what you are doing and rest, try it again, and rest again.

c) The Dimension of Flexibility

What increases the effectiveness of persistence is doing something intelligently. Obsessive persistence coming from blind stubbornness or from gazing at life with blinders on, which is useless. Mistaken, irrational persistence is persistence that is asking for trouble. No good comes from unwise efforts like those of a child who begs to go to the park in the middle of the night.

If we tire, our right arm by turning a stone over, we ought to be able to go on using our left arm. If we tire our minds by studying mathematics for an hour, we ought to be able to go on by studying literature. If the customer doesn't buy our goods with our first strategy, we ought to be able to try a second strategy.

To expand on the point on this, let us ask the following: (1) Am I working toward a reasonable and achievable goal? (2) Is there another road that would help me other than the road I am currently pursuing? (3) Have I tired myself too much, am I about to collapse, should I take a break of a few minutes or a few weeks to recover my physical and psychic strength?

If you clearly understand that your current method for reaching your goal is not effective, stop, think, and try to find another way. Be persistent, but, at the same time, be flexible. Be ready to change tactics, strategies, and even your goals. You do not want to insist on a goal that is obviously impossible or is beyond your limitations. Use your intelligence to understand what is possible for you and what is not. How will you do this?

Please be serious. Do not let a possibility seem like an impossibility. Think that, sometimes, persistence takes us on a narrow pass at the edge of a precipice. When we look from the precipice, the road can appear dark and impossible to pass. There can be many reasons we considered the road an impossibility; for example, because the laws forbid it, the application period has expired, or because nobody will help.

In my life, I have given up great efforts many times because I thought the goal in which I devoted was impossible. However, I would have obtained great results if I had persisted a little bit more. Your goal may be difficult, but do not decide about its impossibility too quickly. Remember, **the secret of success is hidden in persistence beyond the limits of helplessness.**

You can solve some of your problems or reach some of your small goals in a few minutes. But bigger problems may require years of effort. Therefore, if you have big goals, or huge problems, you need to be ready to pay their substitutes. Think about this: If solving something meant saving yourself from death, wouldn't you hold out to the very last breath? Real **persistence means holding on until the last breath.**

I have been defeated, collapsed, and I have given up. Yet, I was sorry I gave up and went back and was defeated once more but I went back again. I repeated to myself: "God willing, I will do it, I will do it. If I don't die, I will keep on trying to do it."

If my brain still works, I still want to do this and I will continue to work on it as soon as I wake up every day. If I do not tear out my heart and throw it away, I will still love it, still, still, still. Until when? Until my last breath, if need be, to the Day of Judgment. Continually and with rest brakes, however short they may be.

Others can try to destroy our hopes, they can be jealous of us, they can look down on us, and they may not show us appreciation. They can pick out one bad thing we have done from amongst ten of our good deeds and wave it in our faces. Life is not a game. To save a life, to add value to life, this is not a game. **To conquer life is superior to conquering the sun and a life to be conquered waits for all of us.**

You will reap weeds from the soil where you did not sow your seeds. If you have not persistently watered the flowers of good intentions within your heart, your heart will turn into an uncultivated field. Your mind will be smothered because you are chasing after useless things.

To truly be flexible and seriously insistent, you need to become as close to your efforts as the flesh is to the bone. Study every day and be concerned every time you talk and love and whenever you look at your goals. **You need to plan your day and you need to become caught up every day with your goals, even if it is only for a minute.**

2. THE REASON FOR PERSISTENCE

There is persistence, patience, continuity, and insistent repetition concealed behind all meaningful successes. Changes in life happen not with disconnected, sudden, and powerful movements but with continuous, slow, and calm movements. The basic ideals, which govern life, force us to persistence.

a) The Concept of Change

When we examine life carefully, we see a series of concepts of change that require persistence:

Many drops make a lake. Mountains rise by inches and lakes fill up by drops. We arrive to all great things by tiny steps. If you eat a plate of potatoes a day, in a lifetime you will have eaten a truckload worth of potatoes. Continuity causes us to build up reserves.

Life changes gradually. If you sow the seed, it takes time for it to break through the soil, take root, sprout, and grow branches and buds. No interference can disturb the relationship of development time that has been established by the Creator. You cannot change the healthy rate of development of a baby even if you place it in a sea of milk.

Change takes place with continuous effect. The flight of an airplane is bound to its being continuously propelled after it has taken off. If a growing plant ceases to be nourished, the plant will die. If you begin a job, then stop doing it for too long, when you return, everything will be overgrown with weeds and decay.

You need to take a reasonable rest to have a continuous effect. Your heartbeats, rests, and beats again. Your stomach fills, waits, consumes, and then needs to be filled again. Your brain works, rests, and then works again. Your body works, it grows tired and sleeps and then works again. In all these cycles, there is a different rest period for each circumstance and every situation. If you cannot find these time periods reasonable, you cannot persist in a healthy way.

So then, you cannot achieve success or produce anything without persistence. Behind all the successes of life lie hidden intelligently utilized persistence. The commerce of the world is under the control of those who persist three times more than others. People who learn to drive, type with ten fingers, and speak foreign languages are those people who work through to the result without abandoning the progress they have made.

b) Striking Effect

Persistence produces a striking effect. If you do ten units of work, piece by piece, you will not even achieve a result but if you work with persistence, you will obtain results equivalent of one hundred units. The seeds of a tree may increase to half a kilo in the first year when it takes root. If it continues to grow at the same rate, it will increase to ten kilos in twenty years and to twenty tons in twenty years. If you keep on nourishing your weak abilities, they will develop profoundly even if you do not notice them and they will suddenly attract attention later. If you try to make a butterfly come out of its cocoon too early, you will kill it.

Most of our abilities have at least a 30% flexibility rate. If you would concentrate your efforts a little more, you could walk faster and read faster. However, if you try to exceed that 30% suddenly, you will stumble and fall. You can develop a double, triple, or a quadruple performance with time. **Everyone can increase his speed in a short time but we have to be aware that it takes years of work to reach super speeds and that only for very few of us.**

The strength of ordinary people may perhaps be sufficient just to direct them but if they work and make good use of the abilities they do have, they can become presidents who direct millions of people.

If you move ahead in persistence, you will suddenly come out of the tunnel. It will be as if the morning had suddenly broken. People who don't move ahead in the tunnel should not hope to see the light. One who keeps on moving ahead should not think that darkness is his eternal destiny.

Some geniuses owe their success to the inspirational wind of a powerful sentence that they have heard while walking. This sentence was an important seed in their intelligences and over time, they generated for themselves a wonderful personality by developing it.

A man advancing a hundred meters in a swamp towards a green valley that lay a kilometer away thinks he has not moved forwards when he looks at the place where he steps. Like this, we fall into the valley of pain. Due to our efforts, our lives are on the point of changing but we cannot see what is to come and we know nothing about the shore we have approached. The day when I was freed from the illness that I had suffered from for years was one of the days when I had thought I would not ever be cured.

c) Protection of Abilities

You know that iron that is used does not rust. An unoccupied house is taken over by spiders. You can obtain value and you can protect value as well. Our ideal should be based on these words: **"If you have planted a tree, water it."**[41]

Currently, there are millions of people who have spent years learning things, yet have forgotten them. They learned foreign languages at the university, yet cannot speak these languages now. They learned war strategies in the military or how to stay fit, yet their bodies are out of shape. They learned songs in elementary school, now they can't even sing as well as crows. They absorbed hundreds of books in their school lives as though they had gone through their digestive systems and now nothing is left in their memories. They learned how to write articles and now they can't even write a letter.

The reason for this is obvious. They did not protect the abilities they gained; they did not use them persistently; they did not make them a part of their lives, whereas even money in a safe will not remain intact. In ten years' time, if the moths on the inside do not eat it up, inflation on the outside will destroy it.

It is difficult to obtain abilities, but is very easy to protect or lose them. We do what is difficult and we neglect to do what is easy. Just as a hungry stomach contracts, the brain that does not work grows weak. The abilities we do not use grow dull over time. If you are a teacher, you need

41 *Mawlana* Rumi , Masnavi, vol. 4, p. 62.

to teach. Once the insect completes its duty, it dies. Whoever closes his or her ears turns deaf. Whoever does not love becomes unable to love.

Your abilities are each divine contracts made with you. People, who break the good faith of their contracts, void those contracts. Those who do not use their abilities as they ought will lose them. Values will be given to those who appreciate them. Look at the destinies of those who are desolate; **their separations, quarrels, and betrayals conceal the same secrets.**

3. THE RECOMPENSE OF LACK OF PERSISTENCE

Those who give up cannot change; they cannot succeed; they cannot overcome their limitations and obstacles.

a) Inability to develop

An effort without persistence is an unstable effort and an unstable effort prevents progress. There is a seed in the human soul that struggles to come forth. It makes humankind work madly from infancy onwards. However, in adulthood, we start to treat our will lazily and in a disorganized way.

Not to develop means to destroy the shell. **The tree that cannot expand its bark will dry up or it will burst.** Baby chickens peck their shell repeatedly to get out of their egg. The first peck expands it, the second splits it, and the third breaks it to pieces.

When a caterpillar emerges from the cocoon that holds it tight to become a butterfly, it is an adventure that lasts for hours. How can those who give up after three tries discover the colorful world?

If there is a cry within you that says, "I want to dedicate myself to higher values," you will reside in a high place. **Lofty spirits fly on high drawing their bodies after them.** If you walk on the high mountains, remember the words of Solzhenitsyn, "One cry can bring down an avalanche."

Some people persist because they do not want to change. Although they appear to want democracy, they act as shocked by its reality as though they had been shot in the heart. They say, "I want to be rich but I don't want to work. I want to be honored but I don't want to have any responsibility."

Pharaoh was so set in his pretense of being a god that he resisted the Prophet Moses (PBUH). With his army, he ran after the Prophet Moses (PBUH) and the believers to the coast of the Red Sea. Even when he saw that the Red Sea parted and the believers passed over it he still silenced his heart and was amazed by this supernatural miracle. He and his army were drowned there. This is the sealing and locking of hearts. When the sea closed again and drowned him and his army and he began to drown, he at last saw the truth but by then it was too late.

The future of proud and closed people is a dark one. Their hearts are locked and change is impossible for them. **If people do not change their knowledge, they cannot change their thoughts, their feelings, their actions, and in the end, their lives.**

b) Failure

Failure is the last option, the final result. If the game continued, nobody would be condemned to lose. Our journey of success goes on until death. The moment a wrestler loses is not when he or she is turned over; he or she can get up. He or she can repeatedly get up for a lifetime and go on. **A runner who continues in the struggle is not considered to have lost.** However, some people may have decided that they can't go on any longer in one of their falls. Then they lose their determination, they become losers.

It is not the tearing of our muscle tissues that make us give up the struggle as healthy humans can give up. What stops our energy is that we do not appeal to the Limitless Power that created our hearts. We submit to defeat or laziness and bow our heads. It is not worthy of us to live like chickens that were raised to have their heads cut off.

The story of a woman who was thought to be a paraplegic during the Vietnam War is an example of this. She was admitted to a hospital for wounded soldiers. They gave the woman the responsibility of answering the telephone. The hospital was bombed and most of the healthy staff were killed. She worked so persistently and sincerely that she forgot all about her illness. After a few days, she got back on her feet and started to walk.

If destiny leaves us hungry, we can suddenly forget our other troubles, but only after we have filled our stomachs and warmed ourselves, hundreds of troubles appear. Spoiled children come from careless situations, a lack of ideals, and love of ease and comfort.

If someone can become interested in something besides illness, many of the roots of his illness will dry up. A useful activity is one of the most effective therapies. Someone who does not shed their sweat in some useful occupation will spend their energy in gossip, jealousy, selfish ambition, and pride. People who fight over simple issues are aimless, without a hobby, lacking in ideals, and vain.

If our deep wish has been lost to our hearts, the goal that it would have led us to is also lost. Once we have lost hold of our lifeline, we will lose much time and progress to take hold of it again amidst the terrible, stormy seas.

One who has lost his goal cannot pick up and go on. **If you start from nothing every day, you will only move forward one day at a time over your lifetime.** The journey of success is not for one day only. A diploma from the university of life will only be given to you with your last breath.

When I was a soldier, I noticed ants running excitedly about. I interfered with an ant that was carrying a bug by putting a rock in front of it. I tried for half an hour to interfere with its progress by putting rocks here and there in its path. Every time after it got past these obstacles, it would get a meter closer to the entry to its nest. I picked up the ant and put it down farther from where it had been. At the first opportunity, it turned around and headed back in its original direction. This is what giving your life to an ideal is about. This is what it means to not give up; this is what continuity is.

4. EXPLANATORY EXPERIENCES

Below, I relate some of my experiences with persistence and the results I have obtained with them.

a) The Exam Example

When I applied to take the exam to become a specialist for the Turkish Parliament, only a short time remained for me to study. I had the responsibilities in a non-profit organization and I was under pressure to deal with all my duties.

The books I had to read were a meter tall when I piled them one on top of another. I had to read and grasp these books while I was still taking care of a half day of errands.

Both things, together, frightened me. After thinking about it for one whole day, I made my decision: I would take care of my business and I would also read the books.

I hurried to my desk every free moment I had. Neither kitchen work, the telephone, the doorbell, nor my work with my students would interrupt my studies. I was back sitting at my desk after quickly dealing with any business that interrupted my reading.

At first, I hid all of the other books except for one. I placed each book in a different section of my mind. In this way, I divided this big goal into smaller parts. The goal that had frightened me as a whole became very small when it was divided into little pieces. I never thought about what I was going to read in the evening or the next day. I simply concentrated on what I was going to read at that time.

What I was able to do in a month was noteworthy. All of the books that I thought I would not be able to go through in a year, I was able read twice. In fact, I even had a chance to do this over again. I divided, took smaller pieces, and swallowed. This study method allowed me to pass my exam.

b) Interview with the Minister

People who were close to me continually told me about certain difficulties they had in a sub-department of the Ministry of Health. The head of the department made the health personnel take care of his private problems, which resulted in the personnel asking for a transfer and fleeing from the district.

I decided to solve the problem and put a stop to the department head. My interviews with the Director of the Province, my informing a representative in the Assembly and my applications to bureaucrats were all without result. I became aware, during my efforts, of how hard it was to prevent the ill intentions and attitudes in bureaucracy and I saw how easy it was for politicians to go astray.

I did not give up my attempts and, in the end; I decided to see the Minister of Health. I made a file of all the information I had gathered. When I went to see the Minister of Health, I had to pass through all the checkpoints from the office of his counsel to his private bureau. However, **I was persistent in my goal. I acted with a firm belief.** I resisted, at every step, those who wanted to turn me away or hand my file to the Minister on my behalf.

After three months of persistence, I caught him at a moment when we were alone in his office and he let me talk to him. I gave him my file and explained the problem. He looked at my face and he must have seen that I was sincere. After reading a resume of my file, he telephoned Director of the Health Ministry, ordered the claims to be investigated, and dismissed the sub-director.

c) Documents

I had to follow up the appointment papers through the provincial Department of Health and the Office of the Governor of Ankara. This could not be resolved through phone calls and the persons who intervened could not solve the problem.

I tried to find the document because it had mistakenly gone to the Assistant Governor's Office. However, when I found that the paper was not written correctly, I took it back to correct. I had to wait because the governor had gone to a funeral. It was an incredible runaround. I held out to the last moment.

Everybody said, "Go away and come back tomorrow" and each time something inside of me tried to make me give up in fear. I struggled with my fearfulness. They would say, "The Governor isn't coming. The papers are not here. Even if he does come, he can't sign them today." Sometimes, I myself would say this but I still wouldn't give up. Then they told me, "There's just ten minutes till he leaves the office. You can't get there in time." But, I persisted.

I got the Governor's signature at 5:22 PM. There were ten minutes until the end business hours for the Health Office. I called the Assistant Director and told him I was on my way. When I rushed to the door, I saw there was a taxi waiting for me. The unbelievable traffic and traffic lights at that hour worked to our advantage, it was as if they had cleared the roads for us. In five minutes, we reached the location that would have normally taken us 20 minutes in that congested traffic. I completed the transaction and realized my goal.

II. HOW CAN WE USE THE POWER OF PERSISTENCE?

1. SPEED CONTROL

A vehicle that cannot control its speed cannot move forward without having an accident: How can you control your speed by resting sufficiently, competing with yourself, and not hurrying?

a) Resting Sufficiently

A competitive racecar that races with another or hurries will remain behind or on the sidelines by a careless accident. The lack of fuel or a burned out motor will stop a car that does not rest. However, the way to advance with stability is to move intelligently, slow down intelligently, and stop intelligently.

Working and becoming tired makes a person active. Iron that is worked on does not get rusty; a person who works stays young and active. However, success in every work lay in its being balanced. For example, a student who sat without moving in front of his computer, died at the end of the day.

I paid dearly every time during periods of my life when I worked without resting. I once worked for a month without stopping. The next month, I was sick, forgetful, unproductive, and could not think. The penalty of my sleepless nights was always that I spent the daytimes like a sleepwalker.

Is your memory becoming weak? Are you unable to learn? Are you suffering from depression? Is your extra work a heavy burden to you? Do you not get any pleasure from life? Can you not put up with anyone? If the answer is yes, the alarm bell is ringing! You need to have overtired your brain or your body beyond what you can tolerate.

Remember the rest periods we previously discussed. Be sure you have rested your brain, your body, your heart in hourly, daily, weekly, monthly, and yearly periods.

To rest is to stop running; it is to leave the work you are doing. The mind is filled with all types of subjects and, if possible, with the beauties of nature and it fills with a renewable energy.

b) Racing with Yourself

If we start with the psychology of surpassing others, we will soon be exhausted. Exhaustion occurs because competition tires your heart by stirring up jealousy and wears your body down by increasing your stress.

If we act with the psychology of surpassing other people, our energy will soon give out because competition fans the flames of jealousy and tires the heart. Additionally, there will always be those who are superior to us. The result of a competitive attitude is fearfulness and exhaustion. It will not benefit us in our lives.

The solution I have found is this: **I will not compete with anyone other than myself.** You can't continue running for very long when you are the very last in a race. The effort you need to exert to show that you are leading is much greater than the effort you use to show that you are not leading. **Those who are always in the lead are those who are only racing with themselves.**

Further, those who compete with others are forced to behave hypocritically; they are encouraged to look attractive and pretend as though they were intelligent and superior. It is tiring for a person to try to conceal his true personality with a false one.

With whom will I compete? Everywhere is filled with people who are more attractive, wealthier, and more intelligent. If I compete with them, they will walk over me. If we compete when we find ourselves failing, our hearts will turn against them and say, "You can't be like that. Stop these vain dreams."

However, destiny does not make one person compete with another. If we were supposed to compete with one another, we would not have been created differently, some tall and some short. Some of us would not have been furnished with strong arms while others have delicate fingers. Some of us cannot see and some of us cannot hold on because we are our own competitors.

It has been revealed to our hearts: "We hold YOU accountable. We gave the duty to YOU and we hold YOU responsible. YOU are the one who is there. We love YOU on YOUR account and not that of others. YOUR **success is in** YOUR **being better than YOU are every day.** YOU **should not have two days that are the same."**

A friend was excited at a speech he heard during a meeting. In a secret jealousy, he told me that he wanted to make just as an effective presentation and proposed this to me. I was aware of the destructiveness of his secret motivation and I warned him: It is very beneficial to imitate successful people but trying to surpass them will cause a person to stumble. We can imitate successful people but we shouldn't compete with them. We can surpass them some day and the soundest way to do this occurs by trying to surpass ourselves every day.

The hardest skill on **earth is to not be jealous of others.** Those who compete with others are condemned to jealousy when they grow weak. People who want to rise in the eyes of others are jealous if they are not the only person standing on the summit for the Master of the universe, the generosity of those who would like to excel resembles to the generosity of the Prophet Mohammad (PBUH): He did not fill himself while others were hungry. because his heart looked out through the window of the mercy of the Creator. He saw all children as his own and loved all mothers like his own mother.[42]

History is filled with the collapse of societies that could not surpass their leaders.[43] Leaders raise us up then they beat their ideologies into our heads. As long as they stand before us, we cannot get beyond the limits of their era. Those who exalt wealthy societies in their worldliness do not exalt their leaders. Rather, they send them to the battlefront that awaits them on the horizon. History is filled with massacres that have occurred because of such leaders.

It is true, some leaders contribute to the world's peace, but they do so by entering and directing our hearts. **Really great leaders have never put to death those who only did not accept their own thoughts.**

Leaders may be great and perhaps we too may be greater than they are but we will never see that we are greater while in the same race because they are superior to us. They raced before we did and while we are still climbing, we are not esteemed worthy of their place. W**anting to surpass great persons is to have the desire to occupy their place.**

42 This is why racism nurtures mercilessness, jealousy, quarrelling, and war. Those who only love their own nations hate other nations. The most beloved human is the moral human who can loves those children of Adam (PBUH) who do not do evil.

43 The unsurpassed leaders were the prophets who possessed supreme leadership and came among us as messengers of Almighty Creator and who conveyed divine orders to us.

c) No Hastening

Our ancestors used to say, "Whoever goes fast goes to his death." This rule is valuable both when driving a car and when ruling your life. So you should move right away, you should not wobble when you walk, but you also should not run along in a panic, almost out of breath. We can take our example from animals of how fast we ought to move.

"If an individual does not hasten, everyone will have their prayer answered. But there are those who are in a hurry and will say, 'I prayed but my prayer was not answered'."[44] "The Almighty Creator loves those who pray insistently."[45]

They who truly want something do not get tired of seeking it. One who is truly hungry does not tire of seeking food.

There are two ways of wanting something: The first way is with belief and enthusiasm, sincerely, with patience and pleasure. The second way is with suspicion, mistrust, exhaustion, collapse, or indifferently. Then you are not ready to obtain what you really do not want.

To give something to the most enthusiastic seeker is to give it to the neediest one. **No one is in more need than someone who seeks something with great sincerity and patience**. The desire of those who are the most needful do not come into their mind once a week or once a month; They keep it alive like a burring flame in a corner of their heart every instant. If you are really thirsty, you will squeeze a handful of dirt to get water when necessary.

No matter how much evil we do, we are the work of a Limitless Power who still does us good and who continually enlightens our hearts with feelings of love. **To grow tired of wanting something from the One who never tires of giving, gives anguish to the conscience.** If He who gives us the sun in the morning has not yet given us some special wish of ours, either we have not insisted on them enough or the time has not yet come for them.

44 The Prophet Mohammad (PBUH), Bukhari, Da'awat, 22.
45 The Prophet Mohammad (PBUH), Jami' us-Saghir 2292, Hadith no. 1876

This means that if you wished for these things, you had received them. You need to trust in the timing of the Creator for when your wishes will be entered into your account. This transfer is sometimes on the first opportunity, sometimes years later and sometimes even in the Next World. Desire itself is the first acceptance which rescues its owner from the monotony of the lack of desire. Haste arises from ambition, from the wish to have everything instantly, and from not knowing what one wants. **"The goal is reached through patience, not through haste."**[46] **"Patience brings people quickly to their goals. The patient bird flies better than other birds."**[47]

The thing you tire of wanting one day is not the thing you really wanted. One must make a decision and pursue it. **History is filled with humans who, while searching for the best, were deprived even of what was bad.**

When I wrote my first book "Think and Succeed," I considered the worst possible negativities.[48]

Whatever was best, I had to finish what I had begun. I owe that book to that obsession and appreciation that the book has met with, which has filled my life with enthusiasm. **What is important is not to do the best but to dedicate yourself to do the best you can.** Indeed, you can't do any better than accomplish your job the best way possible.

People who change their minds at the first sign of trouble should not wait for their lives to change. Victory means keeping your promise and knowing that your promise is as valuable as your life and so you keep it. Those nearest to victory are those who remain faithful to their promises.

You should think carefully when you make a decision. We easily give up the thing that we wanted with uncertainty and indifference. **Every resolution that we frequently change is a sword blow to our will power.**

---

46 *Mawlana* Rumi, Masnavi, vol. 1, p. 319

47 *Mawlana* Rumi, Masnavi, vol. 3, p. 150

48 I might do damage, my mistakes might hurt my reputation, it might dash my hope. We must do whatever we can to avoid risk.

2. THE DIMENSION OF THE INTELLECT

Our persistence, patience, and powers of resistance develop when we develop the awareness of the "here and now" and with the perception of its development.

a) The Intellectual Basis

I shall recommend several exercises to develop our mental capacities for patience, attention, and persistence:

Words: Try to hold any word at all in your memory for a long time. For instance, start with repeating the word "butterfly" hundreds of times. While you are repeating it, various associations will cause your mind to shift to some other area every 20 to 30 seconds. For instance, you will see flowers and valleys where butterflies live, you will behold children playing with butterflies and butterflies emerging from their cocoons and flying amongst the bees. You will recall all the words and images in your mind that are associated with butterflies.

You can make use of these exercises as key words for you ideals: "Computer, commerce, art, PhD, authorship..." you can use these words when you are standing at the bus stop, when you are walking, and in all of your spare time.

Sensory Perceptions: You can activate anything (a door), a sound (a bell), a smell (a rose), a taste (an apple), or a tactile perception (a pen). It is important for these perceptions to be connected to your goals.

Concentrate on a smell you love and try as hard as you can to sense that smell in your consciousness. Bring something to life; for example, imagine a flower in your living room and continually look at that flower in your mind. Close your eyes and imagine for several minutes that you hold a pen in your hand.

Questions: Try to make up questions, and find different and detailed answers to your questions. For instance, you might ask a question such as "What are people doing at this moment?" Search for an answer by wandering in your imagination from Africa to America and from Australia to Asia. Resist being diverted from your question.

Worship: Worship is an activity that develops great patience and concentration. Think of Islamic prayer for instance. The ritual washing before prayer activates and most of the important acupuncture points of the body. The moment you have given yourself over to prayer, you establish a rapport with the Eternal Creator and escape from the world. If you can perceive this, you converse with the highest Authority that can be imagined.

You surrender your body to predefined postures. The point of prostration restricts your visual field. Your mind enters the sphere of the sacred words of prayer. A prayer performed in conformity to the rules is a true prayer and, in a short time, easily creates perceptible spiritual influences.

b) Live in the Here and Now

If we do not allow our attention to be diverted to the pains of the past and the uncertainty of the future, we can think more about the duties of this moment than the results we will obtain and our performance will rise to the skies. The result we hope for gives us encouragement but focusing on the results that we hope for in the future and distancing ourselves from our business of the moment will halt our progress. **You work will be directed toward wherever you focus your attention.** To step on the next step of the stair, you need to look at that step and not at the top of the stairs. **Those who only look at the head of the stairs when they are climbing up them will tumble down with the first step.**

This world is not heaven. If you say, "apple" an apple will not be handed to you through the window. If you want it, it will be given to you but there is a road and a journey from the unknown to the world. The seeds of the fruits you eat this year were planned and planted by the Eternal Creator who is beyond time and space.

Many people turn back from the door of success just when they are standing on its threshold. Wisdom reigns in the world and wisdom requires one to be patient. **If you would wait a second longer, you would**

be number one. Results are the friends of enthusiasm but the enemies of patience. You need both patience and enthusiasm. You need to think of your wonderful future when you do the thing you do now.

We all fall into this trap when we daydream about what we love and avoid the struggle we have to engage in to achieve it. Those **people, who prefer the pleasure of achievement in fantasy to the pains of the journey of achievement, cannot achieve it.**

It is exciting to work to pass an exam, to win an election or a race, but the stress you experience when you exaggerate in your fantasy the size of the thing you are going to gain may make you lose your patience. **Forcing ourselves to be patient promises us victory but loss of that patience warns us of defeat.** If you could see heaven, you would hate the world and you would want to die right away and go there, whereas the way to go there is by living and doing the things that will make you merit it.

Some people imagine when they write a poem that they will become as proclaimed as a poet whose message has spread through the world; however, they forget that for this to happen they must write another poem tomorrow and the next day.

You will not feel the encouragement of work if you cannot imagine the greatness of your results as though you were experiencing them. On the other hand, if the greatness of what you accomplish will make you stop concentrating on your current business, you will abandon what you are doing.

The solution: Let us keep the image of the results alive in our minds, let us allow them to encourage us and keep us patient, but let us also leave their realization to the Limitless Power. **Our duty is to work in reasonable ways.** We cannot create the results but the Almighty can create, Although we may do everything possible, some disaster may destroy our labors. Although we may have prepared ourselves very well, we may fail because of an illness on the day of the exam.

Someone who wants a little crop sows potatoes and reaps a handful of potatoes once. Someone who wants many fruit plants an apple tree and waits patiently, gathering apples for years from its branches. You have the right to wait for the young sapling that you planted bears fruit after a year but you do not have the right to abandon it right away when it does not bear fruit. **What comes later is more valuable. What is more difficult is more beloved.**

c) With the View of Development

To know that we are better off today, we need to know where we were yesterday.

An Azerbaijani student studying in Turkey thought for years under the influence of an experience he had when he was in High School that he was worthless. After reading "Think and Succeed," he shared his experience with me. I asked him what he had succeeded in doing. He had come in 11th in a national exam in his own country, he could have studied in the university, and he was very intelligent. How can somebody think of him-self or herself as being worthless in spite of all the indications of success?

You need two kinds of energy: a) The energy to start over again every day in the race and b) the energy to continue in that same race. The first is given to everyone for free by the Almighty Creator after a night's sleep. However, the actual difference between people is that we have to want the second one.

Modern entertainers steal our precious moments to the point that we cannot find a clear instant to remind us of the purpose of our creation. We cannot think "from where to where" we are going as we move forward in the darkness. **Losers are those who do not look at their maps and cannot control their direction because of their absent-mindedness, which is caused by the vain distractions they have chosen.**

Pick up three blank pieces of paper and a pen. Write the day you were born on the first one and write all the things you have succeeded in doing on the second. On the third, write the particulars of people who are in worse situations than yourself.

The first piece of paper will not be full. You were a helpless baby and you had nothing but a mother who cared tenderly for you. On the second piece of paper, you can see all the obstacles you have overcome. The third piece of paper, concerning all the people who are in a worse situation than you are, however, cannot hold all you could write. There you will see people who have not learned to read or write, people who have never been outside of their villages, the hungry, the thirsty, the orphan, the uncared for youth, and even murderers and convicts.

People who envy the wealth of Bill Gates etc., ought to know that he started on his path years before we did. **A young sapling just planted in an orchard, cannot say, "Why don't I too bear fruit now like the other trees?"**

We must be patient, develop, and flourish. The days will come when we too will bear fruit. Let us continue to grow. One day we too will be one of the examples that will make young trees envious.

3. THE DIMENSION OF ACTION

Persistence demands speedy action and working without interruption, except for rest periods.

a) The Action Basis

You can use the rhythm of music and sports to develop attention and patience.

Rhythm: You can add rhythm to your life. You can use music to develop your brain. You can move your head, neck, and shoulders to the rhythm together with the notes.

Every rhythm causes a different brainwave to activate. Active rhythms cause a mental excitement and courage. Calm rhythms make for an emotional keenness. If you surrender your body to the rhythm, you will achieve complete concentration. In such an environment, you can align your needs in life.

Sports: Swimming, taekwondo, and jogging put the body on the similarly harmonious axis of movements. The power of concentration and the persistence of people who regularly play sports are greater than that of others. Even if you do not play sports, you can practice special exercises at home.

b) Speedy Action

Speedy action is different from hasty action. Speed means not wasting time and moving forward in an orderly manner. Haste means trying to run up the stairs and skipping the steps. The super effective person is the person who does continuously useful work.

If there is no obstacle, we have to do our job in the time it needs to be done. Persistent people start work the minute they decide to do something. I learned this lesson from a Member of Parliament who listened to his constituents. He listened to their problems one-by-one and, afterwards, he did what needed to be done for them.

To postpone something for five minutes causes it to be postponed for one day. To postpone something for a day equals a month and one month means to forget the goal of a lifetime. Because we have postponed the first step, we have deprived ourselves of hundreds of steps. You will never be able to pass through the door you did not open. Whoever does not dive into the sea will never struggle to learn to swim.

If you say "I will start tomorrow" your 'tomorrow" will escape beyond today to the end of time. I have found the real reason behind my failures, it was saying, "I will do it later."

Wanting to accomplish your desires later may cause you to achieve your goals ten years later. If you are not a candidate for presidency now, you will have to wait four years for another election. If you delay in wanting something, you will increase the likelihood of not obtaining it when it does become available.

Perhaps you cannot concentrate intensely on what you deeply desire.

Perhaps you may not have the spare time to nourish the tree you have planted. I once planted a tree and did nothing to nourish it for 25 years. I forgot about it. The day I visited my village and went to that field, I remembered the day when I had planted that tree in that treeless field with my child's spirit. Walking around a huge tree standing alone, I looked for the little tree I had planted when I was a child but that huge tree was the little tree that I had planted.

Something noteworthy happens and you say, "I wanted this to happen years ago." When did you establish your goals? When did you do your first good deed? It is a good deed even to look with love at the soil.

Think of the multiplication effect of your speedy actions: When you teach something to one person and do this regularly, those who learned from you will help your words travel and affect other people. That means if you change one person, this person will go out and, will change at least other five people. If a customer has bought something from you with satisfaction, that customer will also draw in other new customers. **As you see, when you lose out through delay, it means you lose the probable support of other people in the world.**

If **you should live a new day every morning, you should fill your heart "with the same energy every day." It** is the continuity of the wishes that enflame you and ensure the continual flow of spiritual energy over your being. However, if your desires do not lead to action and you act lazily even while you are boiling inside with encouragement, you will either explode or you will extinguish the heart within you.

If **an ideal excites you today, it will also excite you tomorrow. You should then allow it to continually occupy your consciousness.** Abandoning your dream means that you stop your progress. To brake off from your goal means to break away from enthusiasm.

Your dreams are the energy within you. Only your own actions can determine your speed. The obstacles round about you want to lead you into inaction. **Your speed should be high enough to pass beyond those obstacles.** You ought not to hesitate too long on the battlefield of laziness and inaction where the bullets fly. If you hurry forward, those who try to block your way either will run away or be will crushed. **If you are a wind, you will blow through. If you are a typhoon, you will sweep them away before you.**

c) Continuity

We need to develop the habit of long-term persistence. We can't even run for one hundred meters, but life is a marathon. **This is why pausing, except for short rest periods, may cause us to halt and remain stopped in our tracks.** Continuity is more important than speed for progress. It is possible to travel around the world even if you walk with the speed of a turtle.

Illnesses or misfortunes may slow down or cause our efforts to pause, but nothing should stop our dreams, our desires, and our feelings.

I did a radio interview with Stefan Lega, a former mayor from Romania who had vowed to walk around the world in protest of the Bosnian-Serbian War and, together with his wife, had worn out 120 pairs of shoes walking through 40 countries.[49] To tour the world walking is an unbearable journey. Whereas in your 60 year life, you will have walked three times around the world just wandering in your living room and in the streets.

Think of the words of the Prophet Mohammad (PBUH) said, **"Those deeds most pleasing to the Almighty Creator are those that are continuous, although they may be few."**[50] Someone who works one hour every day profits more than someone who works 24 hours yesterday and tomorrow and spends today doing nothing. Success lay in a job that is done continuously even though it is done in a small quantity. If we have a skill, please, don't let us live a day without practicing it.

We must be continuous in a persistent and balanced way. Continuity is not collecting and then squandering something. If you pour a ton of water on a tree in one day and don't water it again for a year, it will dry up.

49 After the live broadcast, I asked him "Can I travel around the world like you?" I was moved by his answer. "IF you want to, you can."

50 Prophet Mohammad (PBUH): Jami' us-Saghir 1:165 Hadith no. 197

If you want your actions to bear fruit, continue what you are doing, even if it is a little. Think about what you want to achieve at least five times during the day. People who do not concern themselves even once a day with their goals, think they know what they want. When you ask them whether they have prayed for something, they remember their dreams of last year.

If you don't work on your projects at least once a day, it will make you not think about them for a week, for a month, for a year, and for a lifetime. Isn't that the way life is? One day you watched television and it made you watch it all your life. Smoking a cigarette one day can make somebody smoke cigarettes for the rest of their lives. All our good and bad habits are the results of the first trial.

I worked on this book yesterday and today I waited impatiently for the night when I would pass in front of my computer to come as soon as possible. When I stopped work one day I felt for weeks as though I had paused doing it for years. If I do not write at least one sentence for one day, I may not be able to open this file for a week.

I owe my success to "not straying from my goal." If I do stray, it will take me days for me to return to it. Before I go to sleep at night, the things I want to do pass before my eyes.[51] Sometimes, I get so excited that my drooping eyelids suddenly spring open and I return to work. If, during the night to which you have entrusted your body, some word or aspiration that excites you pass through your mind, do not wait for it to electrify your soul.

Some people listen to the song of "good morning" from the voice of their most beautiful beloved when they open their eyes. Some start the day in anger at their being together and say "curse this world."

We can develop our ability of continuity through small exercises. We nurture our indecisiveness through little actions: "I will brush my teeth in a little while. Forget it, I will do it later. This evening I won't eat any bread. I changed my mind, I won't do it tomorrow. I was supposed to meet him

51 Are we going to wait for death to take us before we review our lives and ideals? If we live everyday as though we were prepared for that day, we will not experience regret when we leave this life.

at 3 O'clock. Well, he will wait anyhow; I will go at 3:15." **Big indecisions are caused by little indecisions.**

The first way is to allow your ordinary actions develop your will and persistence. "In any case, I am going to chew this piece of food, so I will chew it up ten times exactly. I am going to take a drink of tea in a little while. I am going to swallow it in thirty seconds."

Either you do your job freely or they force you to do them. You need to be active and a real doer. If you rely on your small decisions to do your job, it will be your will that accomplishes the job. However, as much as you use your own will power, you will grow that much stronger.

The second way: You can make simple decisions for short-term actions. For example: "After I finish this chapter of this book, I will take a deep breath. At 6 PM, I will go out on the balcony and sit down."

The third way: Now you need to develop your persistence in following up on your decisions. You will decide to do the same thing in a certain period.

Reading this book will no doubt take hours of your time. What happens if you decide on this time period? "Now, I am sitting down to eat and will read for a half an hour. I will walk in the park for a half an hour. I will count to ten thousand without pause."

Start with short periods; for example, ten-minute periods. Slowly extend these to an hour or two hours. Decide to make this a week and then to make it a month and, finally, a year. These exercises will allow you to take control of your life.

The most tiring part of persistence is the beginning. First one week of persistence is harder than a year of it. This is why you must not allow the difficulties at the start to intimidate you.

4. THE FACTOR OF RECOLLECTION

Some people say, "We get excited in a moment but then we lose the energy we have gained in a few hours or a few days. We can't keep on going in the way we started. What should we do?" We would advise them to rely on the symbols for recollection and incitement that we have added here:

a) Symbols

If you lived in an environment that continually inspired you to excitement, excitement would envelope your entire being. If you abandon your awareness to its own devices, you will become a copy of your surroundings.

If you are aware of what is happening around you but merely talk idly about it, you will be the same as your environment. If you cover your eyes, stop your ears to your surroundings, and concentrate on your own ideals, you will be a copy of the person in your ideals.

The environments where we spend our lives the most are the environments that most inspire us. They are the rooms of our houses where we sit the most, the car we use, the office we work in, the streets through which we pass.

Some people have experienced unhappiness for years in their houses. Associations of stress are attached to every corner, to the faucet in the bathroom, to the fork with which we eat. I would advise such people to move to another neighborhood or town rather than depend on antidepressant drugs.

Omar, the Caliph of Islam, is said to have kept a paid servant with the intention of reminding him that he must die in the end. When his hair started to turn white, he told the servant, "I don't need you any longer." The Caliph, who knew he must give an account to the Almighty Creator in the next world, used the knowledge of death as a means to enable him not to be dedicated to this world and to behave mercifully, with justice, with responsibility, and with sensitivity.

We too can use various reminders as we advance toward our goals. Symbols, words, and pictures can remind us of our duties and purposes. We ought to find a good picture of a car if a car is what we want and if what we want is a house, a fine picture of a villa. We should look for a picture to symbolize these things if we want to have a strong memory. We ought to verbalize the particulars of the things we want. We should engage in conversations that encourage us and give us courage or listen to cassettes with music that does the same.

We ought to hang symbols that we have selected in places where we live, where we can see them; on mirrors, on the walls, on our car, and on our desks.

The reminders will speak to us when we glance at the walls and mirrors and tell us what we want. When we have a chance, even for a few minutes while we are working, we should listen to the motivational cassettes.

b) Activations

You need to develop in your mind a net of relations to activate you. Pavlov's rule of conditioning has become one of the most important strategies for systems of personal development.

In Pavlov's experiment, when a bell rang, the mouths of dogs watered. Even though Pavlov stopped feeding them, the sound of the bell sufficed to cause the conditioned dogs to show the same reaction. All of us have been conditioned in the same way. When you squeeze a lemon, doesn't your mouth water? Don't you remember death when you pass by a cemetery?

You can associate a special position of your body with a feeling or a goal. Then, when you assume that position, you will experience that feeling.

Use every happiness, encouragement, and success that you have experienced as an opportunity, at the moment when you are at the height or depth of feeling.

Pick out a special movement. Snapping your fingers, laughing, winking, making a fist, taking a deep breath, these can all be special moments.

After you have picked out those gestures or others like them, make those gestures in moments of deep emotion. For instance, when you receive wonderful news, consciously smile. Repeat the news and smile again. You should repeat this until it is well fixed in your consciousness. Once you have established the connection, the process becomes complete and your journey to success and enthusiasm becomes automatic.

Any time, especially when you are tired and angry, escape from the destructive feeling in which you find yourself and find feelings of enthusiasm, perform the same movement; for example, smile. Doesn't your feeling change all at once? If it does not, it means that you have not strongly established the activating connection. In this case, continue to find the relationship until it is useful to you.

There could be two reasons for trouble in establishing a connection. One could be that the activation was not adequately clear and repeated with all your feelings sufficiently. The other is that your intellectual health has weakened through poor nutrition, irregular sleep, much like an out-of-shape body.

CHAPTER FIVE:

THE POWER OF CONTENTMENT

I. WHY WE NEED THE POWER OF CONTENTMENT?

INTRODUCTION

If you were a dam, would you ask for the ocean's water? If you were a tree, would you want to hold a mountain? Have you calculated well where to stop? At the end of this chapter, you will discover the importance of contentment in life that has been neglected.

Contentment is the ability to carry the cargo you have loaded into your car. Excessive nourishment will kill a greedy aquarium fish who does not know when to stop. Is the world on your back or are you on the back of the world? T**he content person moves about the world the Creator controls and trusts in the power of the Creator.**

The opposite of contentment is covetousness, which means excessively and culpably desirous of the possessions of others and, basically, depends on selfish ambition.

The covetousness and selfish ambitiousness represents personal strength, but contentment is reliance on the Divine Power that created the universe. The covetous soldier thinks he is an unconquerable hero. However, he is defeated suddenly when he looks at his rivals with contempt.

The covetous person's slogan is, "I will want something and take it by my own force!" Contentment changes this slogan thus; "I will pray and strive for something and trust the Limitless Power will reward me."

Contentment opens the door of the angelic world to the human soul. It presents humans with the names of the Master of the Universe and with His power. On the other hand, covetousness overshadows the Mercy of Almighty and crushes selfish ambitious person like a fly.

A soft plant can break apart hard stones and pass through. It is not important whether we are weak like plants or forceful like rocks. It is whether we rely on the Divine Power. So, let us understand better what contentment is first:

1. THE BASIS OF CONTENTMENT

To be content means to desire passionately, work for, and accept, with happiness, the recompense that comes from destiny. Contentment leads humankind to strive according to the ideals of the Creator and then to trust His divine destiny and timing. A content person is resolute, trustworthy, at peace, and calm. Contentment is composed of three elements: determination, acceptance and thrust. Let us look at them:

a) Determination

One aspect of contentment is determination, which has two aspects: On positive aspect is content and on negative aspect is selfish ambition. Contentment, with determination, results in success and contentment with selfish ambition gives rise to defeat. Let us give more detail:

A divine determination surrounds nature and the human soul was codified so that it has inexhaustible desires. Humans are inspired with determination from inside their souls and from nature outside.

The Almighty Creator created every atom as vast as the universe. The universe is vast externally and atoms are internally vast. **Stars exist throughout the universe and the particles in the atom inexhaustible.** Every heart can encompass the universe. You may read the endlessness of the Limitless Creator in all of His creations.

If humans imagine the sublime nature of the Master of all these works and strive in belief for His destiny, they will live like the roots of the plants that break through passes between the rocks.

Limitless Power does not stop with creating billions of species but He continuously creates, in every moment, new pictures just behind the pictures He had designed.

If few beautiful objects sufficed, what need would there be for a valley to have a different appearance in summer and winter? If wheat was sufficient to nourish humankind, what need would there be to create the eggplant and apple and give each a different color, smell, and taste?

If contended determination means doing the best job possible, then this exists in the functioning of the universe. The Creator sends centuries pass and new species to the earth. The great dinosaurs go and the little birds take their place. Indeed, quadrillions of species were not enough for creation but were sent to the earth in a specific order.

When humans think that they are a part of the universe and a masterwork of the Creator, they will feel inspired to determination. But this determination should be full of contentment, not selfish ambition.

As examples to this, Avicenna who used to pass the nights studying, would drink something and keep on working when he felt sleepy. The famed scholar, Fakhr al-Din al-Razi, read even when he was eating. When he rode his donkey from his house to the mosque, he taught 300 students along the way. Are the results not clear concerning the way in which these persons profited via their time?

On the other hand, people who live by selfish ambition work passionately and can never feel satisfied with the results they get. The selfish ambition of pleasure-loving and calculating persons leads societies to disaster.

So, **in this age in which evil spreads like a cancer, those who do believe in goodness do not have the right to waste their time with worthless works.**

Some people understand that the contentment recommended by religion means not working for a lot and being content with a little. They see our efforts to achieve great wishes and ideals as ambitiousness and find this contrary to their beliefs.

My conception is that the error lies not in wanting something, but in wanting it ambitiously, unthankfully, and ungratefully.

I would like to point out these holy verses: "Say: 'My Lord would not concern Himself with you but for your call on Him'." In addition, "Your Lord says, 'Call on Me; I will answer you.'" "On no soul doth Allah place a burden greater than it can bear. It gets every good that it earns, and it suffers every ill that it earns."[52]

The Prophet Mohammad (PBUH) taught us to ask for abundance. "**When one of you prays for something, you should ask for abundance because you ask it of the Lord.**" "Work like you will never die, but be careful like you will die tomorrow." "My God...I beg you to lead me in the right path." "My God...I beg for your inexhaustible blessings. I beg of you an unending bliss." "My God, exalt me."[53]

However, at the same time he bids us to avoid ambitious selfishness. And says so: "Oh children of Adam, you want things that will lead you to trouble even while you have sufficient good things for your needs. You are not satisfied with little and you are not content with much." He teaches us the difference between contentment, which represents asking much from the Almighty Creator, and selfish ambition, which represents asking from humankind: "The Angel Gabriel (PBUH) came and said to me, 'The honor of the faithful is being content with what Almighty Creator has given them and not expecting anything from humans.'"[54]

52 Qur'an: 25:77; 40:60; 2: 286

53 Prophet Mohammad (PBUH), Jami' us-Saghir 1: 319, No. 532; 2:12, No.1201; 2:130, No.1501; 2:146, No.1537; 2:145,1536

54 Prophet Mohammad (PBUH), Jami' us-Saghir 1: 86 No. 68; 102 No. 89

If certain religious dervishes in history chose to live life in rags to ascend near to the Almighty, this is their own method. Their choice is a precaution against the dangers of worldly life that tries to steal their sincerity. They may also choose this life to avoid falling prey to selfish ambition. However, to reach success in this world and the hereafter, you do not have to avoid riches, science, and art. Our Almighty Creator encourages us to find success and incites us to unify contentment with dedication. This means wanting and working a lot and even in case of failure, still feeling satisfied.

My friend, who was studying in the USA, remarked that, "The students here work to death." Resolution **means to work to death; it unites working "as though you were never going to die and as though you were going to die tomorrow."**

b) Acceptance

The true form of contentment requires acceptance of what you get from the Almighty in your life. You need to unite acceptance with determination to reach true contentment.

The most important result that separates true contentment from selfish ambition is the former keeps a person in a psychological state of satisfaction and the latter causes dissatisfaction.

Think of this example: A child asks his father for chewing gum at night and his father does not oblige, rather makes his son wait for the treat. A content child would say, "My father knows best. I do not know the best reward for my wishes or the right time for them, I do not know better than he does," and feels satisfied with the situation. He esteems his father's love and attachment. But, a selfish child cries out and blames his or her father for being hardhearted.

In the words of the Mawlana Rumi, "**Ask but ask in a proper measure. A plant has not the strength to carry a mountain.**"[55]

55 *Mawlana* Rumi. Masnavi, vol. 1, p. 11

In the same way, content people do whatever they can in their lessons, their families, their jobs, commerce, cultures, entertainment, and religious lives. They do not worry about the results that come from the Creator, but about their own duties. The Creator looks at whether or not people do their best and not at whether they succeed.

We know that what we are required to do is 1) sincerely pray and 2) work with foresight. Almighty Creator will determine how great will be our results in this world. To some He gives great good fortune in this world but to others He gives good fortune by taking them suddenly to Paradise.

Who are more worthy of Divine Mercy? Are they those who accept what come from the Almighty Creator or those who reject it? Is Divine Mercy more piteous to one who accepts the divine plan or to a negative person who continually complains?

The only living being who rebels against the plan of destiny in this world is humankind. They complain with their songs, with their feelings, and with their laziness.

Whereas there are animals that cannot be sly like we are. They are born; they are nourished in a thousand ways. They grow up and are protected in thousand ways. They have not constructed equipment either to feed or shelter themselves. What they have are given to them by the Creator of the universe in response to their contentment and acceptance. So, if we know how to be content like the birds, the world will rush willingly to aid us.

c) Trust

Third, a very important character of true contentment is the trust in the Almighty. To understand this, think that you feel proud of being a citizen of a state that correctly, clearly, and powerfully focus on every issue for the sake of justice and gets successful results. If you have a superb army, you trust in your military and if you have a society that is compassionate, you trust that it will not leave you to live in the street. Just like this example, contentment leads humans to this sort of trust in the Almighty's kingdom of the universe.

I am speaking of a level of contentment that the heart of an atheist can never aspire to. If a meteor falls down, a content believer knows that it cannot strike anyone without the permission of the Creator. If the Creator has so ordered, then nobody can prevent it. So, this kind of contentment causes peace and tranquility.

You can notice the divine operations in nature only with care. When you observe, you will understand that some mechanisms exist to protect the innocent and the weak. The phenomenon of a "Mother's compassion" was created. Thousands of sources of nourishment that struggles to satisfy souls and bodies were established. In spite of the potential of every being, no being can dominate in nature: the gender is balanced and the species are in balance. It is clear that a compassionate, nourishing, powerful Judge who oversees and balances exists. More than this, He is aware even of everybody's fingerprints.

People may comprehend that Divine Power is filled with feelings of complete trust in Him. He sees that they are His guests in this world. They apply themselves to view the beauties of this world because they cannot consume the soil or load the world on their back and carry it home. Even if their bodies are hungry, they are busy filling their hearts.

2. THE GROUNDS OF COVETOUSNESS

Covetousness refers to desiring a lot and being willing to work hard to get. However, at the same time, it signifies not to be appreciative, not to like and not accepting results; it means to be greedy and to disparage everything. Covetousness is basically characterized with selfish ambition and jealousy.

To understand better, suppose that we planted rice in our field and did everything possible to make it grow. When the time came for harvest, the results were low, for whatever reason. If we are angry because of these results, it is because we are greedy and covetous. Or, assume that we did not come in first in the race we had entered. If we feel sorry for this result and become filled with anger, this is where selfish ambition lays.

A little covetousness results in only a little damage, but if it grows violent, it may lead one to suicide or murder. Let us study the reasons for and the results of the disease of covetousness:

a) The reasons of Covetousness

Covetousness is the result of a series of mistaken psychological attitudes that include selfish ambition, competitiveness, currying favor with people, impatience, and arrogance. Let us explain:

-Selfish ambition: "I want to win the car in the race, not my neighbor." "I want to pass that exam and see my schoolmate fail." Having such thoughts causes us to face more competitors whom we will have to overcome. **No one can wish good future for selfish people who do not want for others the good that they want for themselves.**

-Competitiveness: "My poem must be better than others'." "My lecture has to have a bigger crowd than others'." "I have to do what I do first or better than others do." If you compete with others, remember that there will always be a more beautiful woman or a better-looking man somewhere. **Someone who wants to pass everyone will always be running behind someone else. Competitors will be outraged when they lose.**

- Currying favor with people: If you work only to look good to other people, even if you nitpick down to the tiniest detail, nobody will like you. If you are yourself, you will certainly be pleased with yourself. One must live in harmony with the surroundings but a persistent conformism to it is dangerous. We people are not a flock of sheep; we have right and wrong. We can avoid covetousness if when we act, we say to ourselves, not "What will so and so say about this?" but "What does my conscience say, and what does justice and morality say?" Your actions that do not depend on your own values cannot provide lasting value and meaning for you.

-Impatience: We may be in a hurry when performing our duties, but we must be patient when waiting for the results of our efforts. For example, **we must hurry when we sow the field, but be patient when we wait for the crops to ripen.** It is covetousness to say, "I want to get rich quickly. I want the sickness to end now. I want to escape from the pressure of this family. I want to get a job right now. I want to marry right now..." And it is contentment to say, "I will work every day to solve problems and reach goals."

Just stop! Wisdom rules the world. Imagining results only leads us astray. We need to be calm. What is important is to be successful in doing something regularly for our goals every day.

-Arrogance: The most common cause of covetousness is having or displaying a sense of overbearing self-worth or self-importance. Overstepping our limits is daring to think as if we were the creators of the universe. Even though Almighty Creator never gives us a greater burden than we can bear, we load ourselves with various problems.

We cannot save the whole world. We cannot destroy all the evil people. It makes no sense for us to fight against the obstacles that we can never overcome. We may feel sorry at our lack of responsibility, but we cannot take everybody's pain away. Then, everybody has to pay for what he or she has done. **The conscience that is uneasy because of universal justice is the conscience that sympathizes with evildoers.**

b) Results of Covetousness

"He who manifests covetousness, is the loser" in the words of Mawlana Rumi.[56] Covetousness will render us helpless by destroying our interior world. It will hold us back profoundly, alienating us from others and condemning us to unhappiness.

This is because somebody who is working to death with covetousness never feels any satisfaction from any result that he or she has achieved. Working without cease exhausts the body but working without a sense of acceptance and contentment tires the heart and the mind. Psychological exhaustion causes more obstacles by far than physical tiredness. Let us took at this in a more detail:

56 *Mawlana* Rumi, Masnavi, vol. 3, p. 47

-Covetousness **exhausts you: Covetousness is the blind spot, which prevents you from seeing how things are gradually developing.** Covetous patients grow tired of life. A Covetous students who fail their exams lose their strength to study. **People who are unhappy with all existing conditions are condemned to unhappiness, even if they were to become President.**

A covetous attitude concentrates our consciousness on the results and leads us to encouragement and hastiness. People who cannot take their eyes off the top of the stairs where they intend to go cannot climb the stairs safely. **When we progress in a covetous s manner, we will lose our energy through stress, stumble through our haste, or give up because we cannot endure.**

Covetous behavior says to us, "I am struggling but I could not get what I want. I am studying but I could not learn enough. I am being treated unjustly." Note that people who think they cannot do the job will panic. Then they lose more than ever.

If we panic, exhaustion, fearfulness, lack of interest and hopelessness seize us. **Those who endure troubles are resolute and content, but they are not covetous.** If covetous people had to live under the conditions of a sparrow, they would be snowed under apprehension. Covetous behavior conceals their possibilities, progress from people, and reduces them to an unappreciative ingrate.

The physical tension coming from covetous attitudes causes stress and systematic stress results in damage to the nervous system and exerts pressure on the heart and the brain. The chemical elements that allow knowledge to flow through our brains are reduces by stress and our minds begin to grow dull quickly. This process destroys our defense systems and illnesses seize our bodies.

-Covetousness breaks you from inside**:** If you press on the gas pedal and pull the hand brake of your automobile at the same time, you will burn the brake pads. Covetous attitudes are the hand brakes that lock the heart of the human who is trying to advance speedily. The covetous person pulls the brakes from within.

The interior tension coming from your covetous attitude affects your tone of voice, your body language, and all the messages you send. **Those who convey helplessness to others cannot offer help to others.**

I have heard so many times, "A wretch is always a wretch. If you fall, others will also kick you." These phrases are wrong.

Actually, real wretch is the one who is defeated by covetousness. People, who have fallen, fell first from within. s. There is no need to be pessimist. Those who work on calmly can succeed in spite of everything. Those who encounter everything except for evil and perversity with gratitude are unstoppable. Note that covetous attitudes do not allow this philosophy.

Covetousness will increase the pain of defeat and enlarges obstacles in your sight. You cannot resist obstacles that you do not believe you can overcome. As a result, you will see all humankind as evil and selfish.

You can endure a miserable marriage up to a certain point. If it makes you miserable to study, the day will arrive when you will not ever be able to read a book. Expulsion from school might even be the result. Attempted suicides generally exist in such an atmosphere of crisis and depression.

A government minister and the owner of a textile factory have attempted suicide. A professor whom people thought was successful and an artist took their own lives.

If you live a covetous life, no matter what your status may be, whether you are rich or poor, you suffer, and the result is inescapable: to give up in order escaping.

-**Covetousness alienates you:** If a beggar stops you on the street and orders you, "Give me two hundred dollars." what problems arise in your mind? Probably the followings:

Problem 1: You may object, saying, "It's my business whether I give you anything." Problem 2: "Also, it is my business how much I give you. You may tell me, 'I need two hundred dollars.' Problem 3: He is rude to you when he asks for it. He puts on a sarcastic manner. Problem 4: You give it to him but he still tries to take something you did not offer him. For instance, if he took a fancy to your bread and then took it away from you as though it were his own property you would seize it from him. Problem 5: You still gave him the money but he questioned you, "Why didn't you give me more?" Problem 6: After you went away, he slandered you. The covetous person is in the same situation as the beggar both before Almighty Creator and humankind.

You would not give even a penny to an aggressive beggar. However, if you turn away a mother who said, "I need to buy milk for my children." You would feel guilty for the rest of your life. Listen to this voice of love.

Humankind is not and cannot be rich and gracious like the Creator. If covetousness separates us from even the Master of the Universe, it has separated us from friendship with the universe itself. There is no one who is more patient and forgiving than the Creator. When we are stealing apples from an apple tree in our garden, the Creator of the apples does not shout, "Stop, thief!" However, when you enter into the people's gardens, they do not hesitate for an instant to make this accusation.

3. EXPLANATORY EXPERIENCES

Covetousness may cause your efforts to go unrewarded. It may destroy your dreams in the instant when you have drawn near to success. Look at the following examples:

a) Exams I have failed

I had a very busy social life during my third year of university. On the one hand, I participated in activities and, on the other, my classmates and I conducted seminars with young friends from the high schools on the weekends. The efforts of our friends to learn things excited us.

As all this went on, I did well in my classes and I saw my name at the top of the lists when the exam results were announced.

I was filled with vanity and covetousness. Because of my frequent headaches, I could only study for 15-20 minutes at a time at home, but I continued to attend class and I did what I could to make up missed lessons. I thought, "If I can succeed this much by studying this little, I can have the top grades in the department by working harder." My intention was to satisfy my vanity by reaching this goal.

I began working with great intensity for the next exams. I poured over the books and spent every free minute studying; however, I neglected my other responsibilities and I avoided my friends and shut myself in my own study room.

The next exam was on economics and was administered at the end of the month; I had resolved to earn a hundred points. There were ten questions on the test. When I started to solve them, my brain froze. I could not find any answers to the questions that, at the beginning, I had thought were so easy. I sweated, I panicked, I started to tremble with the fear that I would not succeed.

I pulled myself back together toward the end of the exam. I interrogated myself. I saw that I had been covetous and I had made a mistake in identifying the reason for success. Moreover, I had abandoned my other responsibilities in life to be first.

The results of this experience taught me a lesson that I have never forgotten. On my first exam on economics, I earned 90 points, while that of the whole class was 60 points. Now, on the second exam, the class average was 80 points and I only earned 15 points.

After this exam, I gave up my covetous attitude and returned to my old study schedule. I was rewarded immediately. As a result, although I was not the first in the class, I continued to earn high grades.

Covetousness pressures human abilities suddenly and sudden efforts to progress end in stumbling and failure.

b) My Collapse in Reading

One semester term I gave myself over to intensive study to develop myself. Every evening I would take two or three books from library and I would return and ask for new books the next day.

My friends thought I was trying to show off. I really read until morning and struggled with my sleepiness. I would keep from collapsing at my desk with difficulty.

A few months later, I experienced a collapse. I felt a tremendous difficulty reading and right after that I began to hate it. I could not understand anything I read. I reaped the results of the extreme pressure I had exerted on myself and it barred me from reading.

After this experience, I did not go back to my old efforts to read for about two years. I stopped writing because I could not read. I could not develop myself and I could not gain new knowledge or approaches to write or tell people about.

It took me a good deal of time to pull myself back together into a logical system in which I could work without stressing myself. **Covetousness is the opposite extreme of laziness and all extremes harm people. Contentment is exactly the middle of the road and it allows you to move forward in a balanced way.**

c) Some economic losses

I knew a market speculator entertained pleasant dreams of making a fortune in the market. He embarked on various speculations.

He should have built himself up in a stable way and only take risks that he could afford to take. It was not enough that he invested all of his own fortune in the market but he borrowed millions of liras from his friends to invest in the market and lost it all. As a stressful result of this mistake, he found escape in suicide.

The risk you can take is equal to whatever your risk tolerance. If you try for more, then you bring covetousness into the picture and increase the likelihood of loss.

II. HOW CAN WE USE THE POWER OF CONTENTMENT?

To strengthen contentment means to nourish "the resolution, gratefulness, and trust" that we have built up. We have determined our goal of avoidance, selfish ambition, competitiveness, the mistaken desire to please those around us, and overreach our limits.

1. BY CHANGING OUR FEELINGS

To strengthen contentment in our inner persons, we need to persist in thankfulness, against ingratitude, and focus on our works, not the results. Let us see how?

a) Persisting in Thankfulness

As opposed to ingratitude, thankfulness opens to us the way to happiness, happiness to the way of gratitude and gratitude to the way of contentment. On the other hand, happiness that comes from thankfulness opens the way to pleasure, pleasure to wanting even more and that to perseverance.

The meaning of ingratitude is "I don't appreciate it. It is not important to me." The whole life of the ungrateful heart is one that is involuntary. Meister Eckhart says, "**It is sufficient for your prayer through your whole life to be 'thank you'.**"

The Prophet Mohammad (PBUH) says, "**To give thanks to Almighty for benefits is a guarantee against those benefits going away.**"[57] What increases blessings is not ambitious dissatisfaction, but is satisfaction with grateful thanks.

Our behavior to our environment tends to be parallel with our behav-

57 Prophet Mohammad (PBUH), Jami' us-Saghir 3:418 Tradition No. 3836

ior to the Almighty. So, **those who are ungrateful to humans are also ungrateful to the Master of the Universe.**

We are responsible, at least to be thankful, for any benefit we receive. One day we will be reminded of and have to pay back the smallest debt that we have forgotten. We are indebted to our parents, to our teachers, and to many others. If, for example, we give all our fortunes to our teachers, we will never be able to pay them back what we owe. We are indebted to every being that has allowed us to make some positive change in our lives.

Is there not anyone we have to be grateful for the goodness of a tree that sheltered us from the scorching heat of the sun or for a glass of water that has quenched our thirst? Who had created and bestowed for us the trees and water? As long as we are not ungrateful, we will remember that our conscience must seek the greatest Giver of Grace and that we must thank Him.

Do you remember how many times you have given thanks today up to THIS MOMENT? What about your past years? Are you asking, "to whom and for what reason will we thank?" Ok!

With the oxygen we were given today...For the sun beneath which we have warmed ourselves and by whose light we see...for the clouds that have cooled us...For the trees designed for aesthetic beauty that surround us... For the sky shaded with a peace-giving color... for creating the beautiful voices of the birds... For the fragrance of the lilacs... What more can we ask for?

For all the benefits we have received, we need to thank to the Almighty. **"Whoever does not give thanks for little, does not give thanks for much. One who does not feel gratitude to man does not feel gratitude to God."**[58]

Art develops because of years of labor. You need to ascend step-by-step like a staircase. Achieving what is next depends on your being happy with what has gone before. **Beside every sea of success, there is an ocean of gratitude that has collected simultaneously, drop-by-drop.**

58 Prophet Mohammad (PBUH), Jami' us-Saghir 3:279 Tradition No. 3398

If you cannot be grateful for the small values that you now have, forget about imagining greater values. **No intelligent firm would assign the greatest job to someone who is incapable with doing the simplest job. If you do not carry the small values by being grateful for them, how can you await for the greater ones?**

So, to get greater value from the Almighty I suggest that you fill the following three fields with gratitude:

Your personal existence: Your organs, feelings and mental faculties are valuable beyond compare. You ought to thank to the all Merciful One who gave you these gifts. Are you conscious about how valuable your body and abilities are? One day I had an operation for sinusitis and then I understood the worth of my sense of smell when it decreased.

I wanted to feel better about the value of my life. For this, I tried to imagine my friend's eyesight when he struggled to see me after he took off his strong glasses. In fact, people have devices that belong to their bodies and cannot be bought for any price.

Your social surroundings: Your family, relatives, and friends are the most valuable things you can have. You can be happy because they are yours. Even if you do not appreciate them, they surely have some value and you will understand them when you leave this world. Be grateful for them.

Your activities: You struggle to realize yourself and hold on to life. You will acquire new abilities and opportunities in time. We should be thankful that we possess the ability to wander in the parks worldwide where many disabled people are condemned to observe the streets from their windows. We can give thanks for every beautiful thing we are able to do till evening...to write, read, and work.

We can take a lesson from children, **if we observe them** One evening, as I was entering my apartment, a neighbor rushed from behind me and rang the bell of his apartment; the child who opened the door called out as though he were about to enter heaven, "Mother, father is here." The mother hurried to meet her husband, all smiles. It was a happiness filled with feeling.

Are we waiting for the Master of Destiny to give us an automobile every evening to make us happy? Is the sun that He presents us with every morning and the stars that He spreads before us every evening worthless?

Thankfulness is not a gift we offer others. We give an honor ourselves. Ingratitude causes problems and pains to increase.

A patient who says, "Life is worth living, no matter what," tells us how he overcame his cancer thanks to his intense concentration of high morale and love. Who can have a higher morale than someone who is thankful for whatever he or she has?

Gratitude causes love. **You will keep doing better and better in a job you like. You cannot do very well in a class you do not like.** Someone who thinks he is ugly is not aware that he is growing uglier because of his belief. Happiness with oneself increases one's beauty through thinking oneself to be beautiful.

b) Appreciating the Success of Others

To appreciate, approve, applaud, or like something is a sacred endeavor that will help you overcome covetousness. You are easily able do this because everybody has some aspect that is worthy of applause.

If you appreciate the success of others, you allow and accept others to be better than you are. If you do not appreciate others, if you are jealous of others, if you crush others in your jealousy, you will force them to commit immoral acts to retaliate against you.

People who approve of the good aspects of others are great people. Those who belittle others are little people. They are little; therefore, they try to bring others to their level by criticizing them. They give pain...

Those who know their own importance also know the importance of others. When you have been wronged, you understand the importance of helping the victim. This reciprocity is realized in various forms:

First: However much you value the beings that fill your life, that is how much you will value yourself. The better your environment is, the better you are. That is, if the soil on which you walk is golden, you are a person who walks on gold. If nature is precious, then you can see yourself as a part of that precious treasure.

Second: A pure environment reflects the light that shines on it. The answer of goodness is goodness; the answer of love is love. This means, if you value your environment, your environment values you. **The person you most value is the one who most values you. If this is the case,** then do not vainly wait for love from those whom you do not love.

Appreciate the beautiful things in which you believe.[59] Your enthusiasm will increase, you will spread that enthusiasm, and one day you will encounter the support of people you appreciated.

Appreciate yourself: First, appreciate your own successes and good abilities. Every success of yours is worth appreciating. You can feed yourself. You can cut your nails. You found your way home today. You can wash your hair.

On the other hand, everything in your life must not be perfect. When trying to be better, first accept yourself as you are. One who sees their creation and birth as worthless and ugly is insinuating that the Master of the Universe has formed an ugly and worthless work. If I do not like the way I am made, I am insinuating that I do not love the Creator.

Appreciate other humans: Somewhere, a mother can only share her children's pain and nourish them with a flour soup. Somewhere else, a student is studying until late at night to succeed. A little kid is polishing shoes in the street to help support his family.

A few young people in our circle who have determined to lead a pure life try to spread the concept of purity. One youth gave up his seat on the bus to an old man. That other man, who was blind, lives in the street, making his living selling flowers.

---

59 Effective appreciation is directed not at the person but at his or her qualities or activities: it is destructive to say to someone "You are a great poet," but it is constructive to say to him or her, "You wrote great poetry." Believing personal praise is a weakness. If people do not understand why you praise them, they will not trust you. In addition, praise directed at the person makes people arrogant and arrogance is the enemy of success.

A soldier on leave for the weekend tries to pull all his strength together to shoulder the burdens of the next week. A police officer stands at the intersection directing traffic, breathing in the poisonous fumes from your cars under the scorching sun or the chilly cold.

Aren't the people who struggle for their own future, for that of their relatives, their spouse, and children worthy of appreciation? We condemn the heartless mother who leaves her baby in the street but why do we not appreciate the dedicated mothers who give their all for their children?

Perhaps everybody receives a salary for their work; however, can the wages they receive be true compensation for their efforts? The wages you pay are their material compensation, but their spiritual compensation is appreciation. Even if we pay them, our duty is to make them happy because of their services.

Appreciate other creatures: Have you ever had a cat who returned your affection? Can you see the bees who work themselves to death to produce it when you eat a spoonful of honey? Can you envision the trees with their branches full of hundreds of apples when you bite into an apple? It is just as exciting to look behind the scenes of an event as to experience the event itself.

Appreciation destroys arrogance and greed; it wipes away dissatisfaction. **Appreciation surrounds people who are in material poverty with spiritual riches.** Appreciation is the greatest enemy of loneliness. Appreciation is the fuel of love and love is the common value that binds the universe together. **Nobody in your world can hold a greater place than those who appreciate you.** Appreciation is a sensation experienced in the heart. Perhaps you may not have an opportunity to express it. Perhaps you may speak about it twenty times a day. However, in a day, you may feel that there are thousands of praiseworthy people and that the work of thousands of beings is valuable. The first and real fruit of appreciation will flower first in your heart and the result will be gaining the power of contentment.

2. BY CHANGING OUR ATTITUTES

We can turn our covetousness to contentment by competing with ourselves, not with others, and by appreciating the success of others. Let us explain:

a) Competing with ourselves

When we compete with others, someone will certainly be ahead of us and we will frequently see that we are behind. We will be overcome with covetousness and grow discouraged. Not everybody starts on this race at the same time. Not everybody has the same conditions. **It makes no sense for a sapling to measure its height against that of the trees of the forest.**

Some friends said, "Everything, all the wisdom was written in the past. Are you striving to write just to be known as a writer?" These words came from covetousness, jealousy, and perceiving things as worthless.

If it is free to do so, every animal and plant tries to dominate nature through its proliferation. However, the intensive competition of the world of living creatures that produce all these beings is not carried on through a concern for "I wonder what my rivals are up to." Every creature is concerned with its own world and responsibility. The bee competes with itself, the ant with itself. When a bee is gathering honey, it does not damage the hive of another bee.

When we compete with ourselves, we certainly can surpass others. **Indeed, someone who can surpass himself can surpass others.** In fact, someone who surpasses others at the highest speed is someone who is racing with himself generally because he or she is free from heavy stress.

When we do not compete with ourselves, we cannot surpass ourselves. We succumb to covetousness and attempt tactics to trip up those whom we consider our rivals: We resort to slander, defamation, and denigration. No one has the right to denigrate, unjustly; a human whom we know is "created in the most perfect form and shape."[60] People who jealously attack the success of others are losers in the Next World even though they may temporarily appear successful in this world.

Rivalry with others gives rise to jealousy, exhaustion, failure, and alienation. Those who compete with themselves are the first in their own view. They can find time to rest and relax. They are at peace with themselves. They cannot be marginalized and no one in their right senses can be jealous of them. They do not have to show off their superiority and success to anyone.

Many times competition with others is misleading. The Prophet Jesus (PBUH) said, "The day will come when the first shall be last and the last shall be first." You may see those who think today that they are on the summit will be in the depths tomorrow.

"Anyone whose two days are the same is a loser." You can extract meaning from all inspirational messages that "You should try as hard as you can to do your best." However, you cannot demonstrate a divine command such as "You are in trouble if you don't do any better than other people. Be better than others."

In addition, you do not need to compete with your brothers and sisters to be appreciated by your parents. What difference will it make if you please people who discriminate between brothers and sisters? If you want to please somebody, it ought to be someone who is just and virtuous at least.

If you compete, you await applause for your supposed superiority. If you want rewards from humans, selfishness and trading enter the business. Then the Master of Destiny will withdraw and leave you to deal with the ungrateful people whom you expected to reward you. **Whoever competes with themselves relies only on the Creator. For this reason, the Creator guarantees the reward of your labors.** The reward that the Almighty will bestow on you does not even resemble the reward of the most generous person.

60 "We have certainly created man in the best of stature; then We return him to the lowest of the low." (Qur'an: 95:4-5) Those people who commit murder, oppression, violence and theft or who try to spread these are excluded from these principles. But one may not expose or look down on people who are ashamed and try to hide the other personal weaknesses of will to which they have fallen prey.

b) Focusing on our duty

Ferhat was the lover of legend who struggled to reach his beloved Shirin on the other side of the mountain by digging the tunnel. He could succeed in that big job by not focusing on the end result but on the everyday job he should do.

If he had had covetousness, he would have thought, "I have been digging for years and I haven't got through to the other side. Can I hold out working in this tunnel until the end of the world?"

The most enduring people are those who concentrate their consciousness on their job. You will decrease your present strength if you base it on what you think you have done in the past, will do in the future, or what others have done.

You need to concentrate on your responsibility. With that understanding, if you have to leave the world in the middle of your life, you will still have gained. Because when you appear before the One who gave you this duty, you will receive your reward according to your goals and your intentions.

Suppose you are like a soldier waiting for your discharge papers in this world. If you had to leave without finishing your military service, would you be so sorry? It is a great honor to be a martyr, die for your values, if it is needed.

If we are serving goodness, we should be involved with goodness. **If our consciousness separates itself from our duties, it interferes with those duties.** When we lose our focus, we imagine that everybody else has gone astray and we become covetous. After that, covetousness tears us away from the entire struggle.

We need to look to the future because those who imagine what they are going to do over the next twenty years are more likely to succeed in the journey. However, it is dangerous to stick into the future because an insuperable mountain will block the progress of those who look at the next twenty years by not working every day.

If you think about redoing all those things that you have done in the past, you would be afraid, but, in fact, you did do them. The goal you intend to achieve is very great, but if you divide what you are going to do into days and minutes, it will shrink tremendously. It would be difficult to smile half a million times a year. Yet it is the same thing to smile once a minute. As a result, if you concentrate on your duty for that moment, you can calm down and you leave your covetousness.

CHAPTER SIX:

POWER OF SPIRITUALITY

I. WHY WE NEED THE POWER OF SPIRITUALITY?

INTRODUCTION

Did you ever drive a vehicle against a strong wind? Have you witnessed how the spout of a tornado throws everything in the air before it? One cannot be saved from effective spiritual winds or from the results of those winds. Given this is so, where in the spiritual climate do the winds that blow a person to success or to ruin originate?

One of the miraculous aspects of creation is that more than one universe can fit inside of one another with the appearance of a single universe. The material universe houses different universes with different aspects: quantum packages, particles, atoms, molecules, elements, earth, the planets, galaxies, radio, television, and various profound aspects of radiation...

Spiritual life and spiritual bodies are concealed in the spiritual universes that are far beyond the material (physical) universe. We are living intermingled with a mysterious profundity in which there are spirits, angels, Jinns, devils, and other spiritual species.

Our contact with this profound world takes place through dimensions such as the universe of dreams, the universe of visions, telepathy, feeling, the evil eye, and the like. Our physical bodies live in the material dimension and our spiritual bodies including our soul, ego, and conscience live in the spiritual dimension. We are also affected by the spiritual climate from vibrations and the flow of spiritual energy in addition to the heat and cold of matter.

To understand spiritual influence means to comprehend the spiritual system of security. We need to protect ourselves from destructive energies such as the evil eye, curses, hate coming from the spiritual dimension, and embrace the values of prayer, love, and appreciation.

1. THE CLIMATE OF INFLUENCE

The human heart is filled with waves like the ocean. It seldom is static. Every thought, every sight, every event, every environment leads us to a different emotional climate. The real reason for such disturbance of our hearts is the inspirations coming from the spiritual climate.

a) The Flow of Energy

Every drop that falls, every leaf, and every breeze causes a ripple in the little pond. The wings of every butterfly spread a wave to the horizons of the universe. Every moment, from every point, uncounted material and spiritual messages are flowing along.

In the material aspects of the universe, atoms, molecules, and elements have a continual motion and influence. On the spiritual side of the universe human souls, angels, jinni, and spiritual species experience interaction.

Matter is like a puppet. It is dough which is taken hold of and shaped and which does not know where it is going once it has been left to its own devices. Matter has no life, but what moves it in significant ways has a life. Angels represent the spiritual hearts of matter, what is referred to as the natural laws of science. The spiritual body can spread to matter and influence the behavior of matter.

Our souls, which reside in our bodies, receive direction from the spiritual dimension in the forms of visions, dreams, sensations, telepathy, ecstasy, contraction, expansion, and the inspiration of angels and the temptation of the Devil. These kinds of influences are taken from the soul through the channel of cells of the brain specially created to perceive these kinds of contents. Thus, some internal spiritual senses are added to our five senses.

Those who reside in the spiritual depth are immaterial creations like angels, jinni, and devils. Just as there are thousands of species, shapes, and characteristics of living beings in this world, there are very different characteristics of spiritual species.

Depending on the plan of the Creator of universe, some angels have no contact with matter. Others direct inanimate things, plants, and animals. Others take the responsibility to direct animals by inspiration. Others have duties related to people.

A part of the spiritual energy which envelopes our bodies is the result of our prayers, curses, feelings, and worship. Another part is the result of the prayers, curses, and feelings of love or hate directed towards us. Everyone has a body of energy that changes every moment with these sorts of factors.

Spiritual energy can be the gentle breeze of the morning or it can turn into a terrible storm. You can see people who help one another under the influence of compassion but who commit murder when they are shaken by insults. **We live in a world in which people are led to commit murder through friendship with killers and drawn to love virtue through befriending the virtuous.**

In a place where a thousand people pray for you and support what you are doing, you will have the strength of a thousand. If you advance for some day, you will be in the debt of the acceptance of the prayers of people who did not withhold their spiritual support from you.

The flow of energy occurs mostly between people and somewhat between people and angels or jinni. Let us note that plants and inanimate nature are represented by angels.

Every human being carries on a sort of spiritual broadcast to the spiritual world with his or her feelings and thoughts. Spiritual radio broadcasts are made by inspirational angels and tempting devils, if we may make the comparison.

Whoever tunes in to the proper frequency can listen to these radio broadcasts. Some of our readers who became very involved with our books have written that they saw us in their dreams and that they received messages from us. We were not even aware of this.

We may say that when you consider a person important, automatically you open up your spiritual perceptions for that person, or tune into that person's frequencies, and what we said before, is the result of this innate system. And this is a universal divine rule.

Sometimes spiritual broadcasts are directed to definite goals. An invitation from a holy person whom you do not know or with whom you are not involved reaches your heart through the command and permission of God. A holy person in a dream invites you to something good. In fact, that message was directed to some specific people and because your heart was suitable, it heard that message.

On the other hand, the angels can influence people in four ways: with incorporeal spiritual messages and by plants, animals, and inanimate beings. Humans can download constructive energy by listening to the messages in the depths of their spirits (inspirations) and by living close to nature.

You may regard everything in this way even down to every drop of rain that falls, to every particle of light that shines down and the breeze caressing your face. **I would like to remind you that in the appearance of every WORD, the angels carry the light that reaches your eyes.**

b) Energy Load

Many theoretical approaches have been formed concerning the load of spiritual energy. It is theorized that there are flows of energy passing through specific pathways that come together in definite points through the channels of the body with approaches such as chakras, acupuncture, body aura, and bio-energy. Although it is generally known that the body is influenced by the spiritual climate, there exist many different explanations and beliefs about this phenomenon.

We would like to clarify some important points connected with the flow of the energy under discussion, leaving philosophical points aside.

-Spiritual energy is of two opposite types, constructive and destructive. Constructive energy nourishes individual liveliness, energy, enthusiasm, mental and psychic performance. Destructive energy causes a person to tire, be sad, collapse, and experience weakness.

-Constructive energy stimulates wellness or peppiness in the human body. There are, for instance, cases of persons suddenly either becoming sick or getting well which cannot be explained by modern medicine. For instance, a tumor may disappear with a sincere belief, a prayer, or the feeling of trust.

-Humans call forth and live under the effects of the constructive or destructive forces of spiritual energy that they have developed in their environment. In the same way, humans are affected by the positive and negative energy directed to them by the humans in their environment. Everyone's material and spiritual existence is wrapped in a unified bundle of energy that comes from within and without. Sometimes the interior of this bundle is calm and sometimes it is tense.

-Constructive energy is the reward given by the Creator for such behavior as prayer, worship, altruistic love, approval, and acceptance. People receive an advance in positive energy for good attitudes and feel happy immediately. Destructive energy is the divine response given to such negative attitudes and behaviors as curses, selfish love, ingratitude, jealousy, and hate. Everyone receives destructive energy and feels pangs of the conscience and heart immediately for the evil they have done.

-The effect of the energy, which surrounds humans with their success, is very great. There is a radiance, which can be felt by the heart, if not seen by the eyes, which we may call the light of the body, surrounding that person with high energy. This light draws the customer to the merchant, people to listen carefully to the preacher and attracts them to the charisma of the leader. A person with low energy makes people uncomfortable, is repulsive, boring, and ineffectual, and has a dull perception. Cantankerous or mean persons may acquire a strong energy in relation to their selfish arrogance, their self-confidence, and their own affairs. The energy of such people causes disasters like those perpetrated by Hitler.

-The energy which surrounds the universe is positive because the nature of the universe is pure, filled with life and light. The beauty, which is in the waves of the sea, in the ripples of the river, in the waterfalls, in the ranges of the mountains, in the clouds, in the forests, in the winds and everywhere, will attract your attention. This is why the people who work with nature and the soil are happy, strong, and energetic.

-If humankind falls prey to selfishness, it destroys the factor of constructive energy, which the Creator has bestowed upon nature. Selfishness occurs when we want all the light for ourselves; however, whoever absorbs all the light is a dark object. They are darkness and their surroundings are darkness. Whoever says "only for me" has turned themselves into a dry well, a dark cave. Those who only love themselves spread hate outside. The attitude, which will enlighten us, is to wish to share every value of humankind with our spouse, our children, our relative, and our neighbors, with animals, plants and with the whole universe.

Humans have been enriched with many choices to make for themselves a life filled with happiness. Furthermore, our journey of life was begun with a body reflecting the energetic purity of the universe. What a pity that it is a human who gives evil for good and jealousy for appreciation. Much of the time, he or she has chosen evil from among all the possible things he or she could do.

We need to see the love in the universe and, taking it from the Creator who bestows it upon our souls, need to spread it to our surroundings. Then our interior selves will shine and our exterior selves will be illuminated.

People need to look with tenderness at the wind, which cools their hair as if it is saying to them "I love you." They need to listen with love to the birds that seem to say, "We sing with enthusiasm because of the happiness our Creator has spread among us." They exhibit such joyous enthusiasm so that those who look at them might feel love.

2. TYPES OF INFLUENCE

Spiritual influence can be in the form of communication of telepathic messages and transfer of feelings,

a) Communication of Messages

Spiritual influence can be in the form of a communicated message: feelings, inspiration, dreams, and telepathy are of this kind. When you sense an impending decision is the right one and when you are directed unconsciously to a good action, this is the inspiration and sense coming from angels. Sometimes you can even read passages of letters in truthful dreams and sometimes you can establish telepathic communication with your friends.

The writer Marlo Morgan relates this interesting experience: a hunter of an aboriginal tribe was hunting a kangaroo on the other side of the mountains. Morgan says that the tribe suddenly stopped and entered a state of telepathic communication. The tribal hunter, stating that he could not carry the whole kangaroo he was hunting, asked whether he could cut off the kangaroo's tail. The tribe agreed and a little while later, the hunter emerged with the kangaroo with its tail cut off.[61] No doubt, such a tribe would find our cellular telephones ridiculous.

61 See, Marlon Morgan, Mutant Message Down Under, trans. Erin Canady, Istanbul, Dharma, 1999.

Look at this example: I remembered two friends from high school, years later. It had been two years since I had seen these friends. I wanted to see them as soon as possible.

The next day around noon, one of my phones rang. My friend was calling from Istanbul. He saw me in a dream and was worried about me. I told him I had thought about them the evening before and wanted to see the other friend. While I was talking, my other friend called.

I have had many examples of sensation and dreams in my life. I have found that I was unconsciously directed to find many things that I had been looking for over a long period. I have experienced events in dreams years before they happened to me. I received answers to some of my questions in dreams. If we actually paid a little more attention to our lives, we might notice some interesting achievements.

Messages received through spiritual channels have had a very serious influence on human history. Some people have seen in dreams the people they were going to marry, and the affairs in which they were going to succeed – these all arose in their hearts in the form of strong perceptions.

b) Transfer of Feelings

A more common type of spiritual influence is transfer of feelings. You can be sustained by the energy coming from the spiritual climate that has not been put into words and you can feel that energy as negative or positive, according to its load.

Normally we perceive feelings through the hormones injected into our bloodstream. Some forms of thought and some perceptions of feeling in our brains cause us to experience a hormonal rush and related feelings.

There is another hidden spiritual dimension that forces our brains to inject hormones to our blood vessels. That is, sudden waves of feelings can arise from the interpretation of the contents, which are perceived by the spirit, come with telepathy or are felt or experienced in a dream.

In addition to the well-known sensations of joy and sorrow, there are conditions called "wajd" [ecstasy], "qabz" [distress] and "bast" [euphoric joy] and the subtle feeling of "latifa" [divine grace] that may be experienced by very sensitive persons as sensations coming through the channels of feeling.

The advance reward of Almighty Creator for all goodness is joy and the advance punishment of evil is sorrow. If you hurt someone, if you act disrespectfully, if the one you have hurt grieves and sighs at what you have done, it will be as though an arrow has pierced your heart at that moment.

Disorder of the feelings is a medical condition. However, there are tides of joy and sorrow arising from illness, expansion and contractions of the heart and these depend on spiritual causes.

When you do good deeds to your spouse and children, to your mother and father, to your grandparents and if you can, to poor people and orphans, joy and peace will flow into your hearts. However, when you commit a bad deed, you will feel a tension because there is truly a road from heart to heart.

"When Almighty Creator loves one of His creatures, He instills this love in the hearts of the angels. If He hates a human, He places hatred of him or her in the hearts of the angels. Then He casts both His love and hate into the hearts of other people."[62]

Concepts like "light, prosperity, and blessing" indicate constructive spiritual energy. In surroundings having this sort of flows of energy, there are floods of feelings like those of peace, trust, rapture, and joy. People who have strong beliefs, morals, and submission to God emanate a divine illumination. A supportive effect comes from the glances, touch, and prayers of such people.

Furthermore, people can nourish themselves with the spiritual energy of angels in nature when they walk in the rain and on the soil, swim in salt water, and breathe in the clean wind and air. Their bodily contact with nature gives them energy and strengthens them.

62 The Prophet Mohammad (PBUH), Jami' us-Saghir 1:246 Tradition no. 356.

Embracing our spouse and children and touching those whom we love balances our spiritual energy. However, those who have been struck by jealous glances may have their energy sucked up and may fall victim to exhaustion from the evil eye at that moment. Everybody in contact with someone with a low level of energy falls quickly into exhaustion.

3. CHARACTERISTICS OF INFLUENCE

We will study spiritual influence from the aspects of intensity and extension of energy and give some examples of powerful influences.

a) Intensity of Energy

When a stone thrown into a pond is bigger, the ripples will be bigger also. The effect of a whisper is not the same as a scream in the same environment. The result of desiring something is different from the result of begging for it. In a similar way, the experiences and effects carried out by people in their spiritual climate are proportional to the level of their intensity of sincerity.

Every conscious being in the universe has a butterfly effect in the world. The effect of thought carries one high and that of feeling even higher. Feelings, which are accompanied by firm belief and the language of spirituality, are those on the most effective level.

As thought produces feelings and as feelings grow stronger, spiritual energy increases. The seed of thought is turned into a great tree of feeling. **The greatest spiritual energy blossoms through thought transformed into firm belief.**

The energy that accumulates on the road and stretches from thought to opinion and, from there, to belief and firm belief, progressively grows stronger. **The belief coming from feelings is much stronger than belief deriving from opinions.**

At the peak of feelings, spiritual effectiveness is also at peak level. At that moment, the language of speech is the language of pure being. You know the difference between a hungry person's desire for food and that of a person who is full.

The effect you exert with the idea that you express, the method of doing something that you advise or the example you give on a subject, is shaped by certain initial characteristics:

-Do you believe what you are saying? If you believe in the idea you are putting forth, what you are saying does not really matter because people do not generally understand it; they only look into your eyes and decide by the energy they take from your heart whether what you say is true or false.

-Have you experienced something? If you have not experienced it, you cannot give advice about it from the depths of yourself and people are aware of this. If you have experienced something, this is radiated from your whole body and this affects them.

-Are you sincere? Are you being hypocritical? Are you honest? Are you speaking with good intentions or simply trying to ingratiate yourself with others? Pure intent is a magical potion which opens the way to supernatural support in every undertaking, and to spiritual events which affect people.

-Is the effect massive? The energy of one person is not the same as the energy of a group. A thought, a wish or an action is as strong as the number of conscious, sincere supporters of that thought, that wish or that action.

b) Extension of Energy

Spiritual influence can be experienced by those far from one another and those who see or do not see each other. Spiritual energy is not an occurrence like the flow of electric or wind in the material world. Like incorporeal particles that cause gravity, it starts out from the depths among the elements of the spiritual climate.

A mother in the far west of Turkey can establish telepathic contact with her son who is in the far east of the country doing his military service. All humanity can feel the same sensation from hearing the prayers of Mawlana Rumi.

We seldom consciously perceive the constructive forms of spiritual energy. The destructive forms attract our attention more often. In a story I heard from a friend, years ago villagers were building a roadway in Eastern Anatolia with pick and shovel and encountered a huge rock that they could not break up. There was no dynamite available, so they brought a peasant who had a very strong "eye" to the spot without explaining their intentions to him. The "evil eye" of the man, who was amazed by the huge size of the rock, cracked the rock to a degree that it could be broken up in pieces.

There are many more such experiences of psycho-kinesis to be found in various books. **The Prophet Mohammad (PBUH) indicates this with his saying, "The evil eye is real. It can potentially even knock mountains down."**[63]

When people join and spread their beliefs and feelings, the spiritual energy, which is focused in the same direction, grows stronger. Ten people who have joined spiritually are stronger than a million persons who are detached from one another. A million bricks scattered around randomly are only as high as one brick.

No warring society can ever be as strong as a society living in solidarity. **It is not the size of the population that determines its strength but the quality of its spiritual environment.** However many helping hands there are, the work is that much easier. However many helping souls there are, so much stronger will they be. If all souls were to come together and wish for the same thing, the world would suddenly change. The misfortunes that befall nations are because of their own wishes, desires, beliefs, and lifestyles.

Certain religious commentators state that the angels perceive good intentions through sweet smells and bad intentions through bad smells. The human soul perceives spiritual energy; however, much of the time it

63 The Prophet Mohammad (PBUH), Jami' us-Saghir 4:396 Tradition no. 5745.

cannot sense the spiritual environment very well because the human consciousness is focused on the material world.

Prof. Thomas Joiner of Florida State University in the USA suggests that depression is like a psychological cold and passes from person to person like a contagious disease.[64]

Some societies bring the misfortunes of earthquakes, floods, great fires, and terror on themselves by unifying in immorality, injustice, selfishness, and laziness. **When all of humankind joins in error, you may expect Doomsday.**

c) Powerful Influences

Persons with high levels of sincerity spread energy that is more powerful. Let us look at some examples:

Children: Children are extremely sincere and sensitive beings. They love with all their souls and cry with all their being. The sentiments of a child toward his father are as effective and striking as the sentiments of a father toward his child.

The needy: Those who are far removed from the pleasures of this world are closer to the spirits of the needy and their Creator. **Those who cannot achieve physical pleasures, whose effect is temporary, inevitably turn to spiritual satisfactions because this effect is everlasting.** Therefore, pay very close attention to the wishes and desires of needy individuals.

The Sick: People give priority to their spiritual pleasures when they suffer physical pain. The wishes and desires of a sick person may be stronger than those of a thousand well people. Have you used your illness as an opportunity for success? **You will be indebted for many of your successes to the prayers you uttered when you were suffering from an illness.**

Elderly people: The weakness and exhaustion that old age brings gives humans a pure, childlike sincerity. Elderly people are aware of the vanity of the world and they can perceive the limitlessness of the eternal universe.

64 Sabah Newspaper, July 4, 2000.

Parents: The compassion of parents while acting in their parental roles is strong in the highest degree. Naturally, the heartless parents are an exception.

The Oppressed: The oppressed are those who evil doers break. They turn to the Judge of the universe and implore His help with great sincerity. They are helpless; they cannot take revenge; therefore, they turn to the Master of Absolute Justice with claims of injustice. Their blessings are a treasure but their curses are a great disaster.

You will feel the need to support your friends on the road to success. **The spiritual support of hundreds of indifferent and insincere friends cannot be as great as the spiritual support of one true friend.**

If you invite well-deserved curses onto yourself by performing bad deeds, you will fall into a pit. If you invite sincere prayers to yourself, a place for you on the summit will be prepared. See the Prophet Mohammad (**PBUH**) made himself the beloved of the universe with his universal love, which has ascended! Here it is the pit into which Nimrod, who threw those into fire who did not worship him, was thrown!

4. EXPLANATORY EXPERIENCES

Let us mention a few examples to better understand destructive and constructive spiritual influences:

a) Destructive Influence

If you have a superior quality that excites people, you may call down the evil eye upon yourself. **You may pay heavily for not concealing your private characteristics or even for boasting them or perceiving them as grounds for superiority.** You must not expose your values to attacks that you cannot resist. Look at the following examples:

Example 1: I know an older man whose hair was dark black despite his advanced age. An old friend who encountered him commented in amazement, "Your hair is not white yet. It is surprising that you manage to stay so young." The other friend to whom he spoke was stricken by the evil eye and, from that evening on, writhed in the clutches of illness and was saved with difficulty.

Example 2: A government administrator told me a story from his childhood. "I had a young horse that I was very fond of. A neighbor woman saw the horse while it was grazing and said, 'What a nice young foal!' The instant she said this, I looked at the foal. The animal fell down where it stood, rolled into a ditch, and was hurt."

Example 3: A friend, living in Berlin, Germany, visited me in my village in 1988. I looked at his automatic transmission car and I prayed that he might not be influenced by the evil eye; however, I was afraid that this might occur while he was driving around the village. I was afraid, not because the car was so fine, but because the people of the village had not yet seen such a nice car.

I went back to Ankara. My friend began a journey from Trabzon and the car rolled into a ditch near Samsun. The car was ruined but, thank God, my friend got out perfectly unhurt.

I would advise you not to see anybody as being faultless. We should conceal our shames, but if we have small faults, let people know. We are not angels and we should not try to be seen as superior to anybody. A pimple on the forehead of a great beauty serves to protect that face. Appearing faultless causes one to be crushed under the evil eye and the jealousy of others.

b) Constructive Experiences

First, we can receive constructive energy from some sincerely spiritualized people: I have known a number of people with very high levels of spirituality. I experienced one of these meetings in the district of Safranbolu in 1991. At the end of an intensive training program, we visited an elderly holy person who was living quietly in the town.

The elderly woman, who was his wife, sat us down in a corner and we waited. While I was waiting, I experienced sensations that I cannot describe. I felt as if everything in the house had a soul. A pleasant sensation flowed into my heart from the stones and the walls. Just as the energy carried me into a climate of tranquility, the holy man came into the room. When I wanted to kiss his hands, tears began to flow from my eyes for no reason.

He embraced me and, without asking my name, told me I would have to make a change in my last name. May he rest in peace. I was an unknown, shy youth. I left the home refreshed, strengthened, and feeling energized. People like this, those who are bathed in the light of belief, cannot exist in today's crowded, selfish, sinful streets.

Secondly, we can try to approach the spiritual energy of the angels. To perceive the angels, I concentrated on plants and felt excitement every time I tried to read the consciousness in their designs. I experienced great adventures in the forests of Middle East Technical University. One summer at the university, I felt as if I was on another planet, in a city that was more exciting than the images of a cartoon. You become close with time, you talk to the rain, and you embrace the wind.

All the knowledge about the lives of the animals and plants and the workings of nature make you aware of another dimension of angel spirituality. I read some scientific magazines to learn more about this mysterious world. I watched documentaries about nature with excitement and took notes.

II. HOW CAN WE USE THE POWER OF SPIRITUALITY?

We can increase the constructive spiritual energy in our relations with people and avoid the ruin of destructive spiritual energy. We can also try to approach the spirituality of the angels:

1. CONSTRUCTIVE ENERGY

People can experience the spiritual effects that support each other and their surroundings in individual and social forms. We can receive constructive spiritual energy of the angels and humans in general and in targeted forms.

a) General form of energy

Constructive energy, which spreads from your heart to the universe, generally starts from your constructive thoughts and feelings and spreads out everywhere like a radio wave. You can spread the emotional values such as "love, compassion, tolerance, courage" and "honesty, industriousness, justice, respect, belief" and the like ethical values in the form of energy.

You can spread this spiritual energy from your heart in several ways. First, feel good wishes originate within you and pour from your heart. Second, express your energy, feel it from your heart, pass it onward, desire it, even if you do not speak it with your lips. Third, let your messages be broadcasted by the radio, TV, newspaper, courses, and works you have accomplished.

For your message to have a collective effect, it must be imbued in a collective character when it comes from your heart. Your desire for "your child to be happy" will not emerge in the form of energy which will nourish the happiness of all children. Great people aim to enlighten their whole surroundings like the light of day.

People need to form religious, political, and cultural groups for purposes of socialization and activity. However, if these structures cause people to shut themselves up inside and serve to oppress and destroy instead of causing people to interact and enter into reciprocal activity, they do damage. When we support these societies, we must not do so in a mindset of alienating, accusing, and looking down on others.

Religions propose concepts that will allow the faithful to support one another with their spiritual energies. For instance, Islam proclaims all the faithful to be brothers to one another.[65] It demands peace and justice to serve the good and tranquility of all of humankind. It encourages annual and, most importantly, weekly communal prayer and religious holidays.

Which persons, parties, groups, beliefs, or philosophies do you support? Does the energy spread throughout the world by the sports teams you support spread to you also? In this time, people socialize around different goals. I recommend that you research this and use your spiritual support for the good of humankind.

You can support the activities of any fund that works for a clean and green environment. You can at least encourage with your moral support the funds and organizations which work for the poor, the abandoned children, the aged and for law and justice.

The system of social bias is successfully used by ideological states. These kinds of states generally manifest themselves through prohibitions and revolutions. They brainwash the people through systematic propaganda and secure spiritual energy through the worship of ideological leaders.

Oppressive-deceiving systems literally suck out the spirits of the people. An elite class lives like kings, hiding itself behind the leader who represents the ideology without letting the common people know what they are doing. The people who believe they are supporting goodness, liberation, heroism, and national honor grow poorer and weaker year by year and their fortunes are collected in the hands of a minority.

Most people are not very keen about reading and studying. They generally believe whatever they hear and do not criticize it. If they did research things, they would slam the door of reality on the ideologues in a forceful way. In such situations, the truth can only be seen with the eye of good conscience and foresight. When thought, expression, freedom of belief, human virtue and means of democracy grow strong, and then humanity will succeed in freeing itself from these blood-sucking ideologists.

I would like to recall the way in which the leadership of the First and Second World Wars turned people into monsters. On the one hand, the

65 Qur'an: 49;10

Germans greeted the blowing to bits of the children of London with cries of joy. On the other hand, the English watched with feelings of vengeance the image of Elizabeth Zettle, a mother struggling to save her six children from the flames caused by the burning planes that burning Hamburg alive. Everyone is now sorry for these things, but this does not change the reality: **History copies pain from pain and love from love.**

No good can come from any belief or bias that does not work for goodwill, justice, and peace. Almighty Creator who creates human intelligence and the heart is just and merciful. If He holds a human guilty of something, He is considering what he or she understands, what he or she intends and what his or her purpose is.

Many of our conflicts arise from political prejudices. We struggle for our own benefits. If someone does not speak our language, he or she is not a traitor. We cannot judge people because of the papers they read or the societies to which they belong. **A society, which looks down on others thereby to elevate itself, will be degraded.** Nobody has ever been elevated through a condescending and mocking attitude.

b) Targeted form of energy

Another way of spreading the power of spiritual energy is through targeting individuals. You concentrate on a special person or on persons whom you have chosen, one by one, as though done with a spotlight within yourself. To the people you love, to those you are attached, and those with whom you share your life.

You are focusing your spiritual energy on people by: 1) seeing their name and being in your heart, 2) having positive feelings about someone, 3) reciting your prayers for someone, or in a more effective way 4) expressing these things with letters, by telephone or verbally, face to face. You can transfer your energy in the forms of prayers, wishes or appreciation and thanks. To leave a meaningful effect from your energy is to enlist the help of the angels, which depends God's acceptance and orders, and the way to accomplish this is to act sincerely, believing truly that this is the right way.

If you wish, you may pray secretly or you may pray collectively. Research held at 23 Clinics of the University of Maryland has shown that conscious prayer has helped to heal patients.[66] You can also arrange reciprocal prayer with your family and close friends. **A few prayers said together in a moment of the day are more effective than many prayers said in a disorganized way.**

I offer the following suggestions:

-Purity: Your prayer for yourself may embody selfishness or, because of your sins, may not be sincere. On the other hand, the spiritual support you offer for others is usually without opportunistic motives and seldom contains selfishness; it was made with good will and feelings of altruism. **The strongest prayer is that which we offer for another person.** I advise you to pray frequently for your friends in order to achieve effectiveness.

-Answers of the Angels: Angels are the messengers of the physical mechanisms of the material world and they are like the post officer of the spiritual realm. The prayers you direct to the prophets and your various friends do not reach their destinations of their own accord but by means of the angels with the permission from the Almighty. When an angel who is totally pure, who is without sin, filled with love and divine light inside of divine light takes your prayer from your heart, it returns to your heart and then goes away praying for you.[67]

While they carry your prayers to their goal, the prayers of the angels will collect around you. In the evening, you stretch out in the living room and distance yourself from the noise of the day. Suddenly you will feel that those prayers you have made up during the day revolving continually around you heart and mind.

-Expand your heart: When you are praying for yourself, your horizons are limited by your own dimensions. However, as the number of people whom you pray for increases, you turn them into thousands of hearts. One, who prays for the good of thousands of people is exalted, grows great spiri-

66 Aksam Newspaper, June 9, 2000.

67 "When you pray for your brother or sister, the angel (whose duty it is), says, "Amen, may what you requested be given to you twofold." The Prophet Mohammad (PBUH), Muslim Zikr: 88; Tirmizi Birr: 50

tually and a very special glory and happiness is placed in his or her heart.

-Prayer for one's surroundings: Briefly, I recommend that you spread values such as love, prayer, approval, and encouragement to your friends. The Almighty Creator does not sell these for money, rather every heart that desires them and can find them free of charge. What you withhold from others will be withheld from you. It is not only humans but also animals, plants, stones, and soil; even the village child who trembles with cold on his way from school has the right to your compassion. You will even find a reward for the piece of wheat that you give the pigeons that flock in hunger to your balcony. "Judge not that ye be not judged. Do not accuse others so that you may not be accused. Forgive others so that you may be forgiven."[68]

-**Support in the family:** Just look at the disasters of families. Look that those people who cannot get along with their spouses or children, parents who do not pray silently or openly for their children, their elders or couples who do not pray for one another every day. They neglect one another, they criticize one another, and they accuse one another and leave them without support so that their energy fails. Then, as the last straw, they accuse other family members of not getting along with them.

People receive what they give in life. In fact, they receive as much as they give. Whoever loves is loved and whoever gives praise is praised. Support your family members, wish for advancement toward their goals, and desire that each leave behind a wonderful life.

The tears of a single heart that shed all night can save a whole city from destruction. Do not downgrade your heart. **You are as holy as you think; you are weak before the all Merciful Creator. Your prayers can change the flow of history.**

You may not have the time to smile at everyone and listen to everyone's troubles. You may not be able to pay off all of your debts. However, if we want to find a job or pass an exam, give us the kindness that is in your heart. We struggle to succeed. Some of us weep in states of depression. It falls on you to be big enough not to be jealous of us.

68 The Bible, Luke, 6/37.

c) Energy of Angels

It is difficult to connect with the spirituality of the angels because the difference in the levels of spirituality between us and them is relatively great. However, because it is their duty to represent the beings in nature, it is possible for us to contact them through nature and imagine them at least on the level of consciousness. So, possible ways to feel the positive energy of angels are as follows:

-Through inspiration: Some angels bring inspirations from the Almighty to our hearts. The spirituality of some angels is open to mankind. The inspirations that great inventors have received are actually open to everyone. However, we cannot find the time to avoid the noise of the world and listen to this spiritual radio.

If you would sit down in a quiet corner and listen to yourself, you will be able to sense more or less the ugly talk of devils and the moral advice of the angels. If you continue to listen to your conscience in the middle of the night, you will be able to hear your spiritual channels even more clearly.

-Through animals: When you study the lives of animals, you can feel the angels who direct their lives. There are many subtleties in the lives of animals that shed light on the fact that they are directed by angels. For example Prof. Robert Sheldrake of Harvard University studied extraordinary events experienced among pet owners. In one of the examples, Melinda Willis related that one morning she missed the bus trying to restrain the abnormal behavior of her cat and that the bus she missed had a serious accident.

In another example, Jennifer Breton's cat Walter was moving about wildly in front of the TV. When Breton, who was trying to understand what the problem was, turned on the TV, she saw a warning for a great tornado in her region. They immediately went down to her basement and were saved because of the behavior of the cat, from the tornado which twenty minutes later leveled houses.[69]

-Through plants: I believe that plants are the faces of loving angels

69 Hürriyet Newspaper, July 29, 2000.

who smile at the world. In the chapter entitled "Plant Love" in my book "Sevgi Zekasi [Love Intelligence]," I recorded amazing researches on this subject.

Plants use amazing techniques to maintain ecological balance. Some scientists think that plants are conscious. In fact, studies have shown that houseplants react to the changing psychologies of their owners.

For example researchers in Kyoto University in Japan have demonstrated that the defensive genes of Lima beans try to defend themselves against insect pests. These genes warn other plants and permit them to fend off the attacks of the pests.[70]

-**Through inanimate beings:** Physical, chemical and mathematical formulas which describe the universe show that the universe has an inconceivable artistic specificity and displays an aesthetic and symmetrical character.

The geometry of the design of matter is amazing. If you want to make the acquaintance of the angels who were the first admirers of the Almighty-created artistic challenge, which encircles the world, you too may enter the world of science and study matter.

In short, when you establish contact with positive persons, animals, plants and nature, you will be affected by the energy fields of their bodies. Touch nature. Touch stones, the earth, plants, and things and feel it.

2. DESTRUCTIVE ENERGY

Unfair, unjust relations between people cause destruction through "destructive wishes." Sometimes people experience damage through the energy of the evil eye born of negative feelings directed towards innocent persons. Let us inspect the subject:

70 Radikal Newspaper, August 4, 2000.

a) Hatred and cursing

People "who has been treated unjustly, who has experienced oppression, who has been hurt and crushed" feel "sorrow, hurt, anger, the desire to curse and call down evil" against whoever has done this to them. When these feelings have just cause and are directed against someone who deserves them, they are destructive and bring that person to their ruin.

The curses of sorrow from the one you have injured will follow you all your life and will strike you in a time and place you do not expect. There is generally a spiritual curse behind accidents, betrayals, misfortunes, and swindles. People who are cursed wear out their lives wrestling with one misfortune after another. I shall give the following advice:

Theft or unpaid debts: You are encompassed by the psychological stress of people when you caused them financial damage or when you delay repayment of debts you owe**.** Every time they think about the money that is owed them and their financial loss, they fall into a deep grief, excitement and sometimes even into a panic attack of curses. Whoever caused this situation will meet with the misfortune of negative energy and as long as they do not remove the cause for this disaster, their calamity will grow step-by- step.

Forgotten debts are like a tumor in the body. They grow if they are not wiped out. The disaster is not caused by not being able to pay the debt. It is from indifference to it, for avoiding it or not paying it off when you have means to do so. Do not avoid your creditors if you do not have the means to pay. Tell them your situation and agree on a new payment plan with them.

I remember the accidents experienced by someone who was late in their payments. I read about a businessman who became rich off the money of his partners and then committed suicide after he lost his family. I will tell you what I believe: the owners of every business who take a loan with bad intentions or who deliberately do not pay their debts back on the agreed-on dates will one day go bankrupt. No one should think that they could cheat and save themselves by running off somewhere. Not only does the law observe humans, but every step of everyone is recorded by responsible angels. If it does not occur in the near future, Destiny will overtake the offenders with misfortune in hell.

The damage you or your children for whom you are responsible do to the property of individuals or the public causes a similar effect. If you damage someone's garden or scratch someone's car, do not hesitate to excuse. People are sufficiently tolerant to forgive small damages but they do not forgive those who do not ask for pardon. One day when your belongings are damaged, the first thing you are going to ask is: Did I inflict this much damage on someone else's property?

Hostility: Slander, ridicule, disparagement, disrespectful behavior, selfishness and neglect of one's duty can cause hostility among dishonest people. A heart you have broken with injustice grieves every time it thinks of you and the grief of that heart falls on the spiritual realm of your goals like an acid rain. Nobody who has broken a heart should think they could find peace through alcohol or drugs. Drunkenness come to an end but the flow of destructive energy coming from broken hearts goes on.

The misfortunes that come from our tongue are many; many more than those that come from our hands and feet. We invite disaster with idle talk. So, **either do not break people's hearts with unjust behavior or, if you cannot, then totally avoid any communication with people.** The safest way not to break hearts is to control your tongue.

It is slander to talk to people in a way that displeases them. You should speak to people as you would like to be spoken to yourself. **Slander is the seed of misfortune and hate. It is a disease that spreads like a fungus.** People who have important things to do cannot find the time to argue with other people.

Arrogance is foolishness and an ugly form of stupidity that causes mockery. It culminates with the vengeance heaped on those persons who denigrate Divine Honor. **I have never seen people who were criticized as much as those who criticized others unjustly or people looked down on as much as those who looked down on others.** If there are those with whom you are angry, you ought to seek mediators to make peace between you. If you are going to enter into a quarrel, you should not be on the wrong side. If you get angry easily, you need to stay away from other people.

Unjust hate: If you are unjust in your hatred and your hatred results from misinformation, you will deplete your energy. Do not allow hatred to control your heart. Do not immediately respond with hatred to those who hate you. If you are forced to, hate the evil and not the evildoer. The hate of evildoers is harmless but it is not useful either.[71] **If you meet evil with evil, what difference is there between you and the evildoer?"**[72]

If hatred makes someone unhappy and tense and weakens the nervous system, then the hatred is mistaken. Superior people may experience hatred and grief on account of immorality and injustice. They do whatever they can, learn their lesson, and close the subject. People who wander the streets filled with hate have lost their ability to do good to mankind. Islam says to "View Satan as a terrible enemy." But Muslims do not go about frothing at the mouth with hatred for Satan. Their hatred for Satan do not make their hearts convulse with anger, it merely make them feel comfortable.

We do not have to love someone. There are people whom we should not love. **The first way to avoid bad people is to abandon them. We should forget that they even exist.** If they come close and shout at us, we can stop up our ears. We can compare their words to the mewing of a cat but we must not use up our strength in hatred.

Unjust curses: The next step in hatred is turning the curse that is uttered in anger into a malediction. The Prophet Mohammad (**PBUH**) says, "When a human curses something, that curse ascends to heaven and the gates of heaven close, it cannot go in and it comes back again. The gates of the earth are closed as well and it cannot enter. It wanders here and there. It cannot find a place and it goes into the thing that which was cursed. If that thing is worthy to be cursed, it enters into that thing. If it is not, it comes back to the one who uttered it."[73]

71 Two kinds of hatred are useful: The hatred of hatred and of bad behavior. The hatred of good behavior does harm. The hatred the evildoer is useless however. On the other hand, those who do excessive evil have been cursed.

72 *Mawlana* Rumi , Masnavi, vol. 1, p. 125.

73 The Prophet Mohammad (PBUH), Jami'-us-Saghir 2:370 Tradition no. 2069.

When we hear the words “Damn it” in movies or on the streets, we are accustomed to it. Do you want to be cursed because you cursed a rock on which you stubbed your toe? As the number of foulmouthed people increases, social misfortunes also intensify.

You will be the first victim of your curses. If your curse is just, it will find its mark; if it is not, then it will come back to you. What if the person that you cursed has repented of his or her sin, or if he or she made a mistake for some unknown reason or was the victim of a deception or is later sorry and does you some great kindness, or your curse deprives him or her of heaven? I do not recommend curses under any condition other than attacks directed against our belief in the Almighty, our life, or our honor. You should pray for those who curse you so that, if their curse is just, it may not harm you.

I pray that Almighty Creator gives patience to those who suffer greatly. We should defend ourselves but we should also not lose energy through curses. **No one can escape the justice of Destiny that protects those who are not able to defend themselves.**

Look at this example: Someone hit our car in our parking lot and drove away. I asked the neighbors but nobody admitted to the act. When I could not identify who had done the deed, I turned the matter over to the Almighty Creator and closed the issue. The guilty party was revealed the next week. He paid for his hit-and-run behavior with a bigger accident.

b) Destructive Evil Eye

The evil eye is a concept believed in Eastern cultures, but is not proved by positive science and, so, is not well known in Westerner society. I have come to believe in the existence of the evil eye based on repeated personal experiences.

The evil eye means “one human being causing the destruction of another’s spiritual being through a glance or a thought as it might be, that causes his or her illness, misfortune, or death through spiritual energy.”

There are many theories concerning the evil eye. According to some, we are dealing with an infrared or ultraviolet ray that emanates from a person's eyes or brain; according to others, it is an effect of this or that feeling.

I think the evil eye is the process of influence of spiritual energy on the auras of the body. I think it is caused by increases in feelings such as "jealousy, self-centeredness, envy, and self-admiration." I mentioned above the destructive energy of these negative feelings. In this sense, everybody has a grain of the evil eye within them and the manifestation of these feelings is stronger in some people.

I shall tell you the story that Adam experienced in 1996. Adam went to a certain village to "weave" chestnuts.[74] A neighbor asked him to shake down his tree. Adam accepted and began work early in the morning. The neighbor came up to see him around 10:30 AM and admired his performance and poured forth these words: "If this was one of our fellows, they wouldn't have even gotten up the tree. They would have only shaken down half of this."

As soon as Adam heard the words he said, "I suddenly started to black out. I lost my strength and could not hold the pole in my hand. I sank down when my legs began to shake and I held onto the tree so not to fall. I had to stay there for twenty minutes before I could come to. After that, I could only climb down to the ground with difficulty. I felt seriously sick for hours."

After this incident, Adam could not climb a tree for two years. Every time he attempted it, fear and images that fluttered before his eyes impeded him from action. Other's prayed over him and helped cleanse the bad energy from his self. He then could climb trees but he could not achieve his old level of performance.

I have had many such experiences. Sometimes I received a guest who I thought admired me. If I acted as if I were some kind of an angel according to their expectations, I would have a difficult day. My vital energy would suddenly vanish; I would go home half-dead and have to ask my wife to

74 In that region, climbing the tree and shaking down chestnuts with a pole is called "weaving" them.

help me. She would pray for me, with flowing tears and in a half an hour, I would be well. My advice not to cause the evil eye is:

-**Avoid envy and jealousy:** If you observe a characteristic you admire in your friend, try to make him or her happy and pray for him or her. Destructive energy comes from jealous souls but the damage they give themselves is greater than what they give to others. "Acid vinegar corrodes its own pot." **-Be careful with your admiration and envy for people:** A very beautiful, much-liked, attractive work, body or a being actually draws one's heart into it. If you admire someone and especially if he or she behaves according to the happiness your admiration inspires, then your evil eye will strike him or her. However, if you see or feel this being the work of Almighty Creator or express this by saying "masha'allah, what a fine thing Almighty Creator has made," this will destroy the destructive feeling. The admiration for the individual will at once be converted to admiration for the divine art. No matter what it is, nothing must be loved while forgetting Almighty Creator and self-contained sublimity must not be attributed to anyone except God.

Not causing the evil eye does not save one from being struck by it. In particular, attractive people, whose voices and behaviors are liked, who produce effective results, who have high positions in the government, who are rich, who have high social status, who get attention, who are famous, and who have similar characteristics should be more careful. People with rotten teeth, smelly feet or who dress in shabby attire are not subject to the evil eye.

Let us state the following: What people can do to avoid the evil eye:

-Concealment: You need to conceal your children or a capacity that draws attention and has not yet grown strong, especially from those in your close environment who may perceive you as competition. If you are very handsome, beautiful, intelligent, industrious, or successful, do not use these things to brag and boast to people. Not everyone will support you with kind wishes. "If a plant flourishes with pure water, an animal will come and graze on it." "Conceal you affairs even from yourself so that the evil eye may not harm them."[75]

75 *Mawlana* Rumi , Masnavi, vol. 5, p. 62; vol. 2, p. 114.

People who are foreign and a distant land cannot envy you as effectively as your near friends and relatives. The real evil eye comes from someone who knows you well and who sees you as a competitor.

If a young plant makes a great noise and waves about, a goat will come and eat it. If the plant waits until it become a tree, it will not die from losing its leaves.

Many very intelligent children have a hard time when they are grown up because of the evil eye. Their families must conceal those children from public attention.

You need to conceal your special characteristics in the soil of secrecy and they will send out branches and buds when they are stronger. Surely if you are a poet, your poetry will be known and if you are a speaker, your rhetoric will become public. **There is no comparison between a tree that is attacked when it is a young sprout and one that is attacked after it has sent forth branches.**

You are in danger if you have characteristics that attract attention. **If very good people wander about in public too much, they will have very hard lives.** It is difficult and dangerous to be very beautiful, very intelligent, very clever... you need to be careful.

Confuse: Some wise people make mistakes, consciously, in front of other people to avoid the evil eye. For instance, these individuals might talk in slang and behave in an ugly way. In this way, they try to destroy people's admiration and avoid the evil eye. People who try to hide their faults from others and present themselves as angels set a trap for themselves. If you need to, leave a stain on your coat. An evil eye bead does not to deflect the evil eye but, as I have shown, rather serves to deflect and scatter attention. It is a mistake to attribute a power to a bead.

If you have something of value that you are afraid the evil eye will strike, the best thing to do is to add some feature that will make it uncomfortable for people to look at it. Be natural and let them discover you. If they sense your humility, they cannot be jealous of you; they will accept your success sincerely.

To protect yourself with prayer: In Muslim society, sometimes the most common way to protect oneself from the evil eye is to recite verses from the Qur'an. Chapters of the Cow (verse 255), the Down, and the Men (2nd, 113th and 114th chapters) can be recited to ask for protection against spiritual dangers such as the evil eye. You may recite these verses or equivalent ones in your religion. Alternatively, your spouse, your parents, or your friends can recite them as well. Experience shows that not every recitation has the same effect and the recitation of some people is more effective than that of others.

Correction: You can take other steps to correct the balance of energy you might have lost due to the evil eye. These efforts include taking a salty bath or swimming in the ocean, walking on the soil in bare feet, frequent performance of ritual washings, deep breathing, taking long walks in the pure air, having your spouse or someone close to you touch you with their hands. I also think that acupuncture can serve to improve this sort of balance of energy.

People who become too involved in these subjects are inclined to attribute every psychic tension and exhaustion to the evil eye and magic. This is not correct. Everybody can experience stress because of thousands of different physical and spiritual causes. It is a great error to think that the evil eye causes every discomfort. Internet, television, cell phones, noise, and polluted cities are enough to make us experience stress.

We should not attribute the results of an unhealthy lifestyle to the evil eye; a life governed by sufficient sleep, a healthy diet, sports, conversation, socialization, and positive feelings will solve many of our tensions.

CHAPTER SEVEN:

THE POWER OF THE DIVINE WILL

I. WHY WE NEED THE POWER OF THE DIVINE WILL?

INTRODUCTION

Revelations were given to the prophets, but divine inspirations and messages are conferred every moment, in every situation, and to everyone. You only have to open your heart to hear them. What do you have to do today to understand what Almighty Creator wants to say to you? You are right; this is an amazing, fascinating, and unbelievable question.

The divine will represents the alternative roads offered to in your life. The road your car travels on, the earthquake that changes your life, the failure you learn from and the sun lighting your path.

We people of belief, who are searching for the truth, know that our lives will not decay and end. This world is only one in a thousand of the life adventures that await us. Could it be possible that the Almighty Merciful One, who created us for a supernatural purpose, continually nourishes our hearts and brains, might not intervene in our lives? No, it is not possible. We are not aimless beings!

The universe is in absolute control of The Divine Will of the Almighty Creator. What humans do is bound to what Almighty Creator creates. No event in the universe can take place independently from Almighty Creator. Humans cannot create and the process of success in human life cannot be understood without understanding the divine will of the Almighty.

The universe is an orderly and perfectly functioning system established by the absolute will of God. Every development is based on wisdom; everything has a useful purpose depending on the will of God. Almighty Creator is the founder and administer of universal rules, but He is not subject to the rules He has laid down. He can change whatever process He wishes in whatever form He wishes. Our goal in this chapter is to understand: (1) what creation is (2) how future events are determined in relation with the divine will (3) what our responsibilities are in this process.

The secret of success cannot be completely grasped without understanding the purpose of Almighty Creator whose Person is outside of time and space, but who creates everything in time and space, at every point, by the manifestations of His Beautiful Names.

Are you ready to wander in the deep labyrinths of destiny and creation? Let's go on:

1. POWER AND CREATION

The first step to understanding destiny is to understand the relation between Almighty Creator and creation. The questions are these: Is being the universe created? How is it being created?

a) The Activity of Creation

Ninety percent of the world's inhabitants believe in one or more gods. The remaining 10% the atheists live in Western cultures. Since it is not possible to rid oneself of the need for the sacred, the atheist often treats ideologies and science as gods.

The universe either: (1) exists of and by itself, (2) was made by natural laws (causes) or (3) is the work of an Almighty Creator outside of time and space. Reason and conscience demonstrate the unsoundness of the first two possibilities, and our hearts lead us to the idea of the Creator. Let us explain:

1) **Is the universe something unto itself?** It is impossible for something that does not exist within time and space to make itself or any other thing exist. If a being has a beginning in time to exist and stays in existence, it should depend on something outside. So, remember that, according to modern science there was no universe 14 billion years ago.

For the universe to have been brought from nothingness to being requires a power outside of time and space. That being, which began time and space, allows it continue and is independent of time and space is an all Powerful Being and we call Him God. He is the Almighty Creator because He is absolute. He did not come from nothing, He was not born, He will not die, He does not change, and He does not evolve.

2) **Do the laws of nature create?** The laws of nature are the meanings given to the systematized behaviors of matter. These laws emerged step-by-step together with the building of the universe. They have no substance, cannot be touched, and are invisible. It is theorized that there exists graviton particles related to the law of gravity, which is thought to unify bodies. If you truly could destroy matter, there would be no law of nature left.

3) **Is it from the all Powerful Creator? According to our understanding,** the impossibility of the first two options makes the third inevitable. We conclude that the Creator is God. The Almighty Creator lies outside of time and space, which means that He does not come from nothing, He was not created, nor He did not create himself. He exists without beginning and without end

One can see from every point: its mortality, its mutability, and its plasticity, that the universe is not eternal. The Almighty Creator exists in timelessness, was not born, and does not cease to exist. Let us listen to our intelligence, our hearts, our reason, and our consciousness in this matter.

The birth, death, history, and changes in nature show us that nature is like a flowing river. What makes it continuously visible is that it is always nourished from its source. The Almighty Creator cannot be nourished; He can only nourish.

Sensitive balances are concealed in all the details of the universe. All the particles, organs, classes, species, and systems are balanced like individual universes - one within the other and an atom is a tiny solar system. So, according to us, only a single Ruler of the whole system of the universe can establish and preserve the balance that controls the universe.

This means, one who cannot control the sun and its light cannot design the eyes. The One who bestows the faculty of taste to the tongue is the One who gives taste to honey. He balances the ratio between male and female births. The absolute harmony of everything, one with another, shows us a single wise Ruler.

Everything was created both a) in a different view and 2) in the same fashion. That is, all human beings resemble one another; however, no two people are the same, with the same eyes or the same voice. You feel the power of a single Force in every being, in their nourishment, adornment, the way they protect themselves, their harmony, and their planning.

The observable universe was born with an explosion from zero volume and it reached a diameter of 90 billion light years It holds 200 billion galaxies and trillions of stars. Only an Almighty Creator, without limits, could create this limitless horizon from a material nothingness.

Matter is an unknowing, unconscious, unfeeling, plastic stuff. The Designer gives it meaning in the flower, in the glance, in the heart. The One conceals the tears, love, joy, and excitement behind the matter. Matter is stirred from one excitement to another by the hidden textures of the Creator's brush. So then, what must be done to create this matter?

b) Power of Creation

What is the power of creation? To have a real creating power, the Creator must be in and of Himself "eternal, omniscient, omnipotent, having an absolute will." If something has a life, is nourished, and can love, the Creator must also be able to give life, nourish, and feel mercy. Let us concentrate on the four most basic qualities of the creating power:

Eternity: The first condition for being able to create time and space is to encompass all of time and space with one's being. The Eternal Almighty Creator, who has no beginning or end, has no time or space. There can be no other Almighty Creator with a beginning and an end. He is outside of time and space with His Essence. However, He is present in time and space through the manifestations of His beautiful names. Eternal Almighty Creator has neither past nor future. He can create an instant from timelessness and that instant can hold billions of years within it. As such, a whole life can be seen in an instant, from beginning to end, like a flash of lightening.

Divine Knowledge: One who does not know everything can create anything. The creation of the human body cannot succeed merely with knowing the structure of bones, muscles, tissue, cells, molecules, and atoms. One must also know the changes that take place every second of life in the innumerable quantum fields of each atom for the 100 trillion of cells that make up the body.

The existence of the universe took place in time with a beginning; however, its informational body is eternal in the knowledge of God. The wisdom of the Almighty Creator encompasses all time, place, creation, design, and form. It observes the future coming from the past, the past from the future, and all of eternity. It is free from deficiencies such as thinking, learning, holding opinions, and making decisions.

Divine Will: Will power is the independent and sovereign power to choose among alternatives or generate new choices. No one can be considered the true doer of another's deeds when that person has been forced. There can be two kinds of will: One is dependent, other is independent. Creator's Will must be totally independent. The Creator must be one who has ability to choose and do, independently, anything by Himself.

To understand why we cannot be accepted as creators of our actions, we will later discuss the difference between our wills and Will of God and the relation between the two.

Functioning of automated systems in our bodies and in university, depends totally on the will of God. For example a mother does not choose the stages of development for the baby in her body. The digestive system does not operate at our will. The flow plan of the series of the universe and events was and is being shaped under the absolute control of God's Will.

The absolute will of every event belongs to the Master of the Universe. Every event is bound profoundly to the will of the One who controls it. If He does not allow us to exist at this instant, we would cease to be. The blowing of a particle of dust is made possible with His blowing it. Being able to read these words is bound in order to a) "Wanting to read them," b) "His creating your desire" c) "His accepting your desire"and d) "His creating the activity you desire."

Divine Power: The Power that truly creates is the source that is at the basis of all the created powers. No one can be creative by depending on others' power, nor can he or she be enlightened by depending on others' light. The existence of God's Self is the most sublime, transcendental, unlimited, and indefinable. Almighty Creator is the Light of lights and the universe is a tiny shadow of that absolute Light.

So, can a human, a matter or any part of the universe be the creator of anything? As you see, anything or anybody that is made, that is something organized, can never be the creator of even an atom.

The universe is a dark matter towards inside out and a shining light towards the out inside. The intensity of existence increases as it moves from matter to light. Solid matter, as great as the planets, can come from a handful of light. Indeed, wasn't the huge universe created from a point of energy? Almighty Creator is the Light of lights; He is in absolute intensity of existence.

When the electricity of a country is cut off, the lights of the whole country are extinguished. In the same way, the shadow of the names of Almighty Creator has penetrated the existence of the universe.

2. THE FRAME OF DESTINY

The definition and understanding of the concept of "destiny" changes from culture to culture. According to our view, destiny is the overall plan of God for everything in time and space. This universe has a beginning, flow, and an end depending on a divine plan, which is destiny.

Human destiny is a part of the destiny of the universe. The destiny of the universe resembles a flowing river, and the destiny of humankind resembles that of fish condemned to swim with the flow of the river. Individual wills are within the frame of Divine Will as such: When the fish are swimming with the flow of the river, they choose in large measure how they are going to move forward to the right and left and which branch they will swim in.

Our destiny about our life and future is shaped by the intersection of three dimensions:

1) The **compulsory fate** is the absolute determination of God. This is the flowing river that is time/space system and the body of the fish,

2) The **free will** gives us complete free will. This is our way of swimming in the river.

3) The **conditional destiny** is the destiny that we are made to experience for what we deserve through our deeds. We swim on the side of the river that we have chosen in this environment.

Let us expand on these subjects:

a) The Compulsory Fate

The compulsory dimension is making a choice of one of the innumerable alternatives of the universe. It is that you were chosen and were made to happen as one of the innumerable human possibilities. What is compulsory is your innate being, your nature, your basic being that you were not asked about when you were created by God.

Almighty Creator started space and time, and within it, He gives existence to the plan of destiny that He decreed from eternity. He made humankind the most valuable fruit of this project. **Material things flow along existence like individual rivers, which flow from the ocean of Light to matter and the shapes, and forms that have been determined.**

If we could descend to a level beyond physics in the heart of creation, we would encounter the angels which are there according to the plan of the Almighty. A part of the angels represents the laws of nature. **The angels learn from Almighty Creator and relying on God's power, carry out His commandments.**

One sees matter in the exterior of the mirror of the universe and the angels in the interior. According to some it is a stone on which you have stumbled and to us the angel has warned you in the name of God. **According to some, it is an unconscious rose in the garden but according to us, it is an angel smiling with the face of a rose.** Your understanding changes with your viewpoint.

People who view events in a materialistic way see the effects of matter and not the real Maker, God. They cannot see Almighty Creator because He is not material and not of the same stuff as the universe. While they cannot see Him in the universe, they can perceive His Light which is everywhere with the eye of the heart.

We can find the power of the Master of the Universe in the breeze, which strokes our foreheads and the flickering light that plays hide and seek with our eyes. The act of creation of the Eternal Ruler is sometimes the oxygen in our lungs and sometimes the smile on our face. Sometimes His mercy flows from our eyes in the form of tears.

Natural causes could not have prevented our seeing the creation of Almighty Creator if He had created without order or laws. People see the blooming of plants, but they do not perceive what causes this beyond matter. They see how a baby is created, but they do not see the Almighty Creator. The creation of a baby in its mother's womb is as much of a miracle as the creation of a baby in the branch of a tree.

The Almighty created causality not to hide Himself but to make us work and develop in a defined system, deserve success and reward. If the principles of cause and effect had not been given to life, human beings could not operate at any success system. They could not determine their goals and they would not know how to operate. Therefore, for humans to be put to the test, a causality principle had to have been established.

Causality principle operates primarily in the material world and secondarily in the spiritual dimension behind it. We easily know that primary material causes such as natural laws. On the other hand, secondary spiritual causes represented by the angels lie hidden among material causes. For example, the angel called Michael (PBUH) serves at the regulation of nature's climate and Azrael (PBUH) at death.

It is narrated that the angel Azrael (PBUH) said to Almighty Creator, "Your servants will complain about me and be angry at me because of my duty of taking away souls." He received this answer, "I shall hang the curtain of misfortunes and illnesses between you and them so that they may not complain about you and be angry at you."[76]

Nature is passive. It does not make things it is made. It is not the artist, it is the art, it is not the poet, it is poetry. All of the extraordinary internal cycles of nature are directed from beyond nature:

A microscopic life form grows and turns into a larva. It attaches onto a leaf and changes. The body inside the cocoon becomes meaningless, like the shapeless liquid of an egg, and the liquid latter turns into a colored being: metamorphosis introduces a wonderfully beautiful butterfly to the universe. Who made it? The larva? The leaf? The cocoon? The butterfly?

76 Said Nursi, Words, 22, Word, p. 265.

Divine laws designed natural events like the sun, the earth, the wind, the spring. The Almighty Creator has decreed that fire will burn. So long as He does not decree exceptions to this, fire will always burn.[77] He placed the solar system and the Earth in a corner of the universal project that He planned. He determined how the stars would be born and die and how the plants would flower and whither.

The Almighty Creator determined spiritual bases such that the enmity of the cat to the dog and the dog to the cat, the inclination of the male to the female and the tenderness of the mother to her child. A woman cannot negate her nature and take on male personality. Even if one temporarily suppresses and perverts the natural identities by manipulating genetic personalities or by suggestion, emotional conflicts and crises will arise.

Whether you like your compulsory fate or not, you did not create your character, rather it was given to you; what you were born with, the age you live to, and the events you have and will experience. Accidents you may have had or destiny smiling upon you...Not all, because even if we do not choose some of the events in our lives, we may have caused them in the context of our "conditional destiny."

b) Free Will

A peculiarity of humankind in the universe is that "the destiny of humans in part" belongs to their choice. In other words, it is our desire with our prayer, will, deed, and creation of this desire by God. God did not give even the angels much freedom. With the Jinnis, humankind was created as the freest living being in the universe.

Some things in the world lack souls such as statues, plants, and animals and are like robots, for the most part.[78] However, they all play a role that has been fashioned for them from eternity. They are condemned to be what they are, they serve, and their pleasure consists of carrying out their roles.

77 Almighty Creator commanded the fire into which the Prophet Abraham (PBUH) was thrown, "Fire be cool and calm." (Qur'an 21; 69). The specific command changed the operation of a universal law.

78 We may speak of certain animals having very limited will.

On the other hand, we are equipped with material and spiritual tools, and have been given a field of freedom. This is why animals are almost all equal to one another, but abysses separate humans. Some humans remain very primitive, while other becomes illustrious.

We need to understand our free will in relation to and as being different from the divine will of the Almighty and the will of others:

-First, our free will is dependent on will of God. The Almighty granted us a kind of limited will under His total control.

According to Quran "If Almighty Creator does not will it, (that is if He does not grant permission and if He does not so create) we cannot do what we wish."[79] The Almighty Creator granted the freedom to desire and to freely attempt to humankind.

Let us put this into more detail: **Our creator let us have thousands of alternative desires to do something. Then we select among them and God lets us feel these desires in our brains and hearts. Then, if He allows us to do what we desire, He creates the actions of what we want.**

For example, we want to laugh, He makes us laugh; we want to walk, He makes us walk. His will is connected to our will. **We are completely free in some choices and totally limited on others. For example** now, you are free to read this sentence, but even if you so desire, you cannot fly like a bird.

-Second, the Almighty has put our free will under the effect of our environment. Our own wishes and, partly, the wishes of others with whom we share our lives shape our own lives. So, our free will is under the effect of the will of others. That person wanted to marry you; the wish was accepted and you got married. We did not want the Gulf War, but we were affected by it. We did not invent television, but we can all watch it.

Moreover our will is limited by our choices, our abilities, our possibilities, and our environmental conditions. Humans expand their sphere of freedom as they learn science, as they develop their abilities, and as they increase their technical tools.

79 See, Qur'an, 81; 29.

We can be turned into herds that are pushed about by our environment as our ignorance, poverty, and laziness grow. **The people with the lease amount of willpower are the most ignorant people.** Whoever does not know cannot think, and whoever cannot think cannot choose.

-Third, our free will, in some choices, is "under genetic pressure." No one is making you read this book. However, you are free to eat or you are forced to eat by hunger. As the years go by, these pressures and desires, emerge from the hidden chambers of our souls and genetic structures and shape our experiences in this way.

Whatever illnesses our ancestors suffered, and whatever life styles they had, has been passes to us as a genetic inheritance. Peoples' weaknesses concerning sexuality, money, status, and the like are affected by the lifestyles of their ancestors. Everyone has different obstacles to overcome on the road to heaven.

Genetic pressures are not trained. This struggle of training has been left to us so that we may be worthy of heaven. We need to teach ourselves how to use our anger, lust, and intelligence in a balanced way. We need to make our choice in the middle of the positive inspirations from the angels and the negative ones from the devils. Whatever path we choose, the Almighty Creator will make our will stronger.

Humankind is told: "Ask from Almighty Creator what you need within these limits and work. You will be rewarded according to your intentions in the next world for all your prayers and labor. In this world however, Almighty Creator will reward you in a way becoming to His justice. You will be the one responsible for what you achieve, because you were the one who desired it. You will go towards the good in this way and towards the bad in that way."

3. THE CONDITIONAL DESTINY

In addition to natural causality, which are the rules of law we face concerning some interventions in our lives from profound metaphysical dimensions; we call these rule spiritual causality and they are the divine rules of God. We shall now explain the wisdom of the events that change the directions of our lives such as luck, coincidence, accident:

a) Spiritual Causality

Our lives operate under the effect of some hidden spiritual divine rules. The Almighty Creator has given us orders that will confer peace on our social lives. What He has informed us of, by means of the prophets, through such books as the Torah, the Psalms of David, the Gospel and finally the Qur'an, are the principles of spiritual cause and effect.

Let us recite some of the prohibitions and commandments: "Do not commit adultery, do not steal, do not commit murder, do not rebel against your father and mother, do not receive and be paid interest, do not take advantage of the orphan, do not drink alcohol, do not give bribes, do not betray people, do not be arrogant, do not be absentminded, do not bear false witness, do not carry gossip, do not violate the rights of others, do not slander, do not be jealous..." "Aid the poor, respect your parents, study knowledge, work hard, be humble and tell the truth."

Those who deny Almighty Creator, and those who will not behave as His servants, will receive their recompense in the next world.[80] However, they will already start to receive the recompenses of their good and evil in this world in the forms stated above. This dimension makes up the conditional direction of our fate. For instance, "If you rebel against your parents, you will become poor. If you steal, you will have an accident." Be repentant, correct the situation and you will be saved.

This dimension consists of actions spread over days, months and years, it is not a rapid decision. For instance, if you are unjust to your neighbor once, it makes you unhappy, but the recompense of an injustice that continues for five years may be that of being the victim of a murder. Almighty Creator interferes in events and in the minds of humans, so they receive what they deserve, then they come to their senses and are sorry for their

80 The exceptions were the revolts and rebellions against the prophets when they convey the messages of Almighty Creator to people.

wrongs.[81] Mistakes made during drunkenness, adultery or anger can be of this kind.

Because the subject of this book is mostly the world, we shall touch on subjects that concern the world. If you look at a human life in 20-30 year periods, you will be able to understand the recompenses given in this world. Let us consider for instance:

Spiritual Causality Examples

Those who repeatedly do this	***Will be given this recompense***
Those who are kind to their parents	Their lives will be lengthened[82]
Those who do not prevent oppression of others	They will be punished with accidents[83]
Those who continue to tell lies	Their earnings will decrease[84]
Those who socialize with their relatives	Their fortune will increase[85]
Those who repent	Their misfortune shall be taken away[86]

This divine intervention, which guides our lives, generally takes place through accidents and unexplainable occurrences. For instance, a two-year old girl named Veroni fell from the 10th floor of her apartment in Vladivostok, Russia, and only suffered a few bruises on her body. In Mo-

81 The Prophet Mohammad (PBUH), Jami' us-Saghir 1:267, Tradition no. 406.

82 "Almighty Creator lengthens the life of persons on account of their kindness to their parents." The Prophet Mohammad (PBUH), Jami' us-Saghir 2:302 Tradition no. 1910.

83 "If people refuse to prevent oppression, a punishment from Almighty Creator which will cover all of them, is near." The Prophet Mohammad (PBUH) Ibni Maja, Fitan 20.

84 "Lies decrease provisions" The Prophet Mohammad, (peace on him), Jami' us-Saghir 3:199 Tradition no. 3137.

85 "Having good relations with your family increases wealth." Prophet Mohammad (PBUH), Jami' us-Saghir 4:196 Tradition no. 5004.

86 "Prayer turns accidents away. There are two kinds of accidents Almighty Creator has ordained for His creatures: one cannot be changed and the other can be changed," Prophet Mohammad (PBUH), Jami' us-Saghir 3:199 Tradition no. 3137.

lenbeek, Belgium, a 32-year-old woman by the name of Corinne fell 27 floors and lived.[87]

A famous journalist left his newspaper and took up employment with another newspaper. The last thing he wrote on his computer was "I have been transferred to another newspaper. If I had stayed with this newspaper, I would have wanted the corner of the paper where my column is to be empty on the day I died, but unfortunately, this didn't happen." The writer died that day without seeing this article published.[88]

The Prophet Mohammad (PBUH) warns us, "When you ask for something, be careful what it is what you ask for because one does not know which of his or her wishes will be accepted."[89]

Life is not the result of coincidence. We cannot make off from our misdeeds unscathed. Wherever we go, we are always under the eye of the Master of Destiny. When the appointed time comes, every evildoer will be seized. At the same time remember, no torment is forever. Everyone who is patient and struggling will be saved by divine help in the moment he or she least expects. So what kind of process is it to carry out these principles in daily life?

b) Realization of Destiny

Only Almighty Creator knows our destiny that is composed of the aforementioned three intersecting dimensions. As a result, the Almighty interferes with and changes our daily lives by sometimes a) natural causes, b) sending angels, c) guiding us through and showing us dreams or d) inspiring our hearts.

Look at the following example of a dream:

In a dream in the summer of 1999, I observed Anatolia from the skies above Ankara. I looked to the West. The waves of the Sea of Marmara rose to the clouds and they advanced to the East flattening the cities that lay before them. I felt a terrible fear.

87 Radikal Newspaper, June 21, 2000; July 20, 2000.
88 Radikal Newspaper, July 24, 2000.
89 Prophet Mohammad (PBUH); Jami' us-Saghir 1:319 Tradition no. 531.

I saw myself climbing the mountain of Hidirnebi near our village in Trabzon, trying to save myself. I thought of my children and family. I had left them on the Gümüshane side behind the high mountains and they must have been safe.

On one side looking towards the Black Sea, the sea appeared and I calculated my road on the other side. For an instant I noticed that the sea had flooded over the top of the mountain, that it had split Hidirnebi at the base and I was about to slide down with the earth under my feet, die and be lost.

I stopped trying to climb and fell onto the ground and waited for death, saying, "How did I ever think I could escape from God's power and from His universe?" When I woke up in a fright, I gave thanks for a long time that it had all been a dream.

I went on holiday with a feeling I was preparing for a disaster. On August 16, I left the children in my village and went to Hidirnebi Mountain plateau with my three friends. The house I slept in that night was the house of my uncle that was almost directly below the place I had been climbing up in my dream.

I was startled by the news my uncle told me early in the morning: "Get up! Turkey has collapsed," The earthquake we experienced on August 17, 1999, took over 30,000 human lives from this world.

It may be thus written in destiny: Such and such a person will develop cancer in four months from smoking cigarettes; such and such a person who cursed his or her mother will fall off a cliff in two years. Such and such a businessman who gives to charity at every opportunity will do a profitable business deal in five months.

If people who are about to undergo the conditional dimension of destiny change the behaviors that lead them to it, Almighty Creator may at that instant change what was going to happen to them. For instance, if the adult who was condemned to fall off the cliff because of his rebellion had suddenly begged forgiveness from his parents, he might be saved from falling.

Let us see what happened to the people to whom the Prophet Jonah (PBUH) was sent: They rebelled against the Prophet Jonah (PBUH) and the Prophet abandoned them after having warned them once more. After this, the people were aware that disaster was approaching the city in a cloud and abandoned the city after having repented, cried and asked one another's forgiveness. Almighty Creator forgave them and saved them from disaster.

The table below can provide an important impression for you about changes which have happened and which will happen.

Spiritual causality rule	Accumulated actions	Recompense	Change in action	Recompense
The recompense to insistent gossip is to be humiliated.	He gossiped for a year and behaved arrogantly.	He will be humiliated in the meeting tomorrow.	That night he swore to struggle with gossip.	Those who were prepared to humiliate him changed their minds.

There is a detailed file concerning what will happen to us in a metaphysical book that concerns us all. Every day everybody's accounts are entered in it. Not one bit of our actions, our thoughts, our prayers or our attitudes are left out. Everyone is preparing for a future with his or her resume.

4. EXPLANATORY EXPERIENCES

You may sense in a general way the relations between spiritual causality and the intervention of the divine will in the following examples:

a) The Ticket

One Monday evening in 1988, when I was coming from school, the driver of the city bus I asked me for my student discount card. I was being asked for the first time for my pass whereas until that day I never went out anywhere without my card.

"I am a student,' I said. Although I searched what I was wearing thoroughly, I could not find the card. The driver accused me of being a liar and we argued. The passengers shouted, "Cut it short, kid. Buy another student ticket and sit down." I was very ashamed and I was angry. I bought another ticket and the driver and I agreed to settle our difference at the last stop.

I sat in the back row and thought about it. Why was I being shamed like this? I remembered that on that morning, when I was seeing off a friend who had come from Germany to visit me, I had used a discounted ticket for him, even thought he was not a student. Divine Destiny was punishing me because I had misused the rights of the public. I repented when I grasped the situation and quietly got off the bus.

I remembered why I could not find my discount card. The night before when I was digging through my wallet, I had taken out my card and thrown it on the table. This was done to me intentionally as destiny prepared me today's humiliation. It left me without a card today It reminded the driver who had not asked for the cards of the other students to ask for my card just when I was getting on. So, I understood that **when guilty people try to justify their selfishness, it only increases their misfortune**.

b) The Accident

My friend was backing out of his garage in a loaned car and scratched the car parked next to him. He looked around and when he didn't see anyone nearby he grew anxious and wanted to get away immediately. He should have gotten out of the car to see what damage he had done to the other car, at the very least found the owner, and apologized to him.

When he didn't see anybody, he hastily backed up. He was going to leave a damaged car in the garage and when the owner saw it, perhaps he would be angry and curse whoever did the damage.

He was shocked by a terrible racket. Unfortunately, when he was backing up trying to run away, he ran into a truck and his car was severely damaged.

My friend received the recompense of his lack of good intentions immediately. The sins of bad people accumulate and the sinners pay for their actions either with their mortal or with their eternal lives. If we injure someone who does not deserve it, we will surely be made to pay for it.

c) Bribery

In 1988, a relative was sent to Ankara Social Security Hospital to have a kidney stone crushed by laser treatment. Hundreds of patients were crammed into a small area and waited while their paperwork was being processed.

My relative was twisting in pain. He advised me to offer a bribe to one of the employees to hurry the business up. It was a shameful business that I was forced to experience for the first time in my life.

I noticed that some people were calling the employees over to a dark corner and pressing money and documents into their hands. I pressed some money into the hand of one of the employees. I asked him to hurry up processing our paperwork. "Alright, consider it done," he said and went away.

Hours went by, hundreds of people finished their business, and we were still waiting. Office hours finished and everybody's affairs were taken care of. The last patient left but my relative and I were still there all alone. I went out of my mind with anger. We had come early in the morning and we still had not been taken care of. I lost my self-control and rushed into the office. "Where are my papers?" I shouted to the cleaners who were sweeping up paper trash and dumping it into trash bags.

"The people that work here are gone. They didn't leave any papers," they said. I rushed forwards and ransacked the trash for my papers. I then stopped doing it, hopelessly, and thought about how miserable I was. I wept from shame. I suddenly realized I had been punished by the Divine Destiny. I thought that my repentance could save me from this situation. I swore never to pay a bribe again and prayed for salvation from this situation.

The desk pad on the desk next to me was pushed forwards accidentally by my arm. I noticed the corner of a piece of paper under the pad. I pulled it out and saw immediately that it was my document.

I caught the assistant medical administrator as he was heading out the door and asked him kindly to certify my document for me. I had lived through one of my most unforgettable days.

II. HOW CAN WE TAKE REFUGE IN THE POWER OF THE DIVINE WILL?

We are made to wander on earth like migratory birds in the palaces of Almighty Creator. We are guests in this world. Winds from destiny, pleasant odors, sweet attractions, storms, or shocks move us here and there. They even say to us, "Flee from that abyss, avoid that misfortune, fly in this pleasant garden here." However, can we understand what they say in the language of God's universe?

Let us develop two great abilities: the ability to understand the divine messages and the ability to realize what we have to do in response to them. Let us consider the subject:

1. UNDERSTANDING DIVINE INTERFERENCE

Almighty Creator interferes with our lives in different ways. By means of the divine interference He may want to a) protect, b) educate, c) warn or d) punish us. Let us discuss:

a) Divine Protection

The interference of Almighty Creator in our life may be in the form of divine protection. Divine protection can be in the form of hidden help. Think on this example: A fatherless kid with many problems told me his troubles. I helped him with only a little efforts to solve the problems and his wish came true immediately as if the president had ordered it done. I can sense such a protection after I have been with many people. It is easy to aid such people. It is as if destiny will cause them to fly and is only waiting for them to take some small steps. As Mawlana Rumi said, **"If it is Almighty Creator who is protecting human, the bird and the fish as well are his or her guardians."**[90]

The other form of divine protection is prevention. He protects us from the misfortune that we cannot see by not allowing us to reach our goal. For instance, the house we could not buy collapsed or the plane we missed taking crashed. We may have been spared being attacked by losing our good looks or from being murdered by not being united with our beloved. We cannot know these things but Almighty Creator knows. **Some of the obstacles that make us unhappy are angels sent to protect us.**

So, when you are faced with a problem, be patient. Anything that seems bad may be good for your future. Do not decide immediately. Look at this example: A wise old man of a village refused to sell his beloved horse to the king at the very high price that was offered him. The horse was lost. A little while later, fifteen wild horses from the mountains followed him home and the man became rich. The only son who was supporting the old man's family mounted a horse, broke his foot, and had to stay confined to bed for a long while. The family fell into financial distress. Sometime later, a war broke out and soldiers came and took away the healthy young men who were able to bear arms.

The owner of the horse was wise. This was because he had been patient without grieving or rejoicing at the difficulties, that divine destiny had created for him.

90 *Mawlana* Rumi , Masnavi, Vol. 3, p. 264.

Think about this: Are you being protected by some obstacle in your life that looks like a problem? If you are hurrying in life without care, will you fall into an abyss? Don't be angry at your obstacle; rather, think about the results of it in your life.

Sometimes people insist on their error. They know with their intelligence and they understand with their hearts, but they cannot save themselves from the bad habits that are destroying their lives. In that case, an illness would be a guardian angel for them.

A handsome young man was forced into an extramarital relationship by his sexual weaknesses. On the one hand, he facilitated his own fall into the physical trap and on the other hand, he fought against his inner desires.

Suddenly his body broke out in pimples. He developed pits on his face and when he lost his attractiveness, he became undesirable. His first reaction was to be very sad and fall into a depression. He suffered a psychological collapse and became an unlovable, angry, unwanted person. This made him ashamed of his sexual misconduct and he succeeded in overcoming his illicit relationship through internal struggle. He was freed from the pimples in a very short time.

The young man in the story must have prayed a lot to lead a moral life, because the Creator protected the weak willed man from evil with this kind of misfortune.

Worthy youths from time-to-time, ask me various questions about their problems. I try to explain to them what sort of lesson Almighty Creator desires to give them through these trials.

One of these youths has a social shyness problem, but many youths today misuse their courage. One grieves because he is not physically attractive, but if he were, he might have abandoned the competition of life and given himself over to enjoyment with girls. He is deficient in the way in which he is handicapped, but in another direction, he is well protected.

We may recall the journey of the Prophet Moses (PBUH) and the blessed Khidr (PBUH): Without any reason, the blessed Khidr (PBUH) damaged a boat belonging to some poor mariners. The Prophet Moses (PBUH) who was in his company objected, "Did you drill a hole in the bottom so that the sailors would die? You did something terrible."

However, Almighty Creator had commanded the blessed Khidr (PBUH) to damage the boat. It came to be known that the pirates of a ruler were capturing boats that were in good condition and were pursuing the ship. The pirates who eventually caught up with them seized the ship but abandoned trying to seize it when they saw it was damaged.[91]

God's protective obstacles are not permanent. If we can learn how to protect ourselves well from the thing from which we are being protected, then there will be no need for the obstacles or the protection. For example, was the reason we got sick to protect us from getting addicted to narcotics through the pleasure they give? If we successfully combat narcotic addiction, there is no reason for us to get sick. Was the reason we failed the exam to protect us from being arrogant? If we were humble there would be no reason left for this obstacle.

So how can we know whether the obstacle we are experiencing is a divine protection? We cannot be certain in this matter, but we can guess and ask ourselves this question: Was there some use to us from this obstacle or problem? Is there some weakness that holds us back? If this problem had not existed, would we have committed a physical or spiritual misdeed? If we can find the answer to this question, then we shall know whether the obstacle was our guardian angel.

So how can we save ourselves from such an obstacle if it has come about for protecting us? The way to do this is to protect ourselves from that thing from which we are being protected. Does it want to protect us from selfishness? Well then, we must fight our selfishness. Does it try to protect us from immorality? We shall start to fight with our desire for what is immoral.

So then, is Almighty Creator bound to protect us? What does He protects us from and will he always protect us? Almighty Creator only protects those who are worthy, who have a pure heart but use it in a weak way. The

91 Qur'an; 18; 66-82.

others He abandons to the devil that they are so anxious to serve. Nevertheless, if even well intentioned humans break their resolves and continue in their bad deeds, Almighty Creator will abandon them as well after a while. These kinds of people are given a period of complete freedom and ease. When this period is over, the person is seized in his sins and crimes and is taken to the next life.

b) Divine Education

The second kind of interference of the Almighty Creator in our life is divine education by putting obstacles and problems in our lives.

The development of abilities is completely achieved through difficulties. We are in this world to achieve humane values, such as "faithfulness, thankfulness, love of life, honesty, respect, responsibility." These values cannot be achieved alone but through various trials.

No one is exempt from these trials, not even the prophets. In fact, the prophets were trained by having to pass through the heaviest and hardest trials.

Their opponents wanted to kill the Prophet Moses (PBUH), the Prophet Jesus (PBUH), and the Prophet Mohammed (PBUH). The Prophet Job (PBUH) was ill for years and the Prophet Joseph (PBUH) passed years in prison.

There were very serious trials in the lives of many important persons that changed the lives of humankind. Some spent years in prisons and then were elected to be heads of state. Some wise people were put to death by torture and their names are remembered through the ages. As a result of their trials, they were educated, they became educated models for society, we remember their names and we learn from them.

Different lives that contain typical trials have been designated for every human being on this earth. For example a child can be born in a home where the father is a drunk and is brutal to his wife. Somebody can be suddenly paralyzed by an accident for no reason. Another person can be born with a handicap. Someone else may have lost everything he owned in an earthquake. Everyone may have some misfortune or weakness. One person can be struggling with shyness, another with a stammer, another with sexual tensions, or another with an illness. We now know that the Almighty educates us through these kinds of struggles.

"What do we think of when we hear the word 'success': People who have left their marks on life...are those who are always remembered. **If you want to experience an above average life, your journey must be above average.** The marks you left in history are relative to the size of the issues that you combated.

We should think of our troubles as being individual angels who train us. We cannot learn as much from any teacher as we learn from our troubles.

I deeply understood this with following observation: I visited some children in a leukemia ward in a hospital in Ankara. I shrank before the greatness of heart of the children who were suffering from this terminal disease. Troubles serve in an incomparable way to mature those people who are patient.

I hope that Almighty Creator may not give you an unbearable burden: that you may not be left as an orphan or that you may not lose your spouse or your child. You may become depressed and spend your life in illnesses. You may be abandoned, be made a prisoner or go hungry. There is no limit to the bad things in life; man is mortal.

Everyone enjoys the victories, the pleasures, the applause and the appreciations of life, but everyone cannot enjoy the troubles that actually teach and develop us. The truth is clear: "It is possible that ye dislike a thing which is good for you, and that ye love a thing which is bad for you. But Almighty Creator knoweth, and ye know not."[92]

If there were no obstacle, you would have nothing to overcome. If the eagle did not threaten the sparrow, the sparrow would not have become a wonderful acrobat. If we had not needed to hurry, automobiles would not have been produced.

92 Qur'an; 2; 216

Some losses serve to our profit. I was very sorry when I failed my first business exam. Later I learned to be patient and longsuffering. I passed the second exam, which led to a much higher salary. If I had passed the first one, I would not have worked for the second one. When you fall into trouble, immediately move to the examination mode: "I am being tested in this moment. What do I have to do to win?" Ask yourself:

Does the problem come from a mistake of mine? I going broke; is this because I am extravagant? My family is breaking up; is this because I was unfaithful to my wife? Is this misfortune the recompense for a mistake of mine? Did I break someone's heart? Do I have to develop in areas like faithfulness, patience, gratefulness, purity, belief, or kindness? Am I seizing something to which I do not have a right?

If so, how can I correct my error? Shall I give alms? What does the Almighty Creator want to teach me by sending me this misfortune? Does the unfaithfulness of a friend make me think about and correct my insufficient loyalty to my mother? Am I being called on to appear as I truly am through having an oppressive boss? What trouble gives me what lesson?

The Almighty tests us through difficulties in our relations and communications to make us learn each other's true intentions. We too can understand the nature of who we are by looking at ourselves through our relationships. As you know, every car can drive well over a smooth road. One can see the real power of a car on the slopes, on twisting portions of the road, on dips and bumps. Just like this, the person whom you meet every need for will get on well with you. Nevertheless, is that person good or is there a diabolical heart hidden behind that angel face? You can learn a person's real intention only through problems. When you cannot meet a need of someone, look how that person behaves?

One is subjected to insult, he loses his money, he loses his rank, he falls ill, he is betrayed, or he ends up without anyone. **The trial of destiny reveals the hidden reality in which the person finds himself tested like a litmus paper.**

The Almighty Creator knows what is hidden inside of us and shows us to ourselves through trials. Every trial requires an answer: Will the servants of Almighty Creator, who are grateful in prosperity, be patient in poverty? When they are honored, they are devoted to the Almighty Creator, but when they are ill-treated will they abandon their devotion? Are they sincere? For whose sake do they live? Are they opportunist, are they just, are they merciful, are they reliable, are they faithful? Are they diamonds worthy of heaven or do they hide a coal inside of themselves?

c) Divine Warning

The Almighty may interfere in our lives by sending small warning misfortunes that we call "love slaps" to warn us about our mistakes. By sending us little warnings, Almighty Creator wants us to wake up and correct our errors. People who learn from these love slaps quickly correct their mistakes. Those who do not learn will experience worse misfortunes.

Either these slaps terminate in a great divine punishment or Almighty Creator leaves the people to themselves and when their time is up, He puts end to their lives in the midst of their rebellion.

Love slaps are related to our errors. For instance, if you love your car too much, you may have an accident; if you don't give alms to the poor you may have some money stolen, and if you allow selfish aggression to come first, you may lose everything. "**A blow is truly given for a bad habit/It is not the rug that is beaten, beaten is the dust.**"[93]

Look at this example: A friend of mine became very successful in the silver trade. One day when he had many customers, I told him not to forget to give alms to the poor. "Oh, alright" he said, brushing it off. Before long, he threw a bag of silver in the trash by mistake. The silver was piled in a truck and was thrown in the garbage dump.

I heard another story: a man was passing through the town where he was born, but he couldn't trouble himself to visit his mother who was longingly waiting to see him because he wished to save time. He had a flat tire as he was leaving the town. He understood what he had done wrong and as soon as he had repaired his tire, he went back and visited his mother. If

93 *Mawlana* Rumi , Masnavi, vol. p. 26003

he had persisted in his behavior, who knows what accidents would have awaited him?

Thirdly, in 1999, I read of a tragedy that took place in a newspaper. Someone offended the rights of his devoted family by getting into an illicit and adulterous relationship. He moved in with a Ukrainian showgirl, turned his back on his family responsibilities, and disappeared.

First, he was expelled from his military housing. Still he persisted in his sinful ways and was dismissed from the army. Even then, he wouldn't cease and began to have various misfortunes. He went to the Ukraine and lived with the woman. Two months later, they came back to Turkey and were killed in a traffic accident.[94] May Almighty Creator forgive us. **You cannot reach a good goal by using wrong methods.** Good things cannot be done in bad ways.

So, how can we avoid love slaps from turning into divine punishment? What must be done is to cancel the possible sentence for our past mistakes with sincere repentance. The second thing to do is to correct the situation and abandon our errors.

d) Divine Punishment

The result of insistence on sinful errors is divine punishment. We may be deprived of everything which we do not appreciate or which we have misused. Irreparable personal damages are in part special divine punishments for us.

Here is an example: We were in our freshmen of high school. A friend in the last year of high school was well known for his freshness with girls. One day I heard the screams of the girls in the school yard. We all rushed together to see what was the matter.

Our friend had been impertinent to a girl student. When her brother learned he went absent without leave from the army and came there. They

94 If the sergeant's family had deserved this, his punishment might have been postponed to the next life. The punishment of evil deeds done to sinners may be delayed, but the bad deeds of sinners to innocent victims are quickly punished.

both went to the soccer field together, they drank two bottles of alcohol, and then the brother savagely killed our friend.

When I close my eyes, I can still see the empty bottles and dripping blood. Why did the Master of Destiny allow our friend to be the victim of such a murder?

This is another example: A couple went from hospital to hospital for years trying to have a baby. They finally had a healthy baby. The parents and relatives should have felt gratitude to the Master of the Universe for this beautiful gift He had given them. Unfortunately, they celebrated the news of the birth by getting drunk. When they were going home from the hospital, singing songs, their baby was taken from them that very day in a traffic accident.

The All-Powerful Creator gives a period; He educates people and gives them responsibility. Irresponsibility cannot last forever. People who neglect their responsibilities must return the things with which they have been divinely entrusted.

2. CORRECTING THE PROBLEM

After we have understood the message of destiny, we may undertake to "be patient, purify our hearts, make good deeds and give alms" in order to correct our errors." Let us become acquainted with the steps that will lead us from the blow of fate to its support.

a) With Patience

From childhood to adulthood our life transforms like that of a larva in a cocoon to a butterfly. The larva stage occurs only once for the butterfly, but humans can learn new accomplishments every year if they try. Life is like the beats of the pulse. We tense and we relax. We grow comfortable, we get our breath back and grow lazy, and an earthquake wakes us up. We are tried almost every year. We are put to the test by our families, our jobs, our finances, or our health. This reveals what we are made of.

Not all of these trials to develop us are pleasant. Sometimes when we fail these exams, we hate our existence. The purpose of troubles, which are meant to develop us and surround us like a cocoon, is to make us more capable and noble spirited human beings. We will die or become crippled if we burst out of our cocoons too soon.

Humans cannot become finer without a trail and nobody is exempted from the troubles of life. If we are impatient with the trials given by destiny we will die before we emerge from our cocoon. The Mawlana Rumi says, "**If you grow angry at every trouble and every difficulty, if you grow bitter, how will you become a mirror without being first polished?**"[95]

Suppose that you were suddenly slandered and stabbed in the back. Your money was stolen, you developed a serious illness, and you lost something of great value. On the other hand, you have suddenly been offered a wonderful opportunity, an empty promise. In both cases, stop and try to understand the situation, you are being tested. Do not react immediately. Humans are sometimes tested by profit, sometimes by loss.

A woman tried to console herself in her childless condition, saying, "Why me?" After fifteen years, she had a baby. The baby suddenly grew sick and has been fed for the last two years with a stomach tube. The mother has to stay beside the baby 24 hours a day to keep it from choking to death.

While on a television program, I tried to comfort this mother. After the program, she explained to our director that she had beseeched at one time, saying, "My God, give me a child, and I will not leave its side for a moment."

Impatience can cause misfortune and whoever is unfortunate is deeply sunken in their selves. May Almighty Creator not cause us suffering, but we can bear the most terrible suffering. Patience allows us to support, resist, and bear the troubles that come and carry out our responsibilities in spite of everything. If you can demonstrate either your trust in Almighty Creator through patience your pain will be decreased, or you will be delivered from it soon.

95 *Mawlana* Rumi , Masnavi, vol. 1, p. 239.

The Prophet Job (PBUH) suffered patiently for years through a serious illness and through his sincere prayers. Finally, his disease was healed.

I know, it is easy to give advice, but it is hard to live up to that advice. Although this is so, when we face with a problem, we need to think in the following way:

-Ask these questions: "What does the Master of Destiny want to teach me by sending me this suffering? Should I not love the world so much, should I become more involved with my family, should I leave off speaking badly about people?" If you can find out what the spiritual reason is for your condition, and do what you ought to do about it, your troubles will soon end and your problems will quickly be fixed.

-Try your best to increase your level of patience. The strongest soldier is the one who has had the best training and passed through the most difficult tests. If you need to carry the weight of a family and perhaps of a country, you need to learn to be strong.

-Many of us have healthy bodies but our hearts seem to be cancerous. The hearts of those who forget eternal life are counted as dead. The energy that enlivens the human heart the best comes through the window of difficulty. The more you clash with difficulty, the powerful you will be. If a flood or storm passes through a valley where everybody is dozing, won't they all leap from where they are?

-Who is trying you; who is training you? You cannot escape from the training of the Teacher of fate. His endless mercy, even if He may have left you in pain, will present you with a great grace.

-Look at the troubles you lived through from the window of the days to come. Look at your trials from old age, from death, from the bridge that souls must cross to the heaven, from heaven. Do you want to behold yourself as a mother or father who left their spouse and children because they had a serious illness? How do you want your descendants and history to speak of you?

-If people who are in the midst of plenty are miserable because they lack just one thing, they cannot grow. When I was a child, I didn't even have shoes in my village and I was happy. Death exists and we are on our way, we are travelers. We may have something, or not. One day we will have nothing at all. We have the sun, we have the bread we eat, our eyes, our ears, and a million things more we have. Can we not be patient with the pains of this world for the sake of eternity?

We comfort ourselves by concentrating on this moment. We suffer the pains to this moment, but it is not the suffering of a lifetime. No one can escape the suffering of this life. People who are not patient cause themselves more pain. Therefore, may our hearts not join the suffering in the past with that of the future and writhe in the fires.

b) With Purification of Hearts

Every good or bad thing we have done in the past is a seed for the future. A mistake in the past is like a growing tumor or the accumulating interest on a loan. If we can wipe away this evil from our past through purifying the heart, then we can prevent it from soiling our futures.

When the allotted time given by destiny is up for the special testing, of the adult who has unjustifiably rebelled against his parents, misfortunes will fall on him one after the other. We cannot escape paying the penalty for our sins by changing our addresses. We can run away from or plaintiff, but destiny will seize us even if we hide in a cave.

The bad deeds we have done in the past are deeply engraved in our awareness and have affected our personalities. Those who commit continual falsehood, hypocrisy, are arrogance, and are untrustworthy, have furnished their sub-consciousness with moral defects. These stains govern their future and every clean page they try to turn is stained with these bad habits.

Destiny prepares the surroundings for us that we deserve. An old age without respect awaits those who have been disrespectful to their elders. Those who ridicule others will be ridiculed and those who abandon people will experience a future of abandonment.

The curses of the heart, which we have wrongfully injured, encompass us like a nightmare and attack and destroy us where we walk in the most remote corner of the forest of life.

Finally, we may even feel anger and curse those we have injured. If we are not in the right, this offended feeling will also harm us.

We may divide our errors into two groups. The first are errors we have committed against God: Ingratitude, rebellion, denial, worshiping something besides God, indifference to God, disrespect, and neglect of worship. Generally, these kinds of sins are recompensed in the next world and do not affect this life very much.

The other group of sins are immoralities and injustices perpetrated against our neighbors. You know these; they are deeds such as adultery, murder, mistreatment of others, lies, disrespect, treachery. Misfortunes in this world are the recompense of this sort of offense.

I would recommend four vital methods to purify our hearts: (1) repentance, (2) seeking God's protection from Satan, (3) mutual forgiveness and (4) pardoning others.

(1) You can save yourself through repentance from the crushing weight of shameful immoralities big and little if you have committed them in the past and rebuild the feeling of courage and self-confidence. The Prophet (PBUH) says,

Almighty Creator causes the recording angel and even the organs of the sinner's own body to forget the misdeeds of one who begs Him for forgiveness and destroys the traces of that sin from the place where it was committed.[96] Thus in the presence of Almighty Creator there may be nothing to witness to the existence of the sin.[97]

When you beg Almighty Creator for forgiveness sincerely, from your heart and with insistence, He will forgive you and will give you a chance to lead a very pure future life and He will comfort your conscience. Repeated

96 Normally the copy of the energy containing the film of every moment is spread through the universe like a reel and in a heartbeat. Like a ripple of a wave on the shore, copies of everything we do is recorded both on the quantum fields of our bodies and of the spaces where we act.

97 The Prophet Mohammad (PBUH), Jami ' us-Saghir 1:313 Tradition no: 513.

repentance is the most effective opener of the heart's eye. Repentance, repeated repeatedly, is the most effective means of opening the eye of the heart.

(2) The second dimension of heart purification is that of seeking the protection of Almighty Creator from the Devil. This destroys Satan's power over our bodies and will-powers. Sins like acquiring wealth by illicit means, doing things without invoking the name of God, slander, injustices, adultery completely deliver our bodies to Satan. Perhaps devils wander in the blood streams of hundreds of millions of people currently and make themselves comfortable by causing humans to do vile things. Modern technology has placed the devils in a very strong position against mankind. However much you purify your will power from the errors, which nourish Satan, you will strengthen it that much.

(3) We may have done big or small damages to people, knowingly or unknowingly, or we may have committed a fault together with them and caused one another to fall into error. We may beg mutual forgiveness and protect ourselves from future evil coming from one another.

(4) The last step of purification is to pardon others. Rancor causes torment. The cause of many peoples' failure is their unwillingness to forgive small faults or those people who have sincerely repented. People who cannot forgive continually are sad and in the end, their nervous system is destroyed. In these situations, people may become depressed and, if that rancor grows more violent, they might commit a murder, commit suicide, or they die of illness. Either forgive or consign the offence to God's justice. Misdeeds, which are not plots against our life, our religion, our wealth, or our honor, can be pardoned. Someone who feels sincere repentance can find forgiveness.

c) With Good Deeds

If we receive "the slaps of destiny," one after the other, we are being given warnings to "correct our faults". Our misfortune comes from our errors. For instance, errors related to money cause people to fall into financial troubles. If we start from the kind of trouble we are having, we may discover the error we need to correct.

Someone who is pursuing the wrong road to the right goal will be deprived of that goal. You cannot achieve a good objective by a bad path. One cannot gain the respect of one's employer by hypocrisy. One who neglects or worships one's spouse will have family quarrels. Whoever does not give Almighty Creator thanks, will suffer the ingratitude of humankind.

Sometimes you are in trouble and you are wronged, although you are not guilty like a child. If you are a victim, trust in the Owner of destiny that a just recompense will eventually be given for what you are suffering.

On the other hand, sometimes you are in trouble because you make wrong, you commit sins. In these cases, if you do not correct your mistakes, be sure that destiny, which is just, will force you to recompense of what you do.

The results we receive come out of the sum total of our deeds and of our intentions. If we want them to be useful to us, we must correct both our deeds and our intentions.

-The rule for deeds is this: "Do good deeds after bad ones so that the good may erase the badness."[98] If you have grown proud in your error, walk before the Lord in humbleness. If you have broken someone's heart, speak words that will make people happy.

-How you can correct your errors is explained in the related section. You may choose to do what you do because you believe in it and not to deceive people, for the sake of the next world and not for this world, for the sake of truth and not for approval. In the meantime, those who insist on acting irresponsibly may lose their chance to correct their errors.

Look at this experience: I had just started elementary school. I was cruel to the animals in our village. I especially liked to kill insects and flies. One spring day I was wandering in the woods and saw a bird's nest. I climbed the tree and the mother bird flew away. I played with the two eggs

98 The Prophet Mohammad (PBUH), Tirmizi, Birr: 55; Darimi, Rikak, 47.

in the nest. Then they fell and broke. I was startled by the insistent cries of the bird over my head and round about me and I climbed down the tree and hurried away.

The next day I was passing by the same place and I listened to the insistent cries of the bird. It leapt from branch to branch around the bird's nest and cried out continually. I went away from there, but the pangs in my conscience when I heard those cries grew more violent.

The next day the cries were still going on and I could not escape from them because the tree was on the road to our house. When I heard the cries of the bird going on for hours, it was as though I was hearing the sobs of a mother. I hear in my mind the words of a woman, "Whoever destroys a nest will have his nest destroyed."

I had destroyed the nest of a bird. I sat under the tree and cried. I looked everywhere hoping to find a pair of eggs in the grass or branches. There were a few pieces of shell left. There was no other way to correct my mistake than to ask the Almighty Creator to pardon me. The event had so stamped itself on my awareness that I could never again approach a bird's nest. Nowadays I cannot kill so much as a fly or an insect.

d) With Alms

Giving alms to the poor is the most effective means of protection-purification. In this way you can be protected from misfortune and increase your spiritual support.

Divine destiny has put us partially in debt to those for whom we are responsible. Other people have some share in every blessing destiny sends us. In this way atoms unify and become molecules and humans come together and become families and societies.

Destiny has added onto the money you earned today even the sustenance for the cat you are feeding in your home. If your wealth has decreased today, the lack of gratitude of your family will have played its part. Every morning you come to the door of the divine kitchen and nourishment is put in your cooking pan according to the needs of your family. You are one of the bearers of divine graces.

This tradition admonishes us, "If there were no collapsed elders, suckling babies, and grazing animals, misfortune would pour down upon your heads like a flood."[99] This means that we adults generally express ingratitude and irresponsibility toward God, so we look for and deserve troubles from destiny. But, the needy position of elders, children, and animals invites the Mercy of God Almighty and, although we do not deserve, we benefit from this general Mercy.

So in response to their prayer, we are responsible to help the needy. If we do not use our earnings of the day to feed and support those for whom we are responsible, we have committed sins.

The wealth of a father who withholds his wealth from his family and from the poor will find his wealth scattered abroad and lost. To give a correct share of one's earnings to those who deserve it is the same as cutting a cancerous tissue out of one's body. If you don't give it away, destiny will take it and sometimes it may take peoples' lives as well when it is taking their property.

According to the tradition, the Prophet Moses (PBUH) had a poor and religious relative called Karun. The Prophet Moses (PBUH) taught his relative how to grow rich through the art of alchemy. Karun grew so rich with this secret that it took 70 camels merely to carry the keys to his treasures.

When he was told of God's command to give obligatory alms, Karun would not touch his treasure, saying, "This is my wealth." Then thinking it would ease his conscience, he slandered the Prophet Moses (PBUH). When he did this, Almighty Creator destroyed both Karun and all his wealth.

Modern taxation does not absolve one from the responsibility to give alms. In many governments, taxes are spent in the administration and armament of a wasteful state. Whereas everyone lives in a circle of respon-

99 The Prophet Mohammad (PBUH), Jami' us-Saghir, 5:344, Tradition no. 7523.

sibility, which increases as it, moves inward towards one's family. We are responsible in this order: for ourselves, for our families, for our extended relatives, for our neighbors, for our country and at last for all of humanity. If, in this circle, there is some poor person, someone hungry, a student, an orphan, we ought to be able to reach out more or less according to the order given. You can set aside a small share of your income every month for this purpose.

People throw away their fortunes on useless and harmful things like luxury goods and lottery tickets. When it is time to give some money to a charitable foundation or to make an orphan happy, it is too costly for us. What we spend will turn to nothing but that we give to the needy will become our treasure in heaven.

Suppose that your children almost had a fall or you almost had an accident. Such small accidents and little damages are signs that you owe someone from your earnings. If you receive such signs, you need to immediately give alms.

CONCLUSION

You are aware that with the Intelligence of Spiritual Sincerity (SSQ), you have entered a tremendous field of knowledge. You have gained an exploratory overview of out-of-the-ordinary events.

When you study events by relating them over a wide period of time and far-flung places, you perceive the existence of a secret and wise plan. You see that chance, accident, and coincidence arise from divine commands serving secret purposes. You became aware of all this with your belief, your intention, your prayers, your feelings, your submission and the environmental prayers and feelings sent to you.

Life is not the toy of apparent causes and coincidences. When the Master of Destiny commands it, even His laws of nature can work differently. The flow of occurrences could be changed by your sincere prayers.

You have discovered new means to apply to reshape your lives; your belief increases your energy. The message of your heart overflows and is strengthened through your feelings. The Owner of the universe plans your future according to your intentions that represent the essence of your being. If you behave with selfishness, you will lose your power. When your wishes are tested by obstacles, you can show your serious intentions with your persistence. You can change your past through repentance and in this way; you can also change your future.

Those who think life consists of only the material, become blind to the spiritual. People who pass by pretending not to see spiritual causes are the victims of "accidents, chance, and coincidence." Those who cannot recognize the divine warnings that are sent to their lives must meet with divine punishments.

We learned that wisdom governs life. There is a secret purpose sent from destiny for every event in our lives. An illness comes to one person with the message of "value your life." To another an accident is sent to tell him or her, "Give thanks for the wealth you have." The All-Wise Creator talks to each one in the language of the universe and of events. A divine letter is hidden in every joy and sorrow we experience.

You were sent to the world to experience a wonderful life. You came here to love life with enthusiasm and to share in its beauties. You do not exist here to be crushed and suffocated in pessimism. We who are travelers in eternity should think of ourselves as guests in the life that will end soon, whether in a year or a thousand years. we must not try to carry the world on our shoulders, which we cannot do.

As we have learned from the messengers of God, we are travelers in eternity. We do not travel to the ocean depths like Cousteau, to the Moon like Armstrong or to America like Columbus. However, we shall pass by the satellite Voyager that has been on its way for years. Soon we shall travel beyond the solar system and the stars. Some people will lose their chance for the eternal happiness in which they did not believe and for which they did not strive.

We are the most precious living thing that have been sent to this face of the earth. We came from heaven and because of our life here; we will return to heaven or fall to hell. We put on the garments of this world, but our origin is not worldly. We will soon cast off the garments of the mortal body we received in our mother's wombs and wander with the speed of thought on the horizons of the universe.

We, who are the most special of space creatures, ought to demonstrate the supremacy of the Creator to inhabitants of the world, which accepted us to join them. We must not show the shame of rebellion to animals and plants that are perfectly obedient to the Almighty. We must be able to leave behind unforgettable traces and echoes on behalf of the Creator who created the universal journey.

The journey of success will last until the last breath. **Success is ours continually surpassing ourselves relative to the day before.** Those who progress in harmony with their Creator and themselves may be considered to have reached the pinnacle of success.

You have gained a collection of internal tools for the direction of your life. You are walking towards a future that has been determined by your intentions and beliefs together with your material efforts. However much you understand your life from the inside out that is how much you will know how to govern it effectively.

Now we shall put an end to confusion and depression. The mountains that block our way can stop our bodies, but they cannot shake our spirits. **If we can march against obstacles with our hearts, the obstacles will be trodden under our feet.**

Rely on persistence. Persistence is dominant in the universe and those who show persistence are supported by the divine wisdom. Rely on being content, the universe destroys the greedy and aggressive. The stable road of progress is through the bonds of the heart, which you will establish with your stable progress. Persistence has made a drop of water stronger than a rock.

Rely on your positive feelings. A mass of spiritual energy, in the form of excitement, will possess your hearts. Trust in the Creator and behave in surety and submission so that the divine aid will truly open the road for you. Your good deeds should have high intentions. The things that will happen to you in the future will be determined not by what you did but by why you did it.

Study the flow of spiritual energy surrounding you and open your sails to the correct winds. You will see that you will move ahead in the direction you want. Know the laws that govern life and the divine will and causes. In this way, you will come to know the Creator who governs the universe. The highest status is that of knowing the Ruler of the universe.

In this book, you have been acquainted with seven basic fields of power. These fields of power look out from the spiritual to the material universe. **The position of the metaphysical universes relative to the material universe is whatever your heart is relative to your material body.**

In order to understand this book better, you need an inclusive knowledge of destiny and a thorough knowledge of the dimensions of the metaphysical universe.

Our book called "Journey to Eternity" was written to meet this need. We hope that we will support one another's goals together and with new books.

Since this book has been printed, it has been receiving the same intense attention. Our readers share the secret of happiness and success with their loved ones with enthusiasm.

You can make this book the means of improvement of the quality of life for your friends. You can tell them about it or recommend that they read it.

Many readers' letters start with thanks for the friend who let them know about the book. **You will learn as much as you teach others.** What you do not withhold from others will not be withheld from you.

The law of the Master of Destiny is this: As you reap, so shall you sow. That which will return to you many times over are the good deeds you have done. The wealth [or riches] of the world are accumulated by gathering them with the hands; the riches of the world to come are collected by giving to the hand and heart. Whatever you gain for others will be gained for you. The miser will first be destitute himself and the one who does not love will not be loved.

You are a masterpiece who your Eternal Artist says was "created in the most beautiful form." The gate, which was opened for the prophets, is also open for you. Go in through the door of the treasury in the depths of your heart and meet the All-Merciful Artist behind the curtain. This meeting will drown us in light. Every mirror that reflects the sun scatters light.

We are mirrors for you. However, you look at us and we look at you. If you help us to advance, we will help you. If you are light to us, your light will shine back from us to you. If sometimes we become rusty, we break and grow dirty then we may become ungrateful. If we burn out, we will still keep on shining.

Choose to be good even if everybody in your surroundings is bad. The Sublime Creator who speaks to our heart will not cast you away all alone because you, as a "beloved person," are His own creation. When the day comes, He will send a secret winged hand from destiny. You will behold the dawn in the palaces of heaven as the reward of your patience for the dark nights.

We impatiently wait to take peace from your heart, it is the people around you, and it is the trees, the stones, the birds. We are not the sun but have been created as great mirrors that can enlighten like the sun. **According to our appearances, we may seem to be a few bones and drops of blood, but in fact, we are souls created so vast as to ascend into the presence of the Creator who rules over the galaxies and converse with Him.**

www.ingramcontent.com/pod-product-compliance
Lightning Source LLC
LaVergne TN
LVHW051043080426
835508LV00019B/1677
* 9 7 8 0 9 8 5 4 5 2 1 0 0 *